Fountains of Kansas City

Fountains Of Kansas City

A HISTORY AND LOVE AFFAIR

By Sherry Piland and Ellen J. Uguccioni

City of Fountains Foundation   1985

FIRST EDITION
Copyright © 1985 by The City of Fountains Foundation

ISBN 0-932845-04-5 Library of Congress Catalog Card Number 85-72962

All rights reserved. No part of this book may be reproduced,
stored in a retrieval system, or transmitted in any form or by any
means, electronic, mechanical, photocopying, recording, or otherwise,
without the prior written permission of the publisher.

Printed in the United States of America
by The Lowell Press of Kansas City, Missouri

Acknowledgments

Our project began simply as a search for answers to questions for which we held a personal interest. It quickly escalated into an attempt to author the *first* definitive catalog and interpretive history of Kansas City's remarkable fountains. The transition from "interest" to "obsession" was not without its key players who were vitally important in ensuring not only that our enthusiasm was maintained but also that the practical means to publish the book were made available.

Harold D. Rice, President and founder of the City of Fountains Foundation, and the Board of Directors of the City of Fountains Foundation through their energetic leadership and genuine affection for fountain art generously offered the Foundation's support as publisher of this book. We wish to thank Mr. Rice and the board for taking a special interest in the development of the manuscript. The current members of the City of Fountains Foundation Board of Directors are as follows: William E. Reno, vice president; Eugene C. Hall, secretary; Robert J. Wharton, treasurer; Charles A. Garney; Anita B. Gorman; George W. Hawley; Jeannette Lee; James P. Kirk; and Frank Vaydik. Jerry Darter, Director of the Parks and Recreation Department, Kansas City, Missouri, is an advisory member.

Early on it became evident that the manuscript needed to be read not only with a critical eye toward grammar but also with a sensitivity that could discern the critical issues and leave intact the personalities of the authors. We found that person in Patricia G. Boston, a professional editor. We would like to thank Ms. Boston for her good humor, her unflagging efforts, and valuable input as the principal editor of the manuscript.

We owe a special debt to Geraldine Fowle, Ph.D., Professor of Art History, University of Missouri-Kansas City, who served as Ellen's principal thesis advisor during her research of seventeenth-century Roman fountains. That thesis provided us with a background in the special considerations inherent in fountain design and gave us the confidence necessary to undertake this project.

Record keeping in the public and private sectors has been sparse at best; thus it was extremely important that we interview persons who had been directly responsible or involved in the creation of Kansas City's fountains. We would like to thank the following individuals for graciously sharing with us their time and resources, without which this book could not have been written: Stephen Abend, architect; Wallace Beasley, civil engineer; Robert Berkebile, architect; Patti Browne, Executive Director, Municipal Art Commission of Kansas City, Missouri; Norma Christensen, editor; E.W. Corwin, Kansas City, Missouri, Parks Department architect; Tom Colgrove, landscape architect; Jerry Darter, Director of Parks and Recreation, Kansas City, Missouri; Anita Gorman, Kansas City, Missouri, Parks and Recreation Department Commissioner; Lee Fowler, J.C. Nichols Company; Stuart Hutchison, architect; James M. Kemper, Jr., Chairman of the Board, Commerce Bancshares; the late Mayol Linscott, architect; John Lottes, former President of the Kansas City Art Institute and former member of the board of the City of Fountains Foundation; Maurice McMullen, architect; Michael Malyn, landscape architect, Parks and Recreation Department, Kansas City, Missouri; William Nettleship, sculptor; Homer Neville, architect; Miller Nichols, Chairman of the Board, J.C. Nichols Company; William Severson and Saunders Schultz, sculptors; George Tsutakawa, sculptor, Seattle, Washington; Frank Vaydik, former Director of Parks and Recreation, Kansas City, Missouri; and Kenneth von Achen, architect, Eudora, Kansas.

We acknowledge also the assistance of Orville Anderson; Dave Coopersmith (Kim Lighting); the late Jack Furlong; Ken Pepin (Suburban Lawn and Garden); Daniel Hocklander (D.W. Newcomer's Sons); Jimmie Nichols; Gordon Jarchow, architect; and Mrs. Emma Reed.

We also appreciate the assistance of Frank Theis and Ralph Oschner of Oschner, Hare & Hare who generously shared materials and photographs from the Hare & Hare landscape architectural firm; the cooperation of the J.C. Nichols Company in providing research materials and photographs; and the staffs of the Municipal Art Commission and the Parks and Recreation Department for providing us with official minutes of meetings and other research materials.

Area libraries were the primary repositories for our research materials. We appreciate the efforts of the staffs of the Art, Reference, and Microfilm departments and the Missouri Valley Room of the Kansas City Public Library (especially the cheerful cooperation of Sue Dearing, Carol Rosine, and Theora Stevenson); the staffs of the Reference Department, University Archives (especially Marilyn Burlingame), and Western Historical Manuscripts Collection of the General Library at the University of Missouri-Kansas City; the Missouri Historical Society, St. Louis; the Ryerson Library of the Chicago Art Institute; the Nelson-Atkins Museum of Art Reference Library; the archives of the Liberty Memorial (Susan Wilkerson); and the Bryant Library in Rosyln, New York (Anthony M. Cucchiara).

The chapter which describes residential fountains required that we be allowed to photograph and study those monuments on private property. We would like to thank the following individuals for their gracious reception; Mrs. Raymond Hartwig; Mrs. Ewing Kauffman, and Mr. Wade Williams. Our thanks also to Kirk Robinson, who enabled us to have a detailed look at the Royals Water Spectacular, and to Mr. James F. Ryan of the University Hospitals, who arranged a visit to the *Century Club Memorial Fountain.*

We would also like to thank the talented individuals who assisted in the final preparation of the manuscript: Rick Cusick, Jerry French, William Gorman, Barbara Funk, Jeannette Lee, and Payson Lowell. Our appreciation also to Joanne Draney who assisted with the typing of the manuscript.

We have been blessed with supportive families and many good friends who continually expressed interest in our project. While we cannot mention them all by name, the following deserve our special thanks: Elise Guignon Collins, Nancy Davis, and Nell and Jim Howell.

Contents

Acknowledgments   *vii*

Chapter 1. A Singular Art—*Introduction*   1

Chapter 2. A Brief History of the Fountain in Kansas City   55

Chapter 3: Residential Fountains   69

Chapter 4. Reflective Waters—Lakes as a Prelude to Fountains   89

Chapter 5. Mirror Pools   97

Chapter 6. Conventional Fountain Forms   105

Chapter 7. Memorial Fountains   123

Chapter 8. Nature Redefined—

    Fountains That Imitate Natural Water Sources   181

Chapter 9. Courtyard Fountains   187

Chapter 10. Atrium Fountains   211

Chapter 11. The Fountain's Role in Planned Development   219

Chapter 12. Contemporary Fountains   277

Chapter 13. What Might Have Been and What is Yet to Come   303

Epilogue   311

Afterword   313

Appendix I   315

Appendix II   315

General Bibliography   316

Index   317

1 A Singular Art Form—*Introduction*

Though never designated by legal or official means, Kansas City has long referred to itself as "The City of Fountains" in much of its promotional literature. That distinctive slogan is no empty boast as the city has come to be identified with its monumental fountain sculptures. The proliferation of fountains in Kansas City is no coincidence, but rather the result of a collection of factors and personalities, all of which have special signifi-cance in the growth of Kansas City's reputation for fountain art. Our quest for information about Kansas City's fountains began approximately three years ago when it became evident that there was no one definitive source which adequately described all the color, situations, and personalities that surround the construction of these powerful artistic expressions.

Our goal in writing this book has been twofold: first, to provide the public with a source of information that has been lacking; and second, to resurrect and pay homage to the memory of those individuals, long forgotten by contemporary citizens, who made incalculable impact on the style, shape, and substance that characterize our city today. It is our privilege to have the opportunity to discuss these artful creations— symphonies of sound and water—in hopes that the book will not only edify but also inspire and ensure the erection of many other fountains.

One of the questions most frequently asked is "How many fountains are there in Kansas City?" The question cannot be answered immediately, for it needs further refinement. There are an unknown number of private residential fountains; however, their roles relate very much to the reasons for the popularity of the fountain in Kansas City. Likewise, the number of fountains used to embellish the interiors of commercial buildings is increasing rapidly. The fountain has been enormously popular in the huge interior spaces of shopping malls, as it creates an outdoor ambience often desired by designers.

So, this book *still* does not answer the question of quantity in its broadest sense. Rather, we have addressed the fountains which belong to the public sector and have made every effort to provide a representative sampling of private and commercial fountains for their contribution to our story, which spans nearly a century.

In our minds, Kansas City can aptly portray itself as "The City of Fountains" not solely because of their number but because of their excellence. The city has made pioneering efforts in demonstrating not only how an artwork can beautify a cityscape but also in how it can provide a focus and a public recreational space in the heart of a bustling urban environment. From their very beginnings as components of the internationally renowned park and boulevard system, Kansas City's foun-tains have provided its citizens with a legacy unparalleled in any other major American city.

As we move away from simply identifying and listing vital statistics, the personalities which surrounded the inception of the works and the time during which the fountains were designed come into focus. Historic events have played a vital role in the construction of fountains, and that influence must also be considered to fully appreciate the "water wonders" of the city.

We have chosen to organize the book in a way that integrates chronology, geography, and fountain purpose. An overview of the history of fountain development in Kansas City is provided as an introduction to the chapters that follow. Individual fountains are then discussed as they relate to a specific type, purpose, or their relationship to a geographic area. Within each chapter the coverage follows a chronological approach when appropriate. Fountains that have been destroyed and proposals for fountains that were never built are discussed as they relate to specific chapters.

In the discussion, we have applied the broadest definition of the fountain to include drinking fountains, which historically have been enjoyed for both their decorative and functional purposes, without any attempt to make distinctions relative to their use. Today, many of the finest European fountains, designed by some of the most renowned artists, continue to be used as drinking fountains. Some of Kansas City's drinking fountains also included highly decorative designs, often functioning more as works of art than as water outlets. In fact, committees which were organized in Kansas City to establish the form for a commemorative monument to an individual often seemed more comfortable with providing a practical feature to an otherwise "non-functional" memorial. We have, therefore, provided coverage of drinking fountains which combined artistic expression with a memorial function.

Further, we discuss mirror pools and lakes that were only later converted to include a water display. Those water showcases are discussed in the context of their creation, that is, after the jets were added to provide visual and auditory interest.

In conducting research for this book, it immediately became apparent that one of the decisive factors for the lack of any comprehensive treatment of Kansas City's fountains was the dearth of primary source materials. Many of the documents relating to the erection and disposition of the city's fountains either never existed or have been lost. Private fountain development occurred almost exclusively without the acknowledgment of the press or any public involvement, providing little information to the scholar. Public records, such as the early records of the Park Board, were of great value in our research. But they too failed to completely relate the story behind the fountain, as often they mentioned only the conclusion without benefit of the discussions that had to have prefaced that decision.

Our search for documentation led us to persons who had knowledge of those anecdotes surrounding the design and construction of the fountains. We conducted numerous interviews with such persons and corresponded with others who had since left the city. For many public fountains, newspaper accounts provided an invaluable, and sometimes the only, "first-hand" account of many of the fountains.

For comparative purposes we consulted books which described fountain works in other cities by sculptors represented in Kansas City and made inquiries of architects in other cities about those works which had originated outside Kansas City. Various publications which describe the colorful social, political, and economic history of Kansas City were used to arrive at a context within which to place each of the fountain works.

A list of selected publications is provided in the general bibliography, and a list of persons interviewed is included in the Acknowledgments. Unless otherwise noted, quotations which appear in the text are cited from either interviews, correspondence, or newspaper publications.

The works of art themselves proved to be our primary source of inspiration as well as information, as we spent long hours studying the intricacies of their design and the ingenious placement and effects of the water. Our descriptions can serve as no more than a beginning to the enjoyment of these works, as the reader should experience first-hand the delights to which we can only allude.

The vocabulary, which is unique to describing the water elements and jet design, was gleaned from literature provided by major fountain component manufacturers and designers. In most cases, the name used to describe those elements is the same, and where there has been some disparity, we have provided literal descriptions.

The Fountain and Its Water Effects

Any comprehensive discussion of fountain art must begin with a review of the unique aspects of this art form. In the art of the fountain, water is transformed through human creativity into a variety of forms. Water may assume either an active or a passive role and can be exploited for either its reflective, mirror-like qualities or its potential for motion.

A fountain is a singular form of art that can combine sculpture with water and produce both kinetic and sound effects. It is perhaps the most dynamic form of artistic expression, as it possesses the capacity to undergo constant change. Manipulated through the control of pressure and outlets, water can be made to drip, trickle, bubble, ripple, spurt, stream, mushroom, erupt, or gush. The variety of effects is limited only by the intentions of the designers.

The form the water will take is dependent upon the shape of the edge of the lip over which it falls, the size and position of the nozzles from which the water is expelled, and the pressure of the water as it issues from the nozzles. The edge of the lip can cause the water to fall either in droplets or in sheets. If the undersurface of an edge is left flat, the water will run under the surface. However, if a notch is cut under the lip, the water is released and will fall free. Further, if the surface of the rim is rounded, the water falls with a sheeting effect and, if left squared, will break into droplets.

The nozzles of the fountain are the most critical element in determining the form and shape that the stream of water will assume. There are a number of standard forms for the nozzles, and most fountains employ them either individually or in combination to achieve a variety of effects. An aerating nozzle allows air to be combined with the water to produce a frothy effect. The injection of air into the stream tends to cause the water to become even more luminous when sunlight plays upon it. When aerating nozzles are arranged closely together in concentric rings, a massive column of water is produced. The larger the orifice of the nozzle, the larger the column of water. When water is expelled from these aerating nozzles under great pressure, a monumental display of water is created. This arrangement is used to create a "geyser" effect.

The circular mushroom pattern often observed in fountains is produced by a specially designed nozzle composed of a plunger set within a circular shaft. The water pressure, as well as the position of the plunger, affects the height and the diameter of the mushroom that is created.

Patterns can also be created by the placement of the individual jets of the nozzle. "Fingers" of water are produced when jets are arranged in a line across the head of the nozzle. When a swivel is attached, the water will move as the head of the nozzle directs it. In another form, tiers of water, sometimes called "water castles," are created by a nozzle which employs concentric rings of jets that are equipped with internal bafflers to regulate the different heights for the circles of water.

"Bubbler" jets produce mounds of water which are aerated to produce foamy effects. The water does not rise to great heights, and the effect is often preferred by a designer wishing to avoid splash problems. The spray ring is perhaps the most frequently used of all the forms in decorative fountains. The jets of the water outlets are placed in a ring around the circumference of the nozzle and are sometimes set at angles. The jets are arranged so that they produce either an outside fall, an inside fall, or a combination of the two. The effects of the spray ring can range from a dome, to a "basket weave," to a simple circle of water.

The visual qualities of a fountain also change with the atmospheric conditions: when sunlight plays off the glistening beads of water, when rain creates patterns in its reflective pools, or when wind carries the streams in an uncontrolled spray. The result is that the spectator who passes these works is treated to a display that he may not have previously encountered. It is this dynamic quality that guarantees the permanence of the fountain in the cityscape.

Historic Overview

From the time of its earliest appearance, when springs erupted from outcroppings of rock, the popularity of the fountain has not diminished. In fact, the word *fountain* was originally coined to describe the source of a spring or stream but later became associated with the hydraulic and sculptural elements that we use to classify contemporary fountains.

Ancient civilizations can be credited with establishing certain precedents that are still applicable to even the most modern of fountain constructions. Early Greek and Roman artists experimented with the portrayal of water in both its savage and gentle aspects and created a realm of mythological characters to personify the waters. Water held a mystical fascination for these early civilizations as their very existence often depended upon its availability. As a result of early explorations into ways to display these life-sustaining waters, some basic fountain types were established and adapted for use throughout Europe and the Americas during the subsequent centuries.

Fountains are classified by the arrangement of their constituent elements. The wall fountain is a type that uses an architectural backdrop for the water outlets. Niches with sculpture are often employed and give the designer the opportunity to "personalize" the fountain creation. Some of the finest wall fountains ever created can be found in the city of Rome, where they were frequently used as the termination for an aqueduct. The *Fountain of Trevi*, completed during the eighteenth century and popularized in the film, *Three Coins in the Fountain*, is one of the best known fountains of this type.

The pedestal type of fountain is used frequently and has been produced in vast numbers. This free-standing fountain is composed of a bowl or series of bowls supported by a central stem through which water is carried to the summit. The pedestal fountain is appropriate for smaller works and often has been used for the embellishment of formal gardens.

The grotto fountain is another type frequently used as a formal landscaping element. Grotto fountains use rocks and existing topographical features to build an organic form for the placement of the water outlets.

A cascade fountain, a variation of the grotto type, is characterized by a stream of water that falls from an elevated height to a surface below, creating a waterfall effect. The sculptural embellishment in this type of fountain is minimal, as the effect intentionally mimics nature.

The fountain tradition has provided forms and conventions for later designers who adapted them to suit their particular needs. In the twentieth century, technological advances have enabled longer periods of operation, greater variety of effects, and even the creation of some new forms.

Heating elements are available to provide year-round use of fountains, formerly impossible because of damage caused by the freeze-thaw cycle. Because of the advances in recirculating pumps and mechanical systems, fountains can now be made to operate more economically. The control of the water elements has improved as wind sensors can temporarily shut off a fountain if gusts blow the water in unwanted directions. Electricity and colored lenses on underwater lights have allowed the waters to be illuminated with all the hues of the spectrum. Computers can be programmed to cycle the action of the fountain so that the height and force of the water can be changed as often as is desired.

The introduction of new materials such as aluminum, stainless steel, and Plexiglas has given the designer greater latitude in the form and appearance that the fountain will assume. This, along with a progressive stylistic evolution, has resulted in a move away from the mythological subject matter once commonly represented to some very modern, abstract works.

In some modern fountain construction, those elements traditionally associated with the fountain have disappeared. In some cases, for example, the retaining basin of the fountain has been replaced by efficiently sloping floors, cleverly located drains, and recirculating elements, so that the fountain may simply be composed of the water in motion.

The method by which a fountain comes into existence is unique in the realm of artistic expression. Historically, the sculptor has been the sole creator of a fountain, concerned not only with the sculptural elements but also water pressure, placement, and other critical concerns. In more modern times, the creation of a fountain often has been the result of a collaboration between artist, architect, landscape architect, and hydraulic and structural engineers, whose individual talents contribute to the whole. Often, the designer of a fountain begins with a germinal idea that becomes enacted only through the combined professional skills of the architect and engineer. Many of the fountains that have been executed in Kansas City are the result of this kind of collaboration. In charting the course of construction, credit is due individuals who collectively have contributed to the imagery expressed by the fountain.

The principles of a fountain's construction remain what they were centuries ago and can be found in any fountain monument. A recent development has been the organization of companies which specialize in the production of the equipment and expertise necessary to fabricate any kind of fountain that may be desired, often independent of the architect or engineer in a building project. Although there have been companies in the past that also dealt in fountain products, the companies today that specialize in fountains are very sophisticated, creating either the entire fountain design or supplying their individual components.

Many of the fountains in Kansas City derive from their historical antecedents, whereas others differ by their use of twentieth century technology. Two excellent examples of the pedestal fountain can be found at the *Thomas Swope Memorial* in Swope Park and the *Romany Road Fountain* at Romany Road and Ward Parkway. The interior of the Westin Crown Center Hotel exhibits elements of the grotto and cascade fountains in its waterfall and landscaping of a natural cliff. The Alameda Plaza Hotel is highlighted by a cascade fountain that distinguishes the building and draws attention to its corner location. The *William Fitzsimmons Memorial Fountain* at Twelfth Street and The Paseo is a good example of a wall fountain.

Modern elements appearing in the city's fountains include the columns of water which rise from the pavement of Crown Center Square, the stainless steel branches of the *Rain Thicket Fountain* in Oppenstein Memorial Park, and the programmed water display of Royals Stadium.

The return of the waters to Kansas City's fountains for its residents and visitors has become a sure sign of spring and is met with unbridled enthusiasm. Even though the fountain works in Kansas City exhibit a variety of forms and execution, water is the *sine qua non*, a fact which distinguishes them from any other monuments in the city.

Plate 1 **Heritage Fountain**, *detail*

8

Plate 2   **City Hall Fountains,** *detail*

Plate 3 J.C. Nichols Memorial Fountain, *detail*

Plate 4 **Rain Thicket Fountain**

Plate 5 **Rozelle Court Fountain**

Plate 6 **Liberty Memorial Fountains,** *detail*

Plate 7   Muse of the Missouri Fountain

Plate 8 **Eagle Scout Memorial Fountain,** *detail*

Plate 9 Seville Light Fountain

Plate 10 **Westin Crown Center Hotel Lobby,** *detail*

Plate 11 **Northland Fountain**

Plate 12   **Royals Stadium Fountain**

Plate 13 **Spirit of Freedom Fountain**

Plate 14 William Volker Memorial Fountain

Plate 15   Meyer Circle/Sea Horse Fountain

Plate 16 Crown Center Square Fountain

Plate 17 **Kansas City Star Fountain**

Plate 18 Commerce Tower Sunken Garden—Fountain of Life

Plate 19 Loose Park Rose Garden Fountain

Plate 20 Neptune Fountain

Plate 21 **Ward Parkway Mirror Pool**

Plate 22 **Northeast Concourse Fountain,** *detail*

Plate 23 Alameda Waterfall/Diana of Alameda Plaza

Plate 24   **Barney Allis Plaza Fountain**

2 A Brief History of the Fountain in Kansas City

Water has always been especially significant to the citizens of Kansas City, as the city had its genesis at the beginning of the 1800s as a river landing. The evolution into a major metropolitan center progressed slowly, and, as a result, the city's beautification was not an early priority. It is not surprising that some of the first fountains within the city were simple, utilitarian structures provided for the watering of horses. Although often attractive, these fountains were not deliberately intended to be works of art.

One horse trough fountain that was familiar to many Kansas Citians was placed near the Kansas side of the old Intercity Viaduct (completed in 1907). The fountain, which was erected in 1904 by the Humane Society, was designed to provide water not only for horses but also for dogs, birds, and humans. In later years, when horses were replaced by automobiles, the fountain was moved to Eighteenth and Parallel in Kansas City, Kansas.* When that intersection was widened in 1967, the fountain was given to the Wyandotte County Historical Society, where it was provided with a safe home at their museum far removed from the bustling traffic that once surrounded it.

Fig. 1

The fountain is composed of a granite basin, approximately four feet in diameter, resting on a square pedestal (Fig. 1). A block of stone was placed in the basin and equipped with water outlets, although they no longer exist.

*Over the years, the Intercity Viaduct has been upgraded and enlarged several times. In 1969, it was renamed the Lewis and Clark Viaduct at the suggestion of former Kansas City Public Librarian, Peggy Smith. It still serves as the principal link between Kansas City, Missouri, and Kansas City, Kansas.

Another fountain designed especially for horses was the *Faxon Fountain*, once located in the grassy triangle at Fortieth and Main streets in the Westport area of Kansas City. It was during Frank Faxon's tenure as president of the Humane Society, from 1887-89, that the first public drinking basins for horses were provided in Kansas City. Through the years, the basins were criticized for being unsanitary and lacking in artistic design. In 1900, in response to the criticisms, Edwin Weeks, Humane Society president, designed a new fountain for the refreshment of the city's 60,000 to 70,000 horses and its countless dogs and birds. The design was approved by the Municipal Art Commission and permission for construction was obtained from city authorities, but a lack of funds delayed the building of the fountain. In 1909, the Fire and Water Board began turning off the water in the older fountains to prevent the spread of glanders, a contagious disease among horses. This inspired a group of women members of the Humane Society to institute a fund-raising campaign to erect the more hygienic fountain which had been designed by Weeks. Women contributed most of the necessary $400, and on May 29, 1910, the fountain, named after Faxon, was dedicated in ceremonies attended by a group of 100 persons.

In addition to his Humane Society service, Frank Faxon had also served as president of the Commercial Club and as a member of the Board of Education. A number of people representing these groups spoke at the ceremonies: Mayor Darius A. Brown; Faxon, himself; and the president of the Board of Education, Crawford James, who spoke on behalf of horses and children. Emma W. Robinson, a member of the Humane Society, read a poem she had composed for the occasion, including the stanza:

> No camels, kneeling, at this fountain we shall see
> But scores of horses in a day, patient toilers
> Of the streets, shall quench their thirst in silent
> Thanks — in voiceless gratitude.

John Thatcher, a charter member of the Humane Society, spoke briefly on behalf of the dogs in the city. Austin Latchaw responded for the birds: "I am sure that the birds of this neighborhood, big and little, will remember you in their songs."

Fig. 2

Fig. 3

The honor of the first drink from the fountain was bestowed upon a horse named Bonnie Houghton Robinson. Bonnie thrust her velvet muzzle into the fountain and drank "with becoming gusto and gratefulness."

The *Faxon Fountain* was constructed of bronze, and special care was taken in its design to make it "sanitary" through its overflow and drain system. The fountain was a classic pedestal type, standing approximately four feet tall so that horses could drink easily from its deep basin (Fig. 2). A second basin, encircling the pedestal at the base, was intended for use by dogs. The fountain has long since been destroyed.

Engravings in an 1876 centennial publication, heralding Kansas City's progress and accomplishments, reveal that simple fountains were sometimes used to ornament commercial structures or, at least, portray the illustrator's idea of where fountains should be placed. The engravings show simple, tiered basins gracing the landscaped and fenced grounds of the Livestock Exchange Building which was built in 1876 (Fig. 3). The same publication shows jets of water rising from the reservoirs of the waterworks (Fig. 4).

Private Park Developments

Visitors to Kansas City often express their surprise upon finding a lush, green city, expecting instead a flat, sparsely-landscaped wasteland perched on the edge of the prairie. It has not always been so luxuriantly landscaped, for, in fact, the development of parks in Kansas City occurred fairly late in the city's history.

As early as 1878, attempts were being made to convert the town cemetery into a park. From 1847 until 1857, the block bounded by Oak, Locust, Missouri, and Independence streets served as Kansas City's only graveyard, having been donated for this purpose when the land was platted in 1847. For hygienic reasons, additional burials in that location were banned in 1857. Although the green space seemed especially suited for park purposes, this was never accomplished. In 1878 the city engineer

Fig. 4   developed a plan for grading a portion of the block so that a pool of water fifty feet in diameter would be formed with a fountain in the center, but the plan was not acted upon.

The first public park was given to the city in 1882 by William and Catherine Mulkey. This triangular piece of land at Sixteenth Street and Belleview could scarcely be described as a park, for it measured only one-tenth of an acre.

Fortunately, a number of privately owned parks offered recreation and entertainment to Kansas Citians. One of the early private park developments was undertaken by a Colonel Gaston and was known as Gaston Park. This park opened during the summer of 1875 and was probably located in the area that later became known as Observation Park near Twentieth Street and Holly. The five-acre park included croquet lawns, flower beds, promenades, gravel walks, trees, and fountains of "clear and sparkling water." No other description exists of these early fountains. The Corrigan Railway built a line that ran directly to Gaston Park, and eventually private parks were developed almost exclusively by streetcar companies to increase passenger traffic on their lines. The proliferation of trolley transportation in the 1880s was instrumental in the expansion of the city and, as an adjunct, provided an affordable means of entertainment to the general public.

> Thousands of wage-workers with their families daily avail themselves of the opportunities they present for harmless and wholesome recreation. They run in various directions to the beautiful parks, groves and other suburban resorts, and for a nickel at the proper seasons, the poor tired laborer at the close of his day's toil, can enjoy a delightful excursion of miles in extent and hours in duration. (Theodore Case, *History of Kansas City, Missouri*, 1888, 410-11.)

Fountains were occasionally used to embellish these private parks. Washington Park opened in the spring of 1888, the grounds having been purchased for park purposes in 1886 by a group of investors headed by real estate entrepreneur, Willard E. Winner. Winner and his associates had hopes of selling the 2,400-acre park either to the town of Independence or to Jackson County. Winner also constructed a streetcar line that ran from Fifteenth Street and Askew with the park as its terminus. In addition to having a Ferris wheel, merry-go-round, and steam calliope, Washington Park had a reputation as one of the most beautiful sites in Missouri, with abundant wildlife and picturesque grounds. By damming Rock Creek, which passed through the grounds of the park, a twenty-acre lake was formed. At least one fountain graced the grounds. It consisted of a circular basin placed at the intersection of two walkways (Fig. 5). From the center of the basin several jets of water arced into the air. Until its conversion into Washington Cemetery in 1900, Washington Park was one of the city's most popular amusement grounds.

Another turn-of-the-century private park, Electric Park, was also closely related to a streetcar development. Joseph J. Heim, along with his brothers, Ferdinand and Michael, operated a number of Kansas City enterprises, including the Home Telephone Company and the Heim Brewing Company. They built a $96,000 streetcar line (the Fifth Street Car Line) to the neighborhood of their brewery in the East Bottoms. This venture was not profitable but dramatically improved in 1899 when Electric Park was opened adjacent to the brewery. Electric Park was patterned after a German biergarten, with picnic facilities and a beer concession. It also featured bathing facilities, boating, rides, concerts, and a theater for vaudeville and light opera which seated 2,800.

In May 1907, the Heim Brothers opened a new park at Forty-sixth Street and The Paseo and closed the facility in the East Bottoms. Also conveniently located on a streetcar line, the new park opened to a crowd of 53,000 people who had come to enjoy its artificial lake, roller coaster,

Fig. 5

band concerts (which at one time featured John Philip Sousa), and 100,000 electric light bulbs that outlined the buildings and the rides.

A stunning attraction at both Electric Park locations and the subject of numerous reminiscent accounts was the *Electric Park Fountain*. Valued at $75,000 in the 1920s, the fountain was said to be one of only three "Dunlap Illuminated Fountains" in existence. It was reportedly purchased in Europe by Michael Heim, and its display was thought to have been inspired by a similar tableau which had first been presented in Paris. The fountain consisted of a polygonal wooden drum that was equipped with a manually operated lift mechanism. While colored jets of water were sent skyward from the base of the fountain, an operator would raise and lower a platform on which would appear beautiful women in gorgeous costumes, depicting some historical or biblical event. They would pose immobile for the crowd of onlookers, while an announcer explained each group to the crowd (Fig. 6).

In a 1969 newspaper interview, Mrs. Pearl Goelz talked about the fountain and her participation in its displays. For nine consecutive years Mrs. Goelz was chosen as "Queen Electra" of the park's Mardi Gras celebration. This entitled her to lead a parade of 400 costumed attendants and to flip a switch which would light the thousands of bulbs. During those nine years, Mrs. Goelz also appeared nightly in the "fountain pictures," earning $25 for each performance. Mrs. Goelz and three other performers were raised and lowered on the platform. To assist them with numerous costume changes, a wardrobe mistress was available at the base of the fountain, ready to quickly dress and pose the models for their next appearance. Nine scenes were usually presented during each evening's fifteen-minute performance. These presentations were staged elaborately not only through the costuming but also through the use of properties and furniture. The crowd was held spellbound by "the beauty of the girls, enhanced by the colorful, moving lights."

In May 1925, a devastating fire destroyed much of the park, and it was never rebuilt. Although plans were advanced to save the fountain and present it to the city, this was evidently never accomplished and the fate of the fountain remains unknown. The *Electric Park Fountain*, with its combination of mechanics and living statuary, was indeed unique and was never to be duplicated in the city.

The Kansas City Park and Boulevard System

It was not until the 1890s that Kansas City actively began to develop a park system, even though as early as the 1870s some concern had been expressed about the lack of park land in the city. The birth of the park and boulevard system was preceded by a hard-fought and highly-controversial battle. The numerous legal complications that slowed the creation of the system have been carefully chronicled by William Wilson in his book, *The City Beautiful Movement in Kansas City*. Much of the controversy centered on the financial methods for supporting the parks and the method of land acquisition.

In 1892 Mayor Benjamin Holmes appointed a Board of Park and Boulevard Commissioners that overcame the final legal obstacles and are credited with the early success of the system. It was the good fortune of

Fig. 6

Fig. 7

the city that the board selected George Kessler (Fig. 7) to study Kansas City systematically and then to recommend a park and boulevard plan to the commissioners.

Kessler was born in Germany but spent his youth in the United States. He returned to Germany for his education, serving a two-year apprenticeship in the gardens of Weimar while also attending art school. Later he studied botany and technical engineering and completed his education through a period of travel. In 1882 Kessler returned to the United States and worked briefly in New York City with Frederick Law Olmsted, the landscape architect for New York's Central Park. Shortly thereafter, Kessler moved to the Kansas City area to assume responsibility for lands belonging to the Kansas City, Fort Scott & Memphis Railroad Company. In 1893 Kessler presented a detailed report to the park commissioners in which he brilliantly described ways to landscape the many existing hills and valleys of the city rather than try to modify them. Kessler noted: "It would be difficult to find anywhere a locality that can rival the topographic eccentricities of our city." To most, the topography would seem more likely to repel than to attract beautification, but Kessler held fast to his program of converting the bluffs to parks, and the valleys into boulevards that would link the parks. The strength of this plan was its adaptation of the existing topography. The only formal element in the system that would require submission of the land was the design for The Paseo Boulevard, a divided roadway with a 120-foot median strip. The Paseo began near the north bluffs of the city and was projected to extend south for nine miles.

Kessler conceived of The Paseo as a parkway that would serve as a transition between boulevard and park. Its location in what was then the central portion of the city and its intersection with major east-west streets made it important as a passage to the entire boulevard system. In Kessler's words, "It becomes one of the most important and unique features of the whole plan." Its formal design provided a contrast with the more natural state of the other boulevards and parks. Kessler's plan for The Paseo included a pergola, fountains, formal flower gardens, a stone-walled terrace, and a small lake.

In the 1893 report, Kessler mentioned the use of fountains in a general way and actually specified only two locations which would be suitable for their placement. He envisioned the block of The Paseo between Fourteenth and Fifteenth streets as a succession of flower gardens, trees, shrubs, and fountains, "and perhaps water basins for aquatic plants." For the West Terrace Park at about Tenth and Jefferson streets, he conceived the idea of forming two terraces: one was to be adorned with "a central fountain surrounded by flowers and walks," the other to be decorated and arranged in a similar manner but on a lower level.

Within a few years, construction began on two fountains for The

Fig. 8

Paseo. Unfortunately, the first fountain undertaken by the Park and Boulevard Commissioners at Fifteenth Street and The Paseo was a resounding
failure because of technical problems. This failure probably contributed
to the scarcity of decorative public fountains in early Kansas City; however, there was still a strong interest in utilitarian fountains.

Drinking Fountains

Since horses long had been blessed with their own watering places,
drinking fountains inevitably began to be provided for people as well.
Among the earliest were those located in the downtown area (at the
northwest corner of Twelfth and Main streets, the northwest corner of
Eleventh Street and Walnut, and the Eighth Street side of the post office at
Eighth Street and Grand Avenue). All of these fountains eventually were
destroyed.

The Park Department established a shop around 1907 and began
designing and manufacturing concrete drinking fountains for horses and
humans. They consisted of circular basins mounted on bulbous pedestals
(Fig. 8). A proposal for a more ornate drinking fountain was designed by
architect John Van Brunt for the Park Department in 1910, but no evidence exists to indicate whether it was ever constructed (Fig. 9). Utilizing
classical motifs, the design was quite attractive, but one can only speculate that the cost for this marble or granite fountain would have been
prohibitive, especially when compared with the equally utilitarian concrete fountains.

In 1921 the American Legion erected a public memorial drinking
fountain at Ninth Street and Main, which was later moved to the northeast
area of the city. By 1924 all drinking fountains in the downtown area were
out of commission, prompting a disgruntled writer to The *Kansas City
Star* to describe them as "hollow marble mockeries," through which not
a drop of water had passed for years. A more recent critic commented on
the lack of public drinking fountains, noting that in 1982 most of the 101
drinking fountains maintained by the Parks and Recreation Department
were in public recreation areas; and of these, almost one-third were
disproportionately located in Swope Park.

Private Fountain Developments

Ironically, at the same time that drinking fountains were sitting dry in
the downtown area, J.C. Nichols, a major real estate developer, had
started buying and investing in fountains and other art works to beautify
his residential developments in the southwest part of the city. Nichols
also used fountains to enhance the Country Club Plaza, a shopping
district built to serve the needs of his adjacent residential developments.

In the late 1950s a renewed interest in fountains began to develop in
Kansas City, spurred on by the erection of two major memorial fountains:
the *William Volker Memorial Fountain,* dedicated in 1958, and the *J.C.
Nichols Memorial Fountain*, dedicated in 1960. Both of these were located in the vicinity of the Country Club Plaza.

The downtown area was the recipient of three fountains in the mid-
1960s, all provided by the Kemper family: the *Muse of the Missouri* at

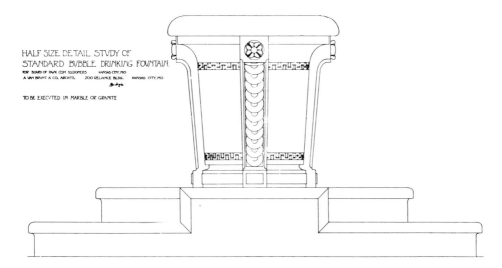

HALF SIZE DETAIL STVDY OF
STANDARD BVBBLE DRINKING FOVNTAIN.
FOR BOARD OF PARK COMMISSIONERS   KANSAS CITY, MO
A VAN BRVNT & CO, ARCHTS.   200 RELIANCE BLDG.   KANSAS CITY, MO

TO BE EXECVTED IN MARBLE OR GRANITE

Ninth and Main streets, a fountain in the arcade of the Commerce Trust   *Fig. 9*
Building, and the *Fountain of Life* in the Commerce Tower sunken
garden.

By the 1960s the fountains in this "City of Fountains" were not
operating to their full potential. In 1959 the high jets of the *Volker
Memorial Fountain* were being turned off from 9 A.M. to 4 P.M. on
weekdays. As a money-saving effort, both the *Volker* and *Nichols* fountains were operated only until 10 P.M. before being shut down for the
night. The fountains of the Liberty Memorial were inoperable because
their pumps were in disrepair. For several summers, the fountains gracing
the south side of City Hall had been inactive because of certain problems:
leaking into the parking garage below and children playing in the pools.

Renewed Park Department Interest

A major renaissance in the concern for Kansas City's fountains came
about in 1964 when Frank Vaydik became Superintendent of Parks.* An
earnings tax, passed that same year, allowed him to institute fountain
repairs and provided funds for the operating costs of the fountains. The
long drought was over for Kansas City's fountains when one of Vaydik's
first decisions was to leave the water running in the fountains as long as
possible each day and each season. Full power was restored to the *Volker
Memorial Fountain*, and the other fountains commenced their longest
operating time (from 7 A.M. until midnight). The Park Department also
began to experiment with year-round operation of certain fountains by
using electrical collars around spray heads which would otherwise
freeze. In 1966 recirculating equipment was installed at the *Meyer Circle/
Sea Horse Fountain* to reduce operating costs, the City Hall fountains
were repaired, and new pumps were installed in the Liberty Memorial
fountains. In 1968 a fountain on the Country Club Plaza was moved to
Seventy-ninth Street and The Paseo to make way for the *Seville Light*

*The Recreation Department, which had been part of the Welfare Department, was
merged into the Parks Department in 1967 during Vaydik's tenure. Vaydik's title changed
from Superintendent of Parks to Director of Parks and Recreation.

Fountain; fountain jets were added to the casting pools at Meyer and Swope Parkway and the Northeast Concourse; and new equipment was obtained for the fountain at Ninth Street and The Paseo. In recognition of his work in "spearheading the aesthetic restoration of the Kansas City park and boulevard system," Vaydik was given an award from the Kansas City Chapter of the American Institute of Architects in its 1965 presentation of the annual Craftsmanship, Allied Arts, and Public Service Awards.

Jerry Darter, who assumed the direction of the Parks and Recreation Department in 1980 when Vaydik retired, continues to place a high priority on the maintenance of fountains and the provision of park land for future fountain construction.

City of Fountains Foundation

The most recent development to ensure the permanence and success of fountains in Kansas City has been the organization of the City of Fountains Foundation in 1973 from a concept suggested by an officer and director of Hallmark Cards. Although other cities have expressed interest in pursuing a similar program, it remains unique to Kansas City. The foundation was organized as a not-for-profit corporation with the goal of conducting a yearly fund-raising drive, seeking annual contributions from each sponsoring member and businesses. Part of the proceeds would be used to construct new fountains. The remainder would be placed in a trust fund to be used to cover maintenance costs. Eventually, the trust would grow to an amount that would lessen the need for annual fund drives to finance additional fountain projects. Public fountains, donated by the organization, were to be kept in good repair by the use of the trust. The City Council endorsed the foundation in a resolution passed in March 1974.

From its inception, the foundation has cooperated with the city to ensure that the city's long-range plans receive consideration. Expertise represented on the original board of the foundation included law, business, banking, construction, art, and public service.

A plan prepared in 1974 for the Municipal Art Commission and the Parks and Recreation Department of the city was reproduced and printed by the City of Fountains Foundation. It identified, for future use, more than 100 possible fountain sites in all parts of the city. Blue Valley Park, on the city's east side, was selected from the plan to be the site of the first fountain erected by the foundation in 1976. That fountain, *Heritage Fountain*, was dedicated to the United States Bicentennial Anniversary.

Since the initial *Heritage Fountain* project, the foundation has been involved in the planning and completion of the *Spirit of Freedom Fountain* (at Cleveland and Brush Creek Boulevard), the *Rain Thicket Fountain* (installed in a downtown park), the *Northland Fountain* (the first Kansas City fountain to be erected north of the Missouri River), and the Barney Allis Plaza fountain.

Fountains in Kansas City are perhaps not as numerous as those in older European cities, such as Rome, Paris, and Stockholm, but during the past two decades notable strides have been made which attest to Kansas City's renown for fountain art. This reputation was gained through quality as well as quantity and is unmatched by any other city in the United States.

The history of Kansas City's fountains is an integral part of the history of the city itself.

Innumerable factors play a role in the life of a fountain, and each becomes a part of its ongoing history. The fountain is one of the most popular forms of punctuation in a cityscape. Like the city itself, fountains experience and reflect the dynamic changes inherent in the urban environment.

We have seen the need to move fountains when they encumbered traffic flow as the city moved further into a motor age. This was the case with the *American Legion Fountain* at Ninth Street and Main, which was moved to the Budd Park Esplanade and Van Brunt Boulevard. Economic considerations have dictated delays in the repair of fountains, have caused their operational times to be shortened, or have resulted in their being turned off completely. Sometimes fountains have simply been neglected because of lack of interest. Such is the fate of the *George Lowry Fountain*, now standing forlornly beside the Linwood Presbyterian Church building that has been vacated by its congregation. Vandals have often taken their toll on fountains, necessitating repairs and, in some cases, new designs, as with the *Volker Memorial Fountain* and the *Meyer Circle Fountain.*

If we are to successfully recount the stories of the myriad fountains that grace the city, then we necessarily must discuss them in the context of the history of the city. Our discussion of Kansas City's fountains does not end with their dedication dates but continues forward to explain their evolution and their present visual impact upon our city.

Fig. 10

3 Residential Fountains

A Nineteenth Century Influence—The Industrial Exposition

The popularity of residential fountains, especially for interiors, can be traced to the industrial expositions of the nineteenth century. During the last half of the century, national exhibitions of industrial products became very popular. Although these exhibitions were conducted primarily to foster international trade, they had two other notable results. First, they provided the impetus for the creation of the large exhibition building, a new type of architecture. Second, they helped to popularize the residential use of the fountain because of its affordability and adaptability for indoor as well as outdoor use.

The most famous building constructed for an exhibition was the large glass and cast iron Crystal Palace, built in London in 1851 for the Great Exhibition of the Works of Industry of All Nations. After 233 plans for the exhibition building had been submitted and rejected, the design Joseph Paxton had prepared in only nine days was selected. Paxton (1801-1865) was a gardener and an architect, an interesting combination of vocations that resulted in this unusual structure which had the appearance of a large, ornate greenhouse.

In addition to showcasing new industrial advances, most of the exhibition buildings erected during this time devoted a large central portion of the hall to a garden and fountain area, attesting to the Victorian love of exotic plants and their burgeoning interest in horticulture. The Paris Exhibition of 1867, for example, featured an oval garden and fountains in the center of the hall.

For the Philadelphia Centennial Exposition of 1876, an entire building, Horticulture Hall, was devoted to the display of plants and fountains. The Moorish-style building featured a handsome marble fountain in the center with a garden, planted with "exotics," running the entire 230-foot length of the building. Eight more ornamental fountains were located at the angles of the building. Among the products exhibited in the hall were fountain basins, trellises, plant stands, window boxes, a revolving flower stand with fountain attachment, and a unique combination of aquarium, plant stand, bird cage, and fernery. The large central marble fountain in Horticulture Hall, by American sculptor Margaret Foley, was restored in 1976 and placed in the rotunda of the Smithsonian's Arts and Industries Building (Fig. 10).

The Paris Exposition of 1889 is credited with introducing the "electric fountain" to the general public. Electric fountains were generally operated by two men concealed in an underground room. Peering out a window that overlooked the fountain basin, one man regulated the electrical lighting effects, and the other man regulated changes in the jets of water.

Artists and mechanics became interested in the possibilities of the electric fountain. As a result, it had neared perfection by the time of Chicago's Columbian Exposition of 1893, where the fountain was a popular attraction. Following this event, several cities constructed electric fountains of their own. One of the most noted was at Prospect Park in Brooklyn, New York, built in 1897 at a cost of $24,000.

Although more regional than international in scope, other communities, including Kansas City, also planned and produced their own expositions. In 1871 an exposition was held in Kansas City, organized by the "Industrial Exposition Association," that brought together products from adjacent territories into one display. The association exhibited in different parts of the city, foregoing permanent grounds. But in 1887, as a private enterprise, James Goodin purchased fifteen acres of land in the eastern portion of the city in the general vicinity of East Twelfth Street and Agnes to build a permanent exhibition hall. Between May and October of 1887, that exposition building, which was modeled vaguely after London's Crystal Palace, was erected on the site. This permanent structure was promoted by Goodin, who finally called upon the public for money to complete the project after many costly delays. The citizens of Kansas City responded with $200,000, and the building was officially opened on October 6, 1887.

Kansas City's Exposition Building encompassed seventeen acres of floor space, and 80,000 square feet of glass formed its roof (Fig. 11). Two architects worked on the design of the building at different times, and although it began as a Romanesque structure, by the time it was finished it did not reflect any particular style.

The total attendance at the 1887 Exposition was 400,000. However, subsequent expositions were not as successful, and the 1892 Exposition ended up losing almost $12,000. The last exposition to be held in Kansas City's "Crystal Palace" was during the fall of 1893. The building burned in

Fig. 11

1901 after it had stood vacant several years with most of its glass shattered by hailstones.   *Fig. 12*

As was the custom, the Kansas City Exposition Building included a bronze fountain on the main floor that was "much admired." The fountain was not a local product, and when it was uncrated in Kansas City, it was discovered that the middle basin of the tiered fountain had not arrived with the rest. After a telegram was sent, the missing piece arrived in short order. Neither a description nor a photograph of the fountain has been discovered; however, it is known that the fountain was flanked on either side by "pyramids of blooming plants."

Conservatories

The gardenlike interiors of these popular exhibition halls no doubt contributed to the popularity of the fountain and to the development of the conservatory as a desirable architectural embellishment for late nineteenth century homes. The conservatory, a glass-enclosed room, was a purely decorative feature and served as a means of demonstrating wealth. Most conservatories were on the first floor adjacent to the main parlor or drawing room. The conservatory was meant to be enjoyed indoors and was replete with plants, fountains, and statuary. Ideally, the conservatory was located on the south side of a residence to receive maximum benefit from the sun. On sunny winter days the conservatory could serve as a solar energy component (long before the idea of energy conservation became popular), repelling the gloom of winter while adding warmth and beauty to the house. Occasionally, a conservatory was constructed to face north and had to be heated by artificial means. The rationing of fuel during the First World War has been associated with the decline of the conservatory. Not many of the early conservatories have survived. Because of changes in architectural style and perhaps because they were difficult to heat during winter months, few were included in homes designed after 1930.

Conservatories were decorated with sculpture, aquariums, fountains, and sometimes even with artificial ponds. Conservatory fountains were usually smaller versions of outdoor fountains and frequently were composed of figures which sometimes served as water outlets, placed in an iron basin about two and one-half feet in diameter supported by iron legs. Very little evidence remains of Kansas City's residential conservatories, although extant photographs document their appearance from the interior (Fig. 12) and from the exterior (Fig. 13).

In 1908, Kansas City architect Clifton Sloan designed a castlelike residence for Dr. Flavel Tiffany at 100 Garfield, overlooking the Missouri River. The fourteen-room stone and reinforced concrete house included a conservatory which opened off the living room through art glass doors and was graced by a fountain. Unfortunately, the fountain no longer exists, and there are no photographs of its appearance.

Mack Nelson Fountain

After the demise of the conservatory, fountains continued to be a popular means of decorating the interiors of houses. Such a fountain played a prominent role in the decor of the Mack B. Nelson residence at 5500 Ward Parkway. Nelson, president of the Long-Bell Lumber Company, commenced construction in 1914 of his lavish Georgian revival mansion from designs by prominent Kansas City architect Henry Hoit. The house was built on a beautifully landscaped site of more than three acres.

Nelson had spent a part of his youth in Mexico and reportedly demonstrated his appreciation of outdoor Mexican courtyards by incorporating an interior, enclosed court into his own home. With its rectangular, marble floor the court became the focal point of the house and remains so today. The perimeter of the second floor level has a balcony/hallway which overlooks the court and provides access to the second floor bedroom suites. Massive wooden columns, painted to resemble marble,

Fig. 13

Fig. 14

support the balconies. A skylight provides illumination and is ingeniously mounted on a sliding track, so that when weather conditions allow, the
interior can be flooded with natural light.

A fountain graces the center of this interior space and takes its cue
from the classical architecture which surrounds it, as it typifies the pedestal form frequently employed in earlier centuries (Fig. 14). Contained
within an octagonal retaining pool, the marble pedestal is supported at
the base by the figures of four upended dolphins. The fluted shaft spring-
ing from their bodies repeats the classical term form (a tapered pedestal
terminating in the bust of a figure). In the Nelson fountain, the shaft
carries a female bust on each of the four sides. A circular saucer rests on
the shaft and serves as a water receptacle and the support for a full length
female figural sculpture, again of classical inspiration. The figure carries a
water jug from which a single stream of water issues to fall into the saucer
and the retaining basin below.

Nelson died in 1950, and his family lived in the house until the death
of his wife the following year. From 1951 until 1956, Mrs. Nelson's sister
lived in the house until she offered it for sale by auction. The purchaser
was Mary Hudson Vandegrift, who bought it as an investment. The house
remained vacant for several years. In 1959, thieves broke into the mansion; they stole chandeliers, hall carpeting, and the figurine at the summit
of the pedestal fountain.

Around 1968 the house was purchased by Wade Williams. He located
the fountain's missing piece and restored it to working order. The fountain continues to add another dimension of beauty to an already beautiful
home.

Nineteenth Century Exterior Residential Fountains

People's homes become reflections of themselves, of their positions in life, and of their tastes. The residence is often used by those of means as evidence of their financial success. Even those of modest means perceive that their home and its appointments directly reflect their worth. The embellishment of the exterior of the home has taken many forms, from elaborate architectural frills, to colorful paint schemes, to meticulous care of the lawn. The finely landscaped yard, complete with garden, ornaments, and fountain not only says something about the dwellers but also contributes an element of beauty to any neighborhood.

Unfortunately, very little is known about early exterior residential fountains in Kansas City. The earliest discovered reference is to a fountain erected in 1875 for L.T. Moore, whose home was in the vicinity of Ninth Street and Locust. Moore was one of the founders of the dry goods firm of Bullene, Moore and Emery (which later evolved into the Emery, Bird, and Thayer Department Store). A fountain gracing his yard was tangible proof of Moore's success as a businessman. The description of the fountain is sparse: "A Venus-capped fountain . . . ready to spout Kaw water." The vases and coping of the fountain basin, erected by local stonecutter Matthew Dunlap, "reflect great credit on that gentleman." The Venus portion of the fountain was probably purchased from a cast iron foundry. An illustration of the fountain (Fig. 15) shows a circular retaining basin with four flower pots around it. A female figure, presumably the mythological goddess referred to in its description, was placed in the middle. Moore's fountain can be considered characteristic of the popular decorative type which once adorned the lawns and gardens of innumerable Kansas City residences.

Before World War I, garden ornaments and fountains were usually mass-produced of cast iron. Their popularity was spread, in large part, by

Fig. 15

the industrial exhibitions held in the late nineteenth century, often featuring manufacturers' exhibitions of fountain products. The J.L. Mott Iron Works of New York had a display at the Philadelphia Centennial Exposition which featured a Renaissance-style fountain of iron (Fig. 16). In 1893 the Mott Iron Works issued a catalog of its products, devoting a special section to fountains. Although the major center of cast iron production was in the northeast portion of the country, Kansas City firms soon added fountains to their lines of products. As early as 1898, the Kansas City Wire and Iron Works was listed under "Fountains" in the classified section of the city directory.

Fig. 16

The decorative treatment of fountains varied little from foundry to foundry. Most models were available with their own shallow iron pools, eliminating the need for lead tanks or dirt ponds.

Fountains of that time period, made from cast iron or bronze, can be classified into two major types. The first type consisted of several basins of decreasing size, mounted on a central stem or pedestal. Sometimes a small iron or lead statue was placed at the very top. The edges of the retaining pools were often decorated with frogs, water lilies, or other water motifs, and the edges of the basins were cut or carved to vary the amount, location, and shape of the spill of water over the rim. Pedestals were frequently decorated with marine motifs such as sea horses, cattails, cranes, and sometimes land-based acanthus leaves.

The fountain located on the front lawn of the Seth Ward residence at 1032 West Fifty-fifth Street is an excellent example of this type of cast iron fountain. Although the house was constructed around 1871, the fountain was probably a later nineteenth century addition.

The fountain is placed in a circular concrete retaining pool and consists of a series of three basins carried on a central pedestal approximately

Fig. 17

five feet high (Fig. 17). Cranes are grouped around the base of the pedestal, and another grouping is around the portion of the pedestal between the lower and middle basins. The lowest, and largest, basin has a curved lip, resembling leaves.

The second type of fountain consisted of a large bronze or lead statue placed on a low base and set within a retaining basin. Common themes portrayed were a boy with a swan, a boy riding a dolphin, a boy with an umbrella, a lady at a well, or a huge water bird. The jet of water usually emitted from the mouth of the animal accompanying the child figure, from a ring of jets around the base of the statue, or from the water jug of the woman at a well.

An example of this second type of fountain was once located at a residence at 2118 Independence Avenue, but unfortunately, it no longer exists. This fountain, probably of cast iron or bronze, had a long history of popularity in the neighborhood and reportedly had stopped more traffic than any other single object in Kansas City. According to Mrs. Robert Gillham, the fountain had been purchased by her husband while they occupied the property in the late 1890s.* The owner in 1934 estimated that requests to purchase the fountain had averaged one every four days during the previous six years.

The fountain consisted of life-size children, a boy and a girl beneath an umbrella, their arms affectionately linked (Fig. 18). The boy held the umbrella while the girl gathered her skirt to keep it out of the range of water dropping from the umbrella edge. A frieze of lily leaves, interspersed with frogs, encircled the edge of the basin. The water apparently spouted from the top of the umbrella, where it also set a small circular element spinning. A woman who grew up at the residence poignantly recalled the charm of the fountain:

For us children, they were not merely little statues, but real

* Robert Gillham, an engineer, built a cable line from the old Union Station in the West Bottoms, up an incline to the downtown area.

people, upon whom we bestowed the most profound affection. . . . That was the age of fountains. Every front lawn that considered itself a front lawn had a fountain. . . . A very popular number being the misshapen obese cupid who, fat face smirking, held in pudgy grasp a writhing swan, from whose upturned throat shot small neat sprays. Or the large nude female figure whose simpering face gazed foolishly over one shoulder at water dripping eternally from a small urn clutched in a tortuous embrace. No right-minded child or adult either could possibly have entertained any sentiment, whatsoever, other than a cold contempt for those stern and aloof creatures . . . my sister and I glowed with honest pride at the attentions bestowed upon "our fountain" by indifferent owners of swans and bare ladies. One of our favorite pastimes consisted of dressing their small figures in our own hats and coats. . . . Never, never, shall I forget the terrible day when an enraged papa stamped angrily up our steps to seize with irate grasp his beautiful gold watch hung with such loving care by his youthful son about the boy statue's neck. We shared our refreshments with our bronze friends too. In the hollow of their little hands were always a few grains of popcorn or melting bits of chocolate. . . . And what fun it was to crouch beneath the umbrella with them when the fountain was on.

The fountain was stolen in the summer of 1935. Widespread publicity following the theft indicated clearly the fountain's factory origin. The

Fig. 18

publicity brought forth remembrances of an identical fountain having embellished the Robert Snyder residence at the southeast corner of Fifteenth Street and Troost. Reports were also made of additional identical fountains at Bethany, Missouri; Richmond, Indiana; Lawrence, Kansas; and near Paris, France.

The popularity of this particular fountain theme can be traced back to the 1876 Philadelphia Centennial Exposition. A fountain of terra cotta, entitled *Out in the Rain* (Fig. 19), was part of the Italian exhibition and was located in the main exhibition building. It was identical to Kansas City's fountain in subject matter and undoubtedly served as the model from which many replicas were made.

There are other early fountains with similar themes, known to us today only through faded photographs. In about 1886 a home was built for Col. David T. Beals on the fashionable Independence Boulevard. Beals, a wealthy rancher and banker, had honeymooned in Europe and returned with a fountain to decorate the grounds of his elegant mansion. The house was set back from the street and was surrounded by landscaped grounds. On his front lawn Beals placed his European fountain, which consisted of a bronze figure of a nude boy riding an eagle positioned in a low retaining basin.

A few years later, in 1899, a mansion was erected at 3000 Troost for William J. Smith, who had financed the Kansas City Cable Railway system. His large home was noted for its spacious, landscaped lawn on which he

Fig. 19

Fig. 20

had placed a low basin fountain with a sea nymph which rose from the center (Fig. 20).

Twentieth Century Residential Fountains

Although these were the two principal fountain types during the nineteenth century, many variations appeared in residential fountains after the turn of the century. An examination of several representative examples will serve to illustrate their differences in style, placement, and water treatment. These examples, dating from 1907 to 1982, attest to the continuing popularity of the residential fountain.

A fountain provided decoration for one of Kansas City's most unusual homes, the summer residence of Col. Daniel B. Dyer. The house was constructed in 1907 on a forty-acre tract at 8100 Wilson Road, on a high promontory overlooking the Missouri River. Colonel Dyer, former Indian agent, real estate investor, and an avid collector, had purchased several exhibition buildings at the conclusion of the 1893 Columbian Exposition held in Chicago, and the 1904 Louisiana Purchase Exhibition held in St. Louis. After storing the dismantled structures for several years, he used various decorative pieces and woodwork from them in the construction of his own home. Kansas City architect James Oliver Hogg was commissioned to assemble these diverse elements into a cohesive design. The product was a large Colonial mansion, featuring columns that decorated a veranda extending around three sides. Floor plans show that an interior fountain decorated a large center hall reception area, which was accessible through the front entrance (Fig. 21).

Another fountain, reported to have been a part of the cascades at the St. Louis Fair, was installed on the landscaped front lawn. Photographs of the fountain (Fig. 22) reveal little detail, although it has been described as a "varicolored glass masterpiece." In 1939, the property was acquired

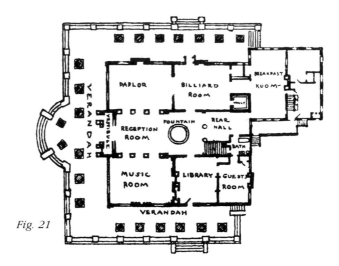

Fig. 21

by the Sheffield Steel Corporation, and the house was razed shortly thereafter. Presumably, the fountains were destroyed at that time.

Proper landscaping was a Victorian concern, evident in the numerous nineteenth-century publications and periodicals on the subject, and interest in beautification extended into the twentieth century. Gardening was immensely popular in the 1920s, and fountains, pools, and other water treatments continued as major elements in formal landscaping plans. A statement made in 1923 by Martha Brookes Hutcheson in a popular periodical of that time, *House Beautiful*, captures the special relationship of water to the garden: "Whether for its reflection or for its sound, to introduce water is to include the fantastic and the intangible, and a garden without it is robbed of poetry and romance."

In Kansas City the art of gardening reached a high point with the development of residential districts by J.C. Nichols. During the period from 1910 to 1940, most of the new residential construction in Kansas City, Missouri, was taking place in the Nichols Company subdivisions in the southwestern part of the city and into the state of Kansas. Substantial

Fig. 22

homes were being constructed in these areas, and fountains or water displays were frequently employed in their gardens. The Nichols Company was actively involved in educating homeowners and stimulating interest in all aspects of gardening, lawn care, and other means of beautifying their homes.

In 1912 the Country Club District Association held its first Annual Lawn Contest, and later, in 1925, the Nichols Company sponsored the Country Club Community Flower Show. The show, which was expected to become an annual event, was held to "encourage better gardening and better acquaintance with flowers." In 1930 the Wornall Homestead Homes Association awarded a pottery piece combining bird bath and fountain to the winner in a lawn and garden contest. The Wellesley Garden Tours, sponsoring annual visits to private residential gardens as a project for raising scholarship funds for Wellesley College, were initiated in 1930 and still continue.

The landscape architectural firm of Hare & Hare worked closely with the Nichols Company in planning new subdivisions and included suggestions for the locations of fountains, parks, and ornamental statuary. The Hare & Hare firm also received private commissions to develop landscape plans for many of the residences within the Nichols subdivisions.

If the grounds were large enough, the firm incorporated a variety of elements. Usually these included a formal garden, a space for growing vegetables, a portion of the lawn screened off by shrubbery for drying clothes out-of-doors, and a rustic area featuring rock gardens and possibly a rill or man-made brook.

The grounds for the Charles S. Keith residence at 1214 West Fifty-fifth Street provide a good example of the Hare & Hare formal landscaping arrangement. The residence was constructed in 1914 for Keith, a lumber executive. The home was set on three and one-half acres. In 1920 the estate was purchased by J.C. Nichols and remained his residence until he and his wife died in 1950. The meticulously maintained grounds featured a variety of ponds and pools, a covered arbor, an outdoor teahouse, and terraced gardens. The lawns provided ample space for Nichols to place statuary and fountains for his enjoyment. One such fountain was a bust of the mythological character Pan blowing his double pipes. This pedestal figure was set in a niche covered with moon vines with a semicircular basin at the base (Fig. 23).

Hare & Hare also provided the lawn and garden treatment for the Italian-style residence constructed in 1918 at 5921 Ward Parkway for Emory J. Sweeney. The original tract covered five acres and included pools, a man-made brook, and a profusion of plantings. The highlight of the grounds was an ampitheater pool, which became a popular gathering place for the many children in the family. Hare & Hare designed the pool, which featured a curving colonnade as the backdrop (Fig. 24). Noted Kansas City sculptor Jorgen Dreyer completed sketches in 1920 for a pair of fountains to grace the pool, and they were installed in 1922.* In his

---

*Jorgen Dreyer was the foremost sculptor in Kansas City during the early twentieth century. He came to Kansas City from Norway in 1903 and worked here until his death in 1948. Among his best known works in the city are the stone lions in front of the Kansas City Life Insurance Building, 3520 Broadway; the sphinxes in front of the Scottish Rite Temple at Linwood Boulevard and The Paseo, and some of the sculptural decoration of the Jackson County Court House, 415 East Twelfth Street.

Fig. 23

design, Dreyer sought to capture the grace, freedom, and joy of child-hood. He created two bronze figures which were to serve as the fountain components placed on each side of the colonnade wall. On one side the sculptural figure portrayed a young girl riding a swan across the waves, and the other side depicted a boy also riding a swan (Fig. 25). The mouths of the swans probably functioned as the water outlets, sending streams of water into the pool. The house was sold in 1928 to Harry L. Dierks who had the pool filled in. The disposition of the playful fountains is unknown.

Between 1919 and 1923, an unusual residence was constructed for U.S. Epperson at 5200 Cherry, outside the Nichols developments. Epperson, an insurance executive who wanted to create a large residence based on various English historic styles, commissioned Horace LaPierre, a Kansas City architect. LaPierre made more than 1,500 drawings in designing this mansion, which is a composite of styles: a central portion that is Tudor-Gothic, a wing that is Elizabethan in character, and another wing inspired by early Jacobean architecture. The house is built on a grade, so that the front (north) and east sides are terraced. The grounds

Fig. 24

are surrounded by a stone and ornamental wrought iron fence with wrought iron gates.

French doors at the east end of the house open onto a flight of stairs to a balustraded veranda. The veranda is built upon a cut-stone wall, and steps connect both sides of the veranda to the front and rear lawns. Beneath the veranda, a fountain is incorporated into the stone work, designed as a deep niche surrounded by a rounded arch. Carved into the keystone of the arch is the head of a lion whose mouth once was the water

Fig. 25

Fig. 27

outlet for the fountain which no longer operates (Fig. 26). Projecting
from the niche is a semicircular basin designed as stylized leaf forms
curling over to form a scalloped rim. Set inside the niche is a smaller
version of the outer basin, which also contained water outlets. The residence is currently owned by the University of Missouri-Kansas City and
used as classroom space.

In 1961 a house at 1211 West Sixty-fourth Street, just west of the *Meyer
Circle Fountain*, was constructed for the Charles E. McArthurs. In the rear
yard they constructed a rectangular pool, approximately twelve feet by
ten feet. In decorating their new home and yard, the McArthurs traveled
to New York City with their decorator, Kenneth Crawley. One of the
purchases made by the McArthurs during the trip was a fountain sculpture
of a marble dolphin (Fig. 27) for the backyard pool. The dolphin is
upended, and water issues from its mouth into a scalloped-shell basin,
then trickles over into the pool. The dolphin is almost identical to that of
the Aleman Court wall fountain in the Country Club Plaza (see Chapter
11). Decorative sculpture and flower arrangements around the pool make
it the focal point of the lovely yard.

Around 1982 the home was purchased by Dr. and Mrs. Raymond W.
Hartwig. Fond of fountains, and unintimidated by the proximity of the
Meyer Circle Fountain visible from the front yard, the Hartwigs placed a
fountain on the front lawn. Mrs. Hartwig likes to think of it as "a comma to
the *Meyer Circle Fountain*."

This fountain is located midway along the walk that leads from the
Fig. 26   street to the entrance of the home (Fig. 28). The concrete sidewalk,

Fig. 28

redesigned to accent the fountain and trimmed with brick at the outer edges, curves around the fountain before continuing to the house. Although similar to other fountains available from lawn and garden suppliers, its tasteful placement and embellishments have made it unique—a good example of how a fountain can be used to enhance a residence.

The fountain is made of cast concrete and consists of a squat pedestal supporting three saucers of gradually diminishing sizes. Water flows from a bulbous plant form at the top and trickles down from one saucer to another, finally falling into the circular concrete retaining basin. This fountain, like the one in the backyard, is equipped with a recirculating pump and lights. Though not operated in the winter, the fountain continues to serve its decorative purpose when covered with foliage and holiday lights.

The Italian Lombard style residence at Mission Drive and Ensley Lane

Fig. 29

Fig. 30

in Mission, Kansas, was constructed in 1930 for Kansas City oil firm executive Ernest C. Winters. The house was designed by noted local architect, Edward Tanner, who sited the residence near the rear of the three-acre estate, to allow for the development of a terraced yard. Winters died in 1962, and the estate was purchased two years later by Ewing Kauffman, a prominent businessman. Kauffman was the founder of Marion Laboratories and is an owner of the Kansas City Royals baseball club.

The Kauffmans installed three fountains on the grounds of their estate. A large circular fountain pool is located in back of their residence, a gift from Mr. Kauffman to his wife for their first wedding anniversary. Mrs. Kauffman had admired a similar fountain during their honeymoon trip.

The fountain is composed of a circular brick basin, approximately fifteen feet in diameter, equipped with a spray ring in the center (Fig. 29). Vertical aerating jets surround the perimeter, adding visual interest and animation to the surface of the water.

The other two fountains on the estate were selected for the Kauffmans by Miller Nichols, who had made frequent trips to Europe and had acquired substantial experience in purchasing works of art. The fountain selected for a terrace in front of the residence was purchased by Nichols from the Romanelli Studios in Florence. This work relies heavily on sculptural embellishment for its maximum effect, and the use of water has been intentionally minimized (Fig. 30).

The polished, brown stone pedestal of the fountain, which provides the support for the sculpture, consists of a composite of geometric forms terminating in a semicircular basin. The basin supports two life-size female nudes seated back-to-back with legs extended over the base. A stylized floral form placed between and extending above the female figures, serves as the channel for the single stream of water which falls over the figures before reaching the circular retaining pool.

The third fountain on the Kauffman estate is more traditional in form and is the focal point for the rose garden on the north side of the residence. The fountain is a copy of a work by Italian Renaissance sculptor Verrocchio, entitled *Eros with a Dolphin* or *Putto with a Dolphin*. Verrocchio earned a prestigious place in art history and worked extensively for the Medici family in Florence during the last half of the fifteenth century. The original *Putto with a Dolphin* was designed as the sculptural component for a fountain in a country estate owned by Lorenzo di Medici at Careggi. Art historian Charles Avery believes that this was the first Renaissance sculpture to "have multiple and merging viewpoints, which provoke the spectator either to rotate the figure or to walk around it in order to fully appreciate its composition." The original work is now located in the Palazzo Vecchio in Florence.

This replica of the playful *Putto* sits on a fluted saucer elevated by a slender marble pedestal (Fig. 31). A single stream emanates from the mouth of the dolphin, then falls back into the saucer and to the basin beneath.

The Kauffman estate illustrates the variety and contrasts that water displays provide to the landscape of formal gardens. This use of fountains, while deriving from antiquity, will no doubt remain a viable and popular way to personalize a private residence.

Fig. 31

4 Reflective Waters—
Lakes as a Prelude to Fountains

In earlier days, before the profusion of fountains, Kansas City had a great number of lakes. The elaborate schemes the Park Board envisioned to beautify those lakes foreshadowed the development of the elegant water displays that we know as fountains. The creation of man-made bodies of water in the urban environment was characteristic of a nationwide trend. A lake is a natural body of water collected in a depression, whereas mirror or reflecting pools are defined as formal, man-made bodies of water that approximate those natural lakes with still and reflective surfaces. Often, lakes and reflecting pools are equipped with pumps and jets to create vitality and visual interest on otherwise quiet surfaces. Many times these lakes and pools were used as formal landscaping elements in cemeteries, parks, and residential subdivisions. Kansas City has several fine examples of these "natural fountain vehicles" but has lost other water displays because many lakes and pools were drained, filled in, and forgotten.

Elmwood Cemetery Lake

In the late nineteenth century there was a concerted effort in the United States to landscape burial grounds so they resembled parks. These became known as "rural cemeteries," a term referring to a location outside of the city. The use of water in various ways was frequently an important means of beautifying cemetery grounds, ordinarily a place which people do not associate with scenic beauty. A lake was created for Elmwood, Kansas City's first rural cemetery, founded in 1872 at what is now Truman Road and Elmwood. At the time of its dedication it was surrounded by a picket fence. A prominent feature of the grounds was a clear brook, fed by several springs. Spanned by a rustic bridge, the brook rushed through a ravine with considerable force.

Ambitious improvements were considered involving alterations and modifications to this brook to create a cascade of water and the addition of a two-acre lake on the grounds. A second brook would be similarly treated with lakes, cascades, and rustic bridges. An 1872 lithographic map of the cemetery shows two lakes and two ponds within the cemetery. The 1891 *Atlas of Kansas City* indicates three bodies of water on the property. A few years later the brook was channeled through a culvert, and water features were no longer used to ornament the grounds.

Park Department Lakes

One of the first lakes constructed by the Park Department was The Paseo Lake, located in The Paseo median strip between Sixteenth and Seventeenth streets. The lake was created in 1898 specifically to collect

Fig. 32

the water used by the Fifteenth and The Paseo fountain, a "waste" fountain in which the water was not recirculated. Although man-made, great care was taken to keep the appearance of the lake as rustic and natural as possible (Fig. 32). The higher, north bank of the lake was lined with rough rocks, the shoreline was irregular, and the entire lake was surrounded by a profusion of vegetation. The lake continued in existence until it was drained, some time after 1908.

The Park Department acquired or created other lakes throughout the years. Spring Valley Park, a tract of thirty-nine acres at Twenty-seventh and Woodland, was acquired by the Park Department in 1902 and in 1930 in two parcels. As the name indicates, a spring was once on this property (Fig. 33). About 1905 the Park Department built a dam as part of a project to form a lake on the site. The lake no longer exists.

In 1907 the Grove, part of the park system at Benton and Truman Road, had a creek channel running through it. The Park Department planned to create a small water basin in the channel and to construct an interesting water garden, filled with aquatic plants. Plans were also under way in 1907 to create a pool and water garden in the quarry and spring located in Roanoke Park, west of Roanoke Road and north of Thirty-eighth Street.

Other lakes acquired or constructed by the city between 1902 and 1951 included the three and one-half acre Troost Lake at Twenty-seventh Street and The Paseo, a three-acre lake in Penn Valley Park, and the two-acre Bales Lake in Blue Valley Park.

Long before the Swope Park swimming pool was constructed in 1941, the Swope Park Lagoon was used as a swimming beach. In 1922 a fountain spray designed by the engineering firm of Harrington, Howard & Ash was added to the lagoon. A central jet forced a stream of water thirty feet into the air, and around the central jet twelve side jets sprayed water twenty feet in all directions.

Fig. 33

Loose Park Lake

When Loose Park was given to the city by Mrs. Jacob Loose in 1927 (see Chapter 12), a small lake was already on the grounds. Over the years, various improvements have been made. In 1934, under the direction of Superintendent of Parks W.H. Dunn, federal relief workers cleaned out and enlarged the lake. At that time, the banks were lined with stone, and an improved drainage system was added to prevent overflowing. Willows and other trees were planted on the banks.

By 1957 sediment had accumulated to such an extent that the water depth was only six to eight inches. The muck was removed, dried, and used elsewhere in the park system as fertilizer. An old storm sewer under the lake was replaced, and the sanitary sewer was removed and routed elsewhere. These improvements increased the depth to three feet—considered shallow enough not to endanger children interested in ice skating. The lake was reshaped, and a small island was created where waterfowl could take refuge from dogs and other marauders.

In April 1964, the lake was rebuilt again and beautified along the lines of a Japanese garden (Fig. 34), the impetus being a gift of $7,500 from the Junior League. The gift commemorated the league's fiftieth anniversary in Kansas City. The work again included draining and dredging the lake, slightly enlarging it, and redefining the shoreline to be more aesthetically pleasing. The west bank of the lake was bordered with sections of used telephone poles. A terrace level was constructed below a rock wall, increasing the visual interest along the west side of the lake. The purpose of the wall was to prevent dirt from washing into the lake, a problem that had necessitated dredgings on numerous occasions. An island with an arched bridge was added to the south end of the lake, and a small peninsula was formed to jut out into the body of water.

Fig. 34   In 1970, Mr. and Mrs. Richard Bloch provided additional funds for improvements, wishing to make the lagoon as enjoyable at night as it was during the day. Bloch at the time was vice-president of H&R Block, Inc. The substantial donation was used to provide night lighting for the lake and surrounding grounds. A single mushroom jet with a diameter of approximately ten feet was also installed in the south-center part of the lake. The improved lighting was cited as the "Lighting Design of the Year" in a commercial competition sponsored by the Electric Association of Kansas City.

J.C. Nichols Company Developments

Although J.C. Nichols is noted for extensive use of fountains and statuary for ornamentation throughout his real estate developments, he was also intrigued with the use of rustic, natural water effects as a landscaping element. The Crestwood subdivision, created by the Nichols Company in 1919-20, had an unusual feature: an "interior" park in the block bounded by Fifty-fifth, Fifty-fourth, Locust, and Cherry streets. The park was in the center of the block with residences on the perimeter. It was named the Happy Woods Park, and contained a pool that was fed by a spring. In essence, the pool was a small pond, and its irregular shoreline was lined with cut stone. Seated in the center on a stone was a small marble figure of a nude child (Fig. 35). The child was depicted laughing at a small bird perched on his knee.

This interior park was never a success. Although other parks and their maintenance could be turned over to the Park Department or to a neigh-
Fig. 35   borhood association, the upkeep of an interior park depended upon the

surrounding homeowners. No one seemed to want to assume the responsibility for the upkeep, and there was even a problem of people dumping trash into the pool. Eventually, the spring that fed the pool ceased to flow, and the pool was filled in and sodded.

In the 1920s, Nichols had as many as twenty small naturalistic dams constructed in Brush Creek and its tributaries to capture water into natural pools, particularly in the Mission Hills and Indian Hills developments in Kansas. The dams were constructed of weather-worn fieldstone and the result was a pleasing combination of quiet pools and rippling cascades.

The Nichols Company was also responsible for the development of two lakes in the Mission Hills area. The construction of one of those, Lake Hiwassee, began in 1924. This large lake, having a shoreline of almost a mile, was located south of Sixty-third Street with Indian Lane on the west and Wenonga Road on the east (Fig. 36). A large concrete dam constructed at Sixty-third Street to form the lake was faced with cobblestone in variegated colors. The lake, its plantings, and ornamentation were designed by the landscape architectural firm of Hare & Hare. The lake had an irregular, curving bank and a rock bottom with a depth of six to ten feet. A bridge over the dam on Sixty-third Street, embellished with four columns supporting stone lions, served as the portal to the Indian Hills subdivision. The lake was large enough to be used for boating, fishing, and ice skating. As on other lakes in the area, model boats were popular. In 1927, seventy-six model boats were entered in a regatta, the owner of each hoping to win a trophy presented by J.C. Nichols. Over the years the lake filled with silt, and the Mission Hills' officials apparently chose not to spend the money necessary to revitalize it. The dam and the bridge of the lions were removed and the lake was drained in the 1940s.

In 1925 Lake Willow was developed in Mission Hills on Ensley Lane south of Sixty-third Street (Fig. 37). Eventually, three homes were built on the lakefront property. In 1936, the Arthur Eisenhowers built the first home at the south end of the lake. Since they personally sponsored the

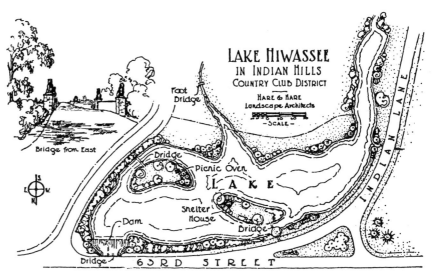

Fig. 36

Fig. 37

maintenance of the lake until the early 1960s, the lake came to be popularly known as "Eisenhower Lake." In 1962, two more homes were built on the lakeshore and their owners shared in the upkeep costs of the lake. Unfortunately, the lake had deteriorated severely by 1966; the water was stagnant and covered with scum. The condition of the lake generated considerable negative publicity, leading to its rehabilitation. It was probably at this time that two large mushroom jets were installed at the north and south ends of the lake.

In 1925, the J.C. Nichols Company turned an old stone quarry into a beautiful, sunken rock garden. The quarry had been used by the Nichols Company to provide stone for bridges, retaining walls, and roads in Mission Hills. When its usefulness as a quarry ended, the firm of Hare & Hare was commissioned to design a rock garden at the site. The Nichols Company hoped the garden would provide a model and inspiration for homeowners in the area to create their own rock gardens.

The finished garden at Overhill Road and Mission Drive had a spring at one end, which was used to send water trickling over the rocks into an irregularly-shaped pool, bordered by jutting rock outcroppings and blooming plants. A stairway of stone led down to the pool's edge, and a little shelter house and benches were incorporated into the garden setting (Fig. 38).

Five years later, Dr. Samuel Roberts had a Mediterranean-style mansion constructed to the north overlooking the sunken garden. Roberts

Fig. 38

had purchased the garden from the Nichols Company, and subsequent owners of the home have restored and maintained it, so it continues to beautify their dwelling as well as to provide a unique garden asset within the Mission Hills community.

5 Mirror Pools

Mirror pools, so named because of the reflective surface of the water contained within their basins, were especially popular during the 1920s. These man-made equivalents of small lakes or ponds were used for a variety of recreational purposes. In effect, the reservoirs of the Turkey Creek Pumping Station served as large mirror pools long before the height of their popularity. As early as 1876, according to published illustrations, these reservoirs were equipped with fountain jets, perhaps used to aerate the water. In 1911, a conscientious attempt was undertaken to beautify the grounds of the pumping station, used for storage, into park-like settings. The lawn in front of the pumping station was sodded, walkways were added, and a fountain became the focal point. The fountain consisted of a circular pool from which several jets propelled water upward.

The same year, 1911, there was a proposal to place a fountain in the middle of the reservoir at Observation Park. The plan was presented to the Park Board by Thomas W. Gilruth, a lawyer who lived in the area, and one hundred petitioners. There are no indications that this project to activate the still waters of the reservoir was ever undertaken.

Vintage photographs show that later mirror pools were used for the "maiden voyages" of toy sailboats and were perfect places for anglers to develop their casting techniques. The pools were sometimes called "casting pools," referring to their use by fishermen.

Kansas City Casting Pool/Gillham Park Wading Pool and Fountain

> And they say it is the cleanest, most fascinating sport in the world, and that when a man has once tried it he becomes a devotee of it for life.

The author of this statement, made in a newspaper article in 1914, was not reflecting on the merits of the sport of baseball, football, or soccer but rather on the "fine art" of bait and fly casting. At one time, there was as much enthusiasm for casting as there is currently for the more "contemporary" sports. Organizations such as the National Association of Scientific Angling Clubs founded chapters on a nationwide basis and held state and national competitions to determine the ranking anglers throughout the country. One of their conventions, held in San Francisco in 1916 during the Panama Exposition, offered prizes valued at $50,000. Chicago was a favorite gathering place for amateur casters in the early part of the century and boasted four specially designed pools constructed for $10,000 each, at that time a phenomenal cost. They were considered to be the finest in the country.

In 1914, seventy-five members of the Kansas City Bait and Fly Casting Club approached the Park Board and requested that such a pool be constructed. They justified their request by noting that without such a facility Kansas City could not hope to compete with Chicago for those contests to be held in the Midwest. Their proposal was accepted with enthusiasm, and plans were made to complete the pool by August of that year.

The *Kansas City Casting Pool* was located at Forty-first Street and Gillham Road, on the site near the present *Gillham Park Wading Pool and Fountain*. Although most pools in other cities were designed with circular basins, Kansas City's was to be designed "scientifically" because expert anglers testified that the secret to accurate casting was always to have the wind at your back. To accommodate this need, Kansas City's pool, 120 feet in diameter, had four triangular grassy peninsulas that divided the pool into channels which then formed the shape of a Maltese cross (Fig. 39). For the maximum effectiveness of his aim, the caster could position himself at any one of the channels, dependent upon the direction of the wind. A target was placed in the center of the intersecting arms of the water channels, sixty feet from the basin's edge, and was equipped with a bell to sound when an accurate cast was made. The channels were lined with concrete and graduated in depth from eighteen inches in the center to six inches at the outer rim.

The art of fly casting is little but nostalgia today as other interests compete for recreational time. The *Kansas City Casting Pool*, though completely rebuilt and enlarged in 1940, saw fewer and fewer fishermen and more and more sunbathers and waders. The unique design of the casting pool was replaced by another innovative design in 1975, this one unconcerned with the direction from which the breezes came.

During Frank Vaydik's tenure as Director of the Parks and Recreation Department, many novel approaches and nontraditional methods were introduced into Kansas City's recreational scheme. A *Kansas City Times* writer remarked that Vaydik "does not believe in rejecting the traditional just to do something different. But a concept that holds the promise of giving the city three benefits from a single improvement holds a strong appeal for him."

The writer made that statement in a 1975 review of a Park Department project, which was called "a novel experience on Gillham." The casting pool at Forty-first and Gillham Road had long since fallen into disrepair with the concrete broken and the pool in a run-down condition. The plumbing of the pool was antiquated and took hours to fill or drain. Because $90,000 of federal revenue sharing money was available, it was decided not to make extensive repairs but instead to construct a new "water experience."

The concept of this project incorporated multiple usage. It would be used as a wading pool, a fountain, and could even be used as a casting facility. Because of the plan's flexibility, the pool could be used beyond the limited summer months. It would embellish the city with another fountain that would be a highly visible element of Gillham Park.

The original design, presented to the Board of Parks and Recreation Commissioners by Park Board architect E.W. (Rusty) Corwin, called for a multitiered basin forming steps which led into a rectangular wading pool. The plan was tabled twice because the board felt that the original design was too dangerous. Commissioner Carl Migliazzo expressed his concern

Fig. 39

by saying, "The children are . . . going to be playing tag and running up and down, and they're going to slip and slide, and everyone of those youngsters is going to end up in General Hospital." Corwin, along with consulting engineer Wallace Beasley of Larkin & Associates, made corrective, though minor, changes to their initial plan, and in November 1975 those plans were approved. Their basic concept remained virtually intact, but important concessions were made for the safety of the public. The changes included widening a step to the water level from eight to eleven feet and separating the steps from the pool so that they would remain dry.

The Gillham Park Wading Pool and Fountain is designed for participation, and its scale, water effects, and location significantly contribute to its popularity. One of the most interesting aspects of the fountain is its integration of a series of water effects. Cascades, bubbler jets, and streams flood the fountain with activity.

The fountain is built in a modified rectangular plan with slabs of concrete that project and form platforms similar to the risers of a stage (Fig. 40). It is built into the rise of a low hill with the wading pool placed at the base and many of the water-producing elements of the fountain located at the summit, where the water can fall naturally to the lower elevation.

Three bubbler jets set within rectangular islands are placed at the north and south ends and in the middle of the fountain construction at its highest point. The jets produce thick, aerated mounds of water, which appear almost as solid forms. Placed at the center of the summit is a concrete slab that overhangs considerably, and water flowing over the slab produces a sheeting effect. Channels for the runoff are provided and contain the water until it accumulates and falls onto the lowermost tiers of the wading basin.

Fig. 40

The fountain is operated from the early spring into the late fall, long after the bathers have left its cool streams. It is illuminated at night and has become a point of reference for Kansas Citians who travel in that part of the city. The "novel experience on Gillham" has proven to be a complete success and is a fitting alternative for a tradition long since displaced by other activities.

Haff Circle Mirror Pool and Fountain

Contemporary citizens of Kansas City, having had the good fortune to enjoy the benefits and facilities of the park system, seldom realize that the whole concept of a park system was once in jeopardy. During the 1890s there was a growing movement for the planning and establishment of public parks, but there was also a considerable, well-organized lobby opposing the plan. That conservative group, known as the "Hammer and Padlock Club," felt that the funds necessary to finance and maintain the parks would lead to onerous taxation, and they made every effort to block the plans of the park supporters.

Delbert J. Haff began work as an attorney for the Park Board in the 1890s. He was solely responsible for resolving the many legal obstacles created by the park opponents and for devising a lawful method for the Park Board to levy taxes for land acquisition. In 1892, Haff drafted a charter amendment which provided for the geographical division of the city into districts, each of which would be taxed separately. Although the amendment was passed, soon thereafter it was declared void by the courts.

Undaunted, Haff redesigned his plan to include an innovative provision which would allow taxpayers as much as twenty years to pay their tax assessments. It would also permit the city to sell Park Certificates, which were actually the same as bonds or notes to be redeemed from future tax payments. In 1895 the voters passed the amendment by a margin of seven to one, and this time the decision was upheld by the courts.

After his success with the charter amendment which gave new impetus to the establishment of a public park system, Haff continued to be a member of the Park Board and served as president from 1908 until 1912. Haff, along with board members August R. Meyer, Simeon B. Armour, Adriance Van Brunt, and landscape architect George Kessler, formulated a master plan for Kansas City's parks and boulevards. During Mr. Haff's tenure on the board, the city entered its decisive phase in land acquisition and development. Established were Holmes Square, North Terrace Park, Penn Valley Park, West Terrace Park, The Parade, Walnut Grove, Independence Boulevard, Benton Boulevard, The Paseo Boulevard, Gillham Road, Armour Boulevard, and Troost Park.

Delbert Haff was born in rural Michigan in 1859. After attending college, he came to Kansas City in 1886 and began a law practice. Haff's conscientious, methodical approach to the law soon won him many clients and an excellent reputation. He became a business associate of railroad magnate Arthur Stilwell and began a long career as a railway attorney. During the expansion of rail lines into Mexico, he became a nationally recognized expert on Mexican law.

The contributions Haff made to Kansas City's system of parks and boulevards were enormous. Because of his achievements, proposals to honor him were made even during his lifetime. In 1916, a leading local sculptor, Jorgen Dreyer, was commissioned to create a portrait bust of Haff. After its completion, it was inexplicably placed in storage and was not displayed publicly until 1967, many years after Haff's death.

He was, however, recognized during his lifetime, for in 1940, when Haff was eighty-one years of age, the Park Board acted to recognize his achievements. They determined that the landscaped circle outside the entrance to Swope Park should be dedicated in his honor. The proposal to identify the circle was initiated by a committee of the Patriots' and Pioneers' Foundation, which had earlier petitioned the board to name a ball park for Mr. Haff. The board felt that designating an athletic field was not sufficient appreciation of Haff's contributions, but they heartily agreed that the 600-foot circle at the junction of Meyer and Swope Parkway, forming a focal point to the entrance to Swope Park, would be an appropriate tribute.

The circle itself was created in 1927 and was landscaped by W.H. Dunn, superintendent of parks. The area was planted with flower beds and shrubbery to make it one of the most attractive spots in the city. Just a few months before the dedication, Works Progress Administration workmen were completing the rectangular mirror pool directly west of Haff Circle.

The pool is virtually identical to the *Northeast Concourse Casting Pool/Fountain* which was constructed several years later. It was designed with a low retaining wall of coursed stone and a shallow basin two and a half feet deep. This pool was also designed with the miniature yacht in mind and was dedicated with a sailboat racing event at which some 250 vessels competed.

In the summer of 1966, the pool was equipped with a center spray ring and seven vertical jets that cycle every ninety seconds, carrying the water twenty-five feet into the air. Colored lights added drama when the display was illuminated at night. The fountain was one of the first to be in operation on a year-round basis; it dazzled its audiences with the effects that were produced in winter when ice formed around the spray heads.

It was mainly through the efforts of former Parks Director Frank Vaydik that the final tribute to Delbert Haff was achieved. Mr. Vaydik expressed his astonishment that nowhere in the city was there a plaque or marker specifically naming the accomplishments of Mr. Haff. Vaydik discovered the long forgotten sculpture and moved swiftly for its installation at the west end of the mirror pool fountain. The bust was installed in June 1967, during a ceremony attended by Mr. Haff's daughter, Mrs. R. Harrison Field. The setting is now complete, as the bust of Mr. Haff looks serenely toward the largest and one of the most beautiful parks in the city—a part of the park system which he was instrumental in creating.

Ward Parkway Mirror Pool and Fountain

In 1924, as part of their beautification efforts along Ward Parkway, the J.C. Nichols Company constructed a mirror pool between Sixty-first Terrace and Sixty-second Street (Fig. 41). The pool measured 250 feet in length and 65 feet in width, with straight sides and curved ends. Four stone baskets filled with flowers carved in relief were placed on the stone *Fig. 41* wall at the junctions of the sides and semicircular ends. Coursed stone

Fig. 42 was used to construct the low retaining wall of the basin. The pool was transformed into a fountain by the installation of a series of water jets arranged intermittently along the center of the basin (Plate 21, page 47).

The original plumbing of the pool deteriorated after many years of operation, and in 1959 a major refurbishing of the fountain was required. Under the direction of the Park Department, the stone walls were repaired, the bottom resurfaced with crushed sand and rock, and new drain pipes installed. The sprays of water, which had been inoperative, were restored to full operating condition.

A second renovation effort was completed in 1965 after an incident in which more than 500 dead fish were found floating in the pool. Although the Park Department was aware that goldfish were being maintained in the pool, the number and the infinite variety of the fish found were a surprise. After removing the fish (many of which were unsolicited donations), new jets were installed, and underwater lights were added.

The fountain is currently equipped with three sets of spray rings. The central group consists of a vertical jet in the center of a spray ring which produces an outside fall. The two rings on either side of it are identical to the central water display but designed to produce jets of lesser height. By focusing attention toward the center of the pool, the designers achieved a symmetry to the composition.

Northeast Concourse Casting Pool/Fountain

In the 1920s and 1930s, the organized sport of miniature yacht racing boasted a huge number of devotees. Young boys would spend hours in shop classes, building these small ships, generally from one to three feet long, which were realistically rigged with sail. There were three locations in the city that were especially suited to racing this flotilla: *Haff Circle Mirror Pool*, *Ward Parkway Mirror Pool*, and *Northeast Concourse Casting Pool* (Fig. 42).

Construction of the *Northeast Concourse Casting Pool* began in March 1939 on the parkway between Gladstone and Benton boulevards, south of the colonnade which overlooked the bluffs. The construction of the 100 x 150 foot rectangular basin with coursed stone retaining walls was a project undertaken by the Works Progress Administration and was ready for use in June 1939. The dedication ceremony, highlighted by a race between 500 miniature ships and presided over by a former World War I naval ensign, initiated the city's first annual regatta.

The pool, enjoyed for its naval races, was also one of the most popular places for young fishermen to practice the fine art of casting. The Parks and Recreation Department frequently sponsored classes where professionals instructed young anglers in their technique.

Over time, all the city's casting pools were converted into fountains. The *Northeast Concourse Casting Pool* was converted to the *Northeast Concourse Fountain*, as the result of a decision made by the Board of Parks and Recreation Commissioners in February 1967. By May 1968 the casting pool had been equipped with multiple jet sprays, adding a new dimension to the pool but disrupting the quiet waters necessary for sailing.

From its construction in 1939, the *Northeast Concourse Casting Pool/ Fountain* has enjoyed a special reputation because of its year-round operation. When it was constructed, the walls of the surrounding basin were equipped with expansion and contraction joints so that it could be used for ice skating in the winter. When the fountain jets were added in the late 1960s, the fountain's reputation for year-round participation was enhanced.

The mirror pool is fitted with a number of spray rings and individual jets that are programmed to cycle from greater to lesser heights. During the winter months the water remains running with the result that every year some spectacular "ice sculptures" are formed by the growing accumulation of ice. When illuminated at night, the ice takes on a magical quality when the colors play off the glistening mounds of frozen water (Plate 22, page 49). The *Northeast Concourse Fountain* has taken on its own special identity relative to other Kansas City fountains as each winter many people make a pilgrimage to see what new frozen water configurations nature has chosen to create.

6 Conventional Fountain Forms

Basin Fountains

One of the simplest fountain forms consists solely of a geometric retaining basin or pool equipped with a series of water jets. Although the basin itself is subject to variations, such as smaller pools within the larger pool, the form retains a basic integrity. The reasons for its continuing popularity include its relatively low installation and maintenance cost and the latitude it gives its creators to employ a multitude of different water effects. The simple fountain pool made its earliest appearance centuries ago, yet it remains one of the most popular of all the fountain conventions.

The Fifteenth Street and The Paseo Fountain

The first fountain erected by the Kansas City Park Department was at Fifteenth Street and The Paseo and was labeled a "white elephant" almost as soon as it was placed in operation. Although the design was ambitious, the fountain was beset with problems from the very beginning, and it was finally torn down in 1941.

The fountain was designed by the father of Kansas City's park and boulevard system, George Kessler. It was one of the decorative elements on formally designed The Paseo Boulevard and was located south of the Fifteenth Street intersection. The fountain was modeled after the classic *Fountain of Latona* in Versailles, France (Fig. 43).* However, the French prototype is much more ornate than the Kansas City version. The unusual tiered design of the Fifteenth and The Paseo fountain is directly adapted from the Versailles fountain, but the figural sculpture around the Versailles basin rims was not included in the Kansas City work, probably because of economic reasons. Instead of a traditional basin set into the ground, this fountain rose above the ground in five circular terraces (Fig. 44). The lowest terrace was eighty-six feet in diameter. The smallest and highest terrace rose fifteen feet above the ground. The pipes from which the water issued were removed from view but were designed so that the water would rise from the inner edges of each terrace, the spray would converge above the center, and then unite with a stream originating at the summit. The water, dropping back, would fall from one terrace to another. Originally, colored electric lights were to be concealed beneath the terrace edges, turning the cascading water into brilliant rainbows of color at night. The plan for lights was abandoned in the finished work because it was thought to be impractical. The fountain was to cost $12,000, and contracts were awarded in September 1898. The project was completed almost one year later.

*The *Fountain of Latona* was constructed in 1665-66, and the figures, by Marsy, were added in 1671. It is one of the major fountains in the formal gardens of Versailles, occupying a place of honor along the main promenade from the chateau.

Fig. 43

On May 14, 1899, after a long session at City Hall, the members of the Park Commission met at the fountain to witness its action for the first time. An account of that observation reported: "A man turned the valves which sent the water rushing through the many pipes, a shaft of water shot ten feet high from the summit and fell back upon the structure's pinnacle with a crash, scores of bubbles played along the rims of the five terraces while numerous sprays shot up from the interior of the great lower basin . . . Then, when the various basins filled, the water fell in cascades from terrace to terrace."

The first of many problems was noticed almost immediately. Instead of water falling over the terraces in a "mountain torrent sort of way," the water simply rippled gently and quietly over the edges. Kessler was optimistic that this fault could be quickly remedied by the addition of more jets and the rearrangement of the sprays. At first a four-inch main supplied water at the rate of sixteen gallons per second. Soon, another main of the same size was added, providing thirty-two gallons of water per second, without noticeably improving the effect.

The Fifteenth and The Paseo fountain was a "waste" fountain; that is, one in which the water simply drained away after its display through the fountain, in this case into The Paseo Lake, 300 feet to the south. Obviously, this made the fountain expensive to operate. Soon after the fountain was completed, Assistant City Engineer Stephen J. Mitchell suggested a way to make the fountain perform more economically. He proposed reusing the water in a bathhouse located at the parade, a level area nearby which had been developed into a playground. Kessler agreed that this was a more practical idea, but there is no evidence to confirm that the idea was pursued.

In 1900, the fountain was operating at least to some degree. An incident that summer focused negative publicity on the fountain when a woman was thrown into it. Outdoor concerts on the site contributed to other raucous activity, and, as a result, the concerts were relocated to a park called the Grove at Fifteenth Street and Chestnut. The fountain continued to operate, but only intermittently, and finally was turned off in 1903.

By May 1908 the people in the neighborhood were complaining to the

Fig. 44

Park Board about the "big, scaly pyramid standing there in idleness and staring dryly back at them." Their suggestions were that it should be either torn down or converted into a flower garden. Hesitant to admit defeat and to have the fountain demolished, the board considered experimenting with the addition of a recirculating pump so that its operation would be less costly. The engineer who was assigned to evaluate this possibility thought that the fountain might be operational, even after its long dormancy, and the water was turned on. Instead, "The fountain awoke from its five-year sleep, stretched, groaned, and burst. About half of the north side of it fell apart with a clatter." That disaster effectively ended the board's plans for revitalization, so it was decided to have all but the lower basin removed and to build that wall a little higher. Lilies, moss, and aquatic plants were to be placed in the water-filled basin with graceful vines trailing over the rim. A water display would remain, consisting of a small stream rising from the center and trickling down over the plants, and a reduction would be made in the size of the remaining jets.

Work was completed on the reconstruction and alteration of the fountain in September 1908. Instead of a fountain featuring aquatic plants as originally planned, a large crowd gathered to witness the first operation of what was now being called a "rainbow fountain" (Fig. 45). Twenty-one jets of water were arranged around the rim of the reconstructed

Fig. 45

basin, sending streams of water twenty-five feet into the air to converge into a dazzling cone of water. When the new fountain was turned on for the first time, the sun had just reached a point in the west so that a rainbow effect was produced by the falling water. The fountain was still not equipped with a recirculating pump, and the spent water continued to be channeled into The Paseo Lake. To minimize costs, the fountain operated only during afternoons and at night.

In 1941, Superintendent of Parks J.V. Lewis reported that a large section of the bottom of the fountain had dropped from its base into a pit below, and the central column had settled, ripping the plumbing apart. It was estimated that it would cost between $1,500 and $2,000 to repair it, which was considered too costly. A decision was made to raze the fountain and to beautify the grounds with a flower bed.

The passing of this once great fountain did not go unnoted. A writer for the *Kansas City Star* reflected that, "There's a place in our cities for such things as a replica of the *Fountain of Latona*. The fact that we had a Latona Fountain here inspired me . . . to go across the seas to France and out to the gardens of Versailles one Sunday afternoon just to see the Latona and her sister fountains playing."

Fig. 46

The Ninth Street and The Paseo Fountain

Fate was kinder to the fountain at Ninth Street and The Paseo, constructed at the same time as the Fifteenth Street and The Paseo fountain. In June 1898, Arnold Sutermeister's bid of $4,115 was accepted by the Park Board for the cut stone and foundation for the fountain, located just south of Ninth Street on The Paseo median strip. According to newspaper accounts, this fountain was designed by George Kessler; however, several of the drawings that still exist for the fountain were delineated by John Van Brunt, who was working for the Park Board as an architect. Because Van Brunt was known as a gifted designer and Kessler must have been very busy in 1898 implementing his master plan for the park system, it seems only reasonable to conclude that Van Brunt played a major role in the design of the fountain, beyond merely drawing the plans. Although the initial concept was Kessler's, it seems clear that the final design was a joint effort.

The first plans were dated May 1898 but were revised in July of that year. Both plans called for a cut stone, oval fountain pool measuring approximately sixty feet in diameter at its widest point. The original plans

were to place the pool close to Ninth Street with a narrow flower garden curving along the north edge of the pool. The revision showed the fountain moved back from the street to give more space for an oval paved court with a similarly shaped flower garden in its center. The fountain was constructed according to the revised plans (Fig. 46).

The south half of the basin featured a cut stone balustrade. Several piers supported either spherical lamps or stone globes at intervals along the balustrade. Steps on the east and the west led from the fountain area to The Paseo and were flanked by ornamental gas lights. A single, two-inch pipe rose from the center of the pool. A large nozzle attached to this pipe sent the fountain waters skyward.

The construction of the fountain was completed by May 1899. Because it was so much simpler in concept and design than the Fifteenth Street and The Paseo fountain, this fountain operated apparently without the difficulties that plagued the other fountain. However, at some point the equipment rusted out, and the fountain basin was simply filled with earth instead of being repaired.

The basin was excavated and repaired in 1970. Working with federal funds earmarked specifically for restoring inner city parks, the Park Board purchased new equipment for the fountain, including a multicolored, sequential light system and a recirculating pump. The fountain is still in operation today, but it has only a shadow of its former beauty. The balustrade has been removed, and the wall clumsily patched; the flower gardens that added color to the area are gone; and the ornamental gas lamps are no longer there. Only an oval basin remains to attest to the charm of this early park system fountain.

Colonnade Fountain

The colonnade in North Terrace Park was completed in 1908 and functioned as an ornamental, visual terminus at the north end of the concourse at Gladstone Boulevard and St. John Avenue. With two wings of classical columns extending from each side of a semicircular central pavilion, this beaux-arts inspired edifice was used primarily as a deluxe bandstand for summer concerts.

A fountain was placed in front of the central pavilion area, probably in the spring of 1909. This simple water display consisted of a circular concrete retaining basin, eighteen feet in diameter (Fig. 47). Five water outlets grouped in the center propelled water into the air. Its designer, Henry Wright, worked in the St. Louis office of landscape architect George Kessler.

Records do not indicate when the fountain was removed. It is probable that when the plumbing rusted out it was simply not repaired. A memorial to John F. Kennedy now occupies the site.

Pedestal Fountains

Another familiar form is the pedestal, or free-standing, fountain. This type, especially popular for smaller settings and ideal within gardens, is composed of one or more saucers surrounding and supported by a main

Fig. 47

stem. The central stem acts as the channel for the water that is carried upward to the highest level.

Many of these fountains are combined with figural sculpture either abutting the pedestal or surmounting the highest saucer. Relief carving has also been employed to add a unique dimension to a standard form.

The pedestal fountain is frequently found in combination with a reflecting pool that has been equipped with a series of water displays, thus adding to the dialogue of the waters.

Scottish Rite Temple Fountain

During the fall of 1928, ground was broken for the massive Scottish Rite Temple at the northwest corner of Linwood Boulevard and The Paseo. The $1.5 million structure, utilizing classical architectural elements, was designed by Kansas City architects Keene & Simpson. The building was completed and dedicated in December 1930, and it is still occupied by the Scottish Rite organization.

Before the automobile became the prevailing means of transportation, when most of the members of the temple still used streetcars, the principal entrance to the building was from the Linwood Boulevard side. The ground area in front of this side of the building was paved with concrete. In more recent years, a side entrance next to a parking lot has become the primary entrance. In view of this change, it was decided in the late 1970s to remove the concrete apron in front of the building and to landscape the grounds.

Orville Anderson, longtime member of the temple and Potentate of the Ararat Shrine in 1950, decided to contribute to the beautification of the temple grounds by donating funds for a fountain. Anderson, an insurance executive, has a long history of civic and political involvement. In 1911 he and his brothers L.C. (Andy) and Dallas established Anderson Photo Company, the oldest photographic company in the city. Dallas Anderson died in 1948, and L.C. continued management of the firm until his death in 1952. Orville Anderson then assumed active management of

Fig. 48 the firm until selling the company in 1977. Dallas and L.C. Anderson were also active members of the Scottish Rite Temple. In fact, when several items were placed in a box and sealed into the cornerstone of the temple in 1929, one of those items was a small piece of stone from King Solomon's quarry, a gift from L.C. Anderson. Anderson had acquired the stone during one of his many trips abroad.

On bestowing the fountain, Orville Anderson dedicated it to his brothers. It was designed by Jack Furlong, an aeronautical engineer, who was the executive secretary of the Scottish Rite Temple. This is the only fountain designed by Mr. Furlong, and he created a representation of the fraternal organization itself. His creation is built with a series of basins which gradually diminish in size as they ascend from the base of the fountain, culminating in a bronze square and compass, the symbol of the Blue Lodge (Fig. 48). The smallest basin at the top represents the York Rite; the middle basin, the Scottish Rite; the bottom basin, the largest, represents the Shrine. Water flows from the bronze square and compass at the top, then trickles from bowl to bowl to be recirculated. Flowers are planted within the stone retaining walls surrounding the fountain, which is illuminated for nighttime viewing.

The bronze piece at the top was fabricated by a member of the Shrine from Sedalia, Missouri. The bowls were purchased from a local stone company. The fountain and its surrounding circular stone retaining walls were erected in 1979 by members of the temple who donated their labor.

The fountain is a good example of the pedestal type but is unique in its purpose. Not only does it provide a remembrance of members of a well-known business firm who were active in the temple but it also represents the Shrine itself.

Newport Apartment Fountain

A pedestal fountain graces a small, landscaped area in front of the Newport Apartment Building at 3536-42 Baltimore Avenue. The fountain is intriguing because so little of its origin and history is known (Fig. 49).

The current owners of the apartment building purchased the fountain from the old St. Joseph Hospital at Linwood Boulevard and Prospect. The fountain was one of the many objects of salvageable material sold before demolition of the building began in 1980.

At one time the fountain had been placed in a formal rose garden setting at the hospital. In scale and design it is remarkably similar to the horse-trough fountain that was located at the Kansas end of the Intercity Viaduct (subsequently removed to the Wyandotte County Historical Society Museum in Bonner Springs, Kansas). The similarities are so strong as to foster speculation that perhaps this fountain was also a horse-trough fountain before being placed in the hospital rose garden.

Since its relocation at the Newport Apartment, the owners have added a sculptural embellishment, consisting of a small boy struggling to hold a bird. The water elements of this fountain are no longer intact.

Fig. 49

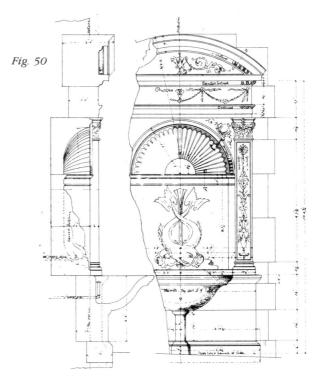

Fig. 50

Exterior Wall Fountains

Wall fountains share a special relationship to architecture because the wall functions as an architectural backdrop and becomes an integral part of the fountain itself. The best-known example of its type is the legendary *Fountain of Trevi* in Rome, Italy. Kansas City's wall fountains have been somewhat more modest in concept and scale.

The first mention of a wall fountain to be erected in the city was as part of the formal scheme for the embellishment of The Paseo Boulevard. The median strip between Eleventh and Twelfth streets on The Paseo was purposely designed not to follow the grade of the street (which is several feet lower at Twelfth Street than at Eleventh Street) to allow construction of a tall, curved, stone retaining wall at the Twelfth Street end of the median. Stone stairsteps on each side of the wall provided an entrance to what was essentially an elevated plaza. From the summit of the plaza, the spectator would have a perfect vantage point to view the elaborate sunken flower garden that was located on the next block, between Twelfth and Thirteenth streets.

The original plan of the Park Department was to affix a large, decorative drinking fountain to the south end of this stone wall. This wall fountain was designed by Park Board architect John Van Brunt in February 1899. Evidently the fountain was never constructed, but Van Brunt was not to forget either the site or his plans. Nineteen years later he had the opportunity to design the *William Fitzsimons Memorial Fountain* and to recommend its installation at this site. His design for the *Fitzsimons Memorial Fountain*, which was dedicated in 1922, is remarkably similar to his proposed design of 1899 (Fig. 50). Both have strong classical influences expressed in the decorative relief panels on the sides, terminating in decorative capitals, in the egg and dart molding, and in the rounded pediment. Van Brunt simply had to alter some of the details to convert his earlier plan into the *Fitzsimons Memorial Fountain*. The swag relief in the curved pediment was replaced with a carved eagle. The entwined dolphins beneath a semicircular shell, from which the water was to flow and which took up the center portion of the work, were replaced by an inscription panel.

Observation Park Fountain

During his tenure with the Park Board, John Van Brunt had another chance to create a wall fountain in the improvements to Observation Park. The city employed the New York-based National Waterworks Company to develop its water system in 1873. The main reservoir of the waterworks was in the vicinity of Fairmount and East Twenty-fourth Street. With Turkey Creek flowing just to the east, the plant was called the Turkey Creek Pumping Station. Water was pumped from the Turkey Creek reservoir to an upper reservoir on an elevated site between Twentieth and Twenty-first streets, Jarboe to Holly. From here, aided by the force of gravity, the water would flow into the homes built at lower elevations. When the city bought the waterworks in 1895 and instituted municipal

Fig. 51

operation, this upper reservoir was included in the purchase. The portion not taken up by the nine-million gallon reservoir itself was given to the Park Department in May 1899 for its development as Observation Park. As the Park Board noted: "Its unique position on a high point on the western bluffs, with lower ground all around, makes it a central point of observation and presents from its summit a perfect panoramic view of the southwestern part of the city."

The two-acre park overlooked the Kaw Valley and the confluence of the Kaw and Missouri rivers. Within a few months after its acquisition, the Park Department had developed a master plan for the park to include a main entrance at the north end, on West Twentieth Street; a comfort station and bandstand near the middle of the park, just north of the reservoir; and a southern entrance on West Twenty-first Street, with an observation tower approached by a flight of steps.

The main entrance featured a cut stone wall, flanked by a double staircase. Mounted on the stone wall between the stairways was an ornamental drinking fountain. Plans for the fountain were drawn by John Van Brunt in November 1897, and it was probably constructed around 1899. The fountain was composed of a round arched niche with a relief carving of a lion placed in the center (Fig. 51). A single stream of water issued from the lion's mouth to fall into a projecting semicircular basin. A relief floral carving was executed for the semicircular area surrounding the lion's head.

Observation Park reached the zenith of its popularity at the close of the nineteenth century principally because of the commanding views it provided. The park eventually became underutilized, plagued by vandalism, and by 1939 was essentially abandoned.

Today the park is again being used. The reservoir has been filled in, and baseball diamonds are where it used to be. Some of the stone retaining walls remain. The stone wall and double staircase now lead up to the ball diamonds. The fountain basin has disappeared, but the stone lion's head still remains, although badly weathered.

Hall's Plaza Fountains

The animal-head motif was especially popular for wall fountains and in more recent years was the theme chosen for the wall fountains that grace Hall's Plaza store, a specialty department store. Hall's, which opened in 1965, was designed in a Spanish-Moorish style to continue the theme of the older Plaza architecture. Mexican craftsmen were employed for many of the exterior embellishments of the building, including the iron grillwork, the mahogany entrance doors, and the exterior wall fountains.

Three wall fountains set in arched niches are affixed to the exterior of the building. Each of the arches is different, and their designs were reportedly inspired by the Alhambra, a fine example of Moorish architecture near Seville, Spain. The two fountains on the south wall of the building also derive their inspiration from the Alhambra, for the animal figures that are part of these fountains are modeled after the famous Alhambra *Court of the Lions Fountain*.

At the east end of the south wall of the Hall's building is a fountain consisting of a rectangular niche containing a lion figure of black volcanic stone, whose body seems to be emerging from the stuccoed background of the niche. The lion issues a single stream of water from its mouth into a projecting semicircular retaining basin of red stone, approximately one and one-half feet deep. The pediment of the niche exhibits a curvilinear baroque treatment, and the keystone is inscribed with a decorative motif (Fig. 52).

An identical basin and lion figure compose the fountain at the west end of the south side of the building. The only differences are the use of a voluted pediment and the side panels of the rectangular niche, which have shields carved in relief upon them.

The third fountain, located on the west side of the Hall's building, exhibits an entirely different treatment and is set within a tiled niche surrounded by a horseshoe arch. The fountain has two basins: one of red stone which rests on the sidewalk and another of black volcanic stone which is placed above it and affixed within the center of the niche. Placed above the smaller basin is the protruding head of a cat, which is also carved in the volcanic stone material. Although this fountain is no longer operating, it was designed so that a single stream of water would flow from the mouth of the cat into the smaller upper basin, and then overflow to the larger red stone basin. Both basins are now planted with flowers.

Fig. 52

Proposed Pershing Road Fountain

A variation of the traditional wall fountain is created when a backdrop is built specifically for the application of a fountain element that bears no integral relationship to a building itself. Such a "fabricated" wall was proposed for a fountain at McGee Trafficway and Pershing Road in 1939. Although this fountain was never constructed, it represents an early use of this "free-standing" wall fountain (Fig. 53).

Fig. 53

In the late 1930s, the east side of McGee at Pershing Road had the appearance of an unsightly clay bank, from which an old spring poured out a steady stream of water. Mayor Bryce B. Smith and City Manager H.F. McElroy were anxious to embellish the east end of Pershing Road in some way, especially since the site was visible from Union Station and played a part in every visitor's initial impression of the city. Homer Neville of the architectural firm Gentry, Voskamp & Neville drew a presentation sketch for the mayor and city manager who were anxious to initiate the project. The work was to have been carried out with Works Progress Administration funds with the city supplying some materials, including rock quarried from Penn Valley Park. The total cost to the city for this fountain would have been only $2,000.

The plan called for a graceful curved rock wall twenty feet in height. Openings near the top of this wall would allow three streams of water to gush out and fall into an elliptical retaining basin, twenty feet at its widest point at the street level. Extending on each side of the central wall would be three terraced wings of native stone with plantings of decorative shrubs. The overall length of the fountain would have been 164 feet.

Unfortunately, the Works Progress Administration funds necessary for the project were never received. Mr. Neville speculates, "The authorities for these funds may have remembered that we, as architects for the old Municipal Auditorium, had used the largest WPA fund ever given at that time for a public building. They may have thought then that Kansas City had had enough."

In the early 1960s, a fountain was eventually installed on Pershing Road at Main. This was a project of the Stalcup Company, a firm specializing in outdoor advertising. The simple fountain consisted of a raised basin, with smaller basins placed inside. It was demolished when the development of Crown Center began.

Fig. 54

Old American Insurance Company Fountain

More modern versions of the "free-standing" wall fountain have been erected. A wall fountain was part of the original design of the Old American Insurance Company building at 4900 Oak Street, designed in 1959 by the Kansas City architectural firm of Voskamp & Slezak. Here the fountain is incorporated into a granite upright, approximately thirty feet long, that carries the words identifying the building. A row of water outlets, placed perpendicular to the wall, issues a gentle cascade of water. The resulting waterfall pours into the recess of a rectangular retaining pool where it is recirculated (Fig. 54).

Nichols Restaurant Fountain

Another variation of this kind of wall fountain is located at the southwest corner of Thirty-ninth Terrace and Southwest Trafficway, decorating

Fig. 55

the Nichols Restaurant parking lot. Formerly known as Nichols Lunch, the restaurant was founded by Frank Nichols in 1921. Nichols, a native of Linistaina, Greece, died in 1962, and the restaurant operation was continued by his son Jimmie Nichols. The parking lot for the popular restaurant was built in 1971, at which time the fountain was erected (Fig. 55).

As a tribute to his father, Jimmie Nichols commissioned a duplicate of a fountain in his father's native mountain village in southern Greece, which was used for drinking water and for washing. The result is a novel fountain for Kansas City, incorporating traditional metal lions heads with mouths spouting water; classical design elements that recall Nichols' Greek heritage (the Greek fret frieze); and a variety of stones that could serve as a geology lesson. The surface of the wall is inset with lava rock, pink marble, petrified wood, malachite, chryscolla, pyrite, and obsidian. A common toilet tank mechanism simply, but effectively, provides part of the fountain's mechanical system.

Interior Wall Fountains

A wall fountain is especially adaptable for interior use. It can provide the pleasing, restful sight and sound of water without taking up as much space as a fountain basin. There are innumerable wall fountains in Kansas City that decorate not only residences but also commercial buildings; however, a few representative examples can illustrate their particular charm.

J.C. Nichols Company Fountain

A wall fountain was used to decorate the offices of the J.C. Nichols Company at 310 Ward Parkway on the Country Club Plaza. In the company's headquarters building, constructed in 1930, the wall fountain is

Fig. 56

Fig. 57

located on the east wall of the first floor lobby (Fig. 56). It is composed of an arched niche approximately six feet high and four feet wide. The arch is faced with decorative colored tiles from Mexico depicting knights in armor alternating with tiles illustrating heraldic crests. In the center of the niche was a metal lion's head whose mouth served as an outlet for a single stream of water which was carried into a semicircular basin below. In more recent years, the fountain was disconnected because water occasionally overflowed. The basin was filled with growing tropical plants, the niche was veneered with cork, and only the colored tile arch remains.

D.W. Newcomer's Sons Funeral Home Fountain

Another distinguished example of a wall fountain within a commercial structure was the interior wall fountain at D.W. Newcomer's Sons Funeral Home at 1331 Brush Creek. D.W. Newcomer's was organized in 1893. Between 1898 and 1925 the company was located in a building at 2107-11 East Ninth Street, where it established a reputation as one of the most progressive burial firms in the Midwest. In 1916, while at the Ninth Street address, they added the first crematorium and columbarium (vault) rooms in Kansas City. The three columbarium rooms consisted of compartments for the permanent or temporary storage of several hundred urns. A deliberate attempt was made to lessen the funereal aspects of these rooms by means of their decor. The floors were of red tile, the walls and woodwork were painted a light color, and Turkish rugs and cream-colored wicker furniture further brightened the space. On one wall were two recesses lined with jutting rocks over which water fell constantly into shallow basins containing goldfish.

Fig. 58

In 1925 a new D.W. Newcomer's facility was constructed at 1331 Brush Creek. This building underwent a major expansion in 1936. Edward Buehler Delk, early designer of the Country Club Plaza, was employed as architect during both phases of construction of the Newcomer's building. He designed a wall fountain for the columbarium room, a part of the addition. This fountain, which is no longer operational, consisted of a jet installed within a ceramic-tiled arch, seven feet high and five feet wide (Fig. 57). A rectangular basin projected at the base of the tile panel. A decorative panel at the basin level features a cat-o'-nine-tails design. Near the top of the arch is a lion's head, which serves as the water outlet. The components for this fountain were purchased from standard stock patterns of the Mueller Mosaic Company in Trenton, New Jersey, at a cost of $150.*

D.W. Newcomer's Sons also has an interesting exterior wall fountain in the recessed courtyard area on the north side of the building. This fountain is set into a shallow, round arched niche (Fig. 58). The fountain consists of a protruding semicircular marble bowl at the base and a smaller basin above. Between the two basins is a carved relief depicting the head of a bearded man. His mouth is used as the water outlet for a stream of water which falls into the larger basin. Mounted above the smaller, upper basin is an upended dolphin, whose tail curls in a decorative loop. The dolphin's mouth provides the outlet for water to flow into the upper basin. Water trickles out of the upper basin, over the head of the man, into the lower basin, from which it spills out into a semicircular retaining basin below.

---

*The Mueller Mosaic Company also provided the metal lion's head that serves as the water outlet for a rectangular reflecting pool in the courtyard on the north side of the building.

7 Memorial Fountains

The development of the park and boulevard system in Kansas City and the publicity which resulted from its success undoubtedly boosted the city's self-image because during the early twentieth century a new awareness and appreciation for the beauty of the city emerged. Editorials in local newspapers helped to formulate this aesthetic conscience. By evaluating beautification efforts undertaken by other major cities, Kansas City hoped to emulate their successes and avoid their failures. A 1904 *Kansas City Star* article applauded the use of fountains, gateways, arches, and benches as suitable embellishments to the cityscape. The article went on to criticize the overabundance of statues honoring individuals, which had failed to provide an element of beauty or to memorialize the individual appropriately. The article pointed to Kansas City's advantageous position by stating:

> With the community's active interest and the possibility of taking
> advantage of other cities' errors, there is no danger that the streets
> and parks will be littered with the figures, sometimes grotesque,
> that are scattered about Washington and New York.

Although it was recognized that there was a need for monuments that were designed to honor the memory of a particular individual, the editorial was quick to advocate the avoidance of "stiff-legged men standing on blocks of stone."

Newspapers occasionally illustrated successful memorials located in other cities. Within two decades, memorials in Kansas City demonstrated some remarkably similar qualities. For example, the *Farragut Monument* in New York City (1876, St. Gaudens, sculptor) features a bench which, as described in a contemporary newspaper account "served to make the whole a thing of beauty." The overall concept of Kansas City's *Alfred Benjamin Memorial Fountain*, placed in Swope Park in 1927, is quite similar, particularly in the integration of the bench into the total artistic scheme. Compare, too, the *Richard M. Hunt Memorial* in New York City (1898, Daniel Chester French, sculptor) with the *Thomas Swope Memorial*, also located in Swope Park and begun in 1917. Both the Hunt and Swope memorials rely heavily on classical architectural precedents which had merely been updated to serve their particular purpose.

During the late nineteenth century, New York City realized there were a number of unattractive "works of art" on its streets and in its parks, and the city took steps to correct that unacceptable state of affairs. In 1898, a municipal art commission was established, one of the first such commissions in the country. The commission's purpose was to approve the designs of monuments before they were erected and placed on public property.

Kansas City moved quickly to emulate New York's example when in

1906 an art commission was established by ordinance under the administration of Mayor Beardsley. However, that commission and the others that followed had no real power, rarely met, and ultimately faded into obscurity. A provision for the formation of another art commission was included in the city's 1925 charter reform, but under the administration of the Pendergast "machine" years, it was once again ignored.

Although the commission continued to exist during the intervening years, it was to experience a major renaissance when Mayor Ilus W. Davis took office in 1963. One of his first decisions was to revive the activities of the Municipal Art Commission. He noted that "it could be a real force for making our city a more attractive place to live." His first appointees to the commission were persons tenacious in their insistence that the Municipal Art Commission become an active participant in city government.*

In 1965, the commission engaged a consultant to help identify the issues in which it should become involved. Although plagued by a small budget and resistance from other departments within City Hall, by 1966 a vigorous and active commission had evolved. Both the public and city officials had come to realize that "the art commission is part of the regular process, and they [the applicants] go through it so their project won't have to be sent back."

The art commission has played an active role in approving the designs and placement of fountains that were erected in more recent years. Until that time, professional judgments were primarily limited to the persons directly involved with the art work's commission and execution. One of the tasks that the Municipal Art Commission would face was to determine what constituted an "appropriate" memorial to an individual or event. They would have, as part of the basis of the criteria from which they were to judge, a number of memorials that had been previously erected in Kansas City for some particularly noteworthy events and persons.

World War I became the catalyst for the creation of some of the city's earliest memorials. In 1921, two fountains were dedicated to honor the American Legion, and the following year the Kansas City American Legion proposed that a statue or memorial be placed in the city every year during the next decade. Dr. Paul Wooley, a member of the William Fitzsimons Post of the American Legion, remarked: "Kansas City is far behind other cities of the country in statues to America's distinguished dead. . . .The posts of the American Legion are going to do all they can to encourage the movement." Although a number of memorials were erected in the 1920s, including the *Liberty Memorial* and the *William Fitzsimons Memorial Fountain,* the goal of a yearly project was soon abandoned.

In 1927, a critical observation of the status of Kansas City's monument art was offered by Phillip Hewitt-Myring of the *London Daily News.* Hewitt-Myring was temporarily on the staff of the *Kansas City Star* as a participant in an exchange program sponsored by the Walter Hines Page Fellowship. The quality of the monuments and statues in Kansas City was

*The mayor's first appointments to the commission were Mrs. James Lally, Lynn Bauer, Andrew Morgan, Mrs. Moulton Green, Jr., Henry E. Scott, and William Schuler. The late Lynn Bauer had a long and distinguished term on the commission, serving from his first appointment until his death in 1983. He served as vice-chairman during his entire term. The mayor is chairman of the commission.

much higher than he had anticipated, which perhaps indicates that he, along with some other visitors to Kansas City had often prematurely assumed that the city was an underdeveloped, unsophisticated frontier town. Hewitt-Myring's general impression was that there was, in fact, room for more public art work "if the present high quality is maintained."

Kansas City has an interesting and diverse collection of memorials that incorporate the use of water in their design. These memorial fountains can be categorized into two types: those that are war memorials and those that honor the memory of individuals. Fountains have proven to be exceptionally popular design vehicles to provide recognition of persons or events that have had great impact on the community.

Capable of conveying an unconscious reverence for life and possessing universal symbolism, water has strong connotations as a life-giving and rejuvenating natural element. It has been especially appropriate in honoring the memory of Kansas Citians who have given their lives in the defense of their country.

Memorial fountains that honor specific individuals illustrate a great diversity. Almost without exception, they avoid depicting the physical likeness of the person. More commonly, they are allegorical works stressing the deeds of the honored person. Ranging from small, simple drinking fountains to elaborate and grandiose works, these fountains not only memorialize noted citizens but also provide a dramatic addition to the cityscape.

War Memorials

The William Fitzsimons Memorial Fountain

When the United States entered World War I, the shock of global warfare along with the realization that man had within his grasp the power and the will to provoke and witness total destruction changed the lives of the citizens of Kansas City. All energies—emotional, physical, and industrial—were expended to ensure that the war would be won. Kansas City quickly geared up for the action and anxiously awaited news of the battles, triumphs, and defeats.

When the Germans bombed an Army hospital in France on September 4, 1917, the terrible reality of war came home to Kansas City with the announcement of the death of a Kansas City physician. First Lieutenant William T. Fitzsimons, United States Army Medical Corps, became the first American officer to lose his life in the war.

In May 1918, the Board of Parks Commissioners was asked to support a proposal by the Dr. Fitzsimons Memorial Committee to erect a monument. John Van Brunt, Park Board architect and brother of Park Board Commissioner Adriance Van Brunt, was commissioned to create its design. Van Brunt selected the site at Twelfth Street and The Paseo, and all but $500 of the amount needed to construct the fountain was raised through public subscription.

Major Paul M. Wooley, who dedicated the fountain on May 21, 1922, some five years after Lieutenant Fitzsimons' death, said this:

It is my hope that all who pause here to drink will reflect that

Fig. 59

THIS FOUNTAIN IS ERECTED
IN MEMORY OF
WILLIAM T. FITZSIMONS
1st LIEUT MEDICAL CORPS U.S.A.

KILLED IN FRANCE · · · ·
SEPTEMBER SEVENTH
NINETEEN HUNDRED
SEVENTEEN · THE FIRST
AMERICAN OFFICER TO
GIVE HIS LIFE IN THE
GREAT WORLD WAR ·
· · · FOR LIBERTY

many have lost their lives in the defense of their country since the beginning of this Republic, and that this fountain is dedicated to one of these.

The fountain is one of a small group that are affixed to a wall surface (see Chapter 5). The Fitzsimons *Memorial Fountain* is applied to the end wall of the Terrace at Twelfth Street and The Paseo, which was constructed during the city's beautification of the boulevard system in the late 1890s. The rectangular monument of Dakota stone consists of a tablet bearing the Army Medical Corps emblem in bronze with an inscription dedicating the monument to William Fitzsimons. Flanking the tablet are two Corinthian columns which bear relief swag carvings. Above the tablet is a semicircular lunette carved with an eagle in its center. The swag motif is repeated on either side of the eagle. The water-producing elements of the fountain are restricted to the base and consist of a bronze lion's head spout from which issued a single jet of water. The fluted basin, supported by a pedestal, unfortunately has been destroyed, and the fountain is no longer operational. The sculpture was executed by Jorgen C. Dreyer, a Kansas City sculptor (Fig. 59).

In choosing the location for this fountain, architect Van Brunt had to consider the existing architectural elements in his design of the tablet and basin fountain. The semicircular balustraded wall of coursed ashlar was divided into bays by projecting stone piers placed intermittently along the wall surface. The tablet with basin beneath was fitted into the central bay enframement by the flanking piers. The rounded, scalloped lip of the central basin repeated the shape of the urns which had surmounted the balustrade (but which are now gone) and perfectly integrated the fountain into the context of its predetermined architectural setting.

The American Legion Fountains

In 1921, the American Legion held its national convention in Kansas City. One of the highlights of that convention was the dedication of two fountains, gifts from the city under the administration of Mayor James Cowgill to honor the American Legion posts. With a $20,000 appropriation, the city had intended to erect eight fountains, one for each post within the city, but actually only two were constructed. By providing these monuments, the city sought to pay public tribute to those who had served their country and ultimately ensured the final success of the war effort.

One of the two monuments, a drinking fountain, is located in Swope Park north of the main shelter house. The fountain was constructed of Tennessee marble at a cost of $8,000. It takes the form of a rectangular slab approximately six feet high, buttressed by shorter, projected wings (Fig. 60). The focus of the monument is a bronze relief panel that extends across it horizontally. A product of sculptor Robert Merrell Gage, the work employs varying depths of carving to create a space-defining scene of American soldiers entering a war-ravaged French village. On the right side of the panel, the emancipating soldiers approach the villagers on the

Fig. 60

left, who are depicted as wounded and as refugees. The water-producing elements of the fountain are isolated in the center of the panel at the bottom and consist of a spigot that pours into a fluted, scalloped receptacle basin. The dedication of this fountain on October 31, 1921, was attended by a throng of people who vied for the honor of being the first to drink from this monument which honored these heroes.

Two days later, the second American Legion fountain was dedicated at Ninth and Main streets. Three Medal of Honor winners participated in the ceremony. The fountain, installed in front of the Westgate Hotel (later known as the Kay Hotel and eventually demolished), was a focal point for the streets which radiated from it (Fig. 61). As vehicles gradually displaced the cable car and pedestrian traffic, the fountain became more and more isolated from the people it was to have served. Since it stood in the middle of this busy hub, it became a great problem in the management of area traffic.

It is interesting to note that the site of the fountain had been exceedingly appropriate. Its predecessors included first a well, from which firemen had filled their buckets when fighting a downtown blaze, and then later a horse trough. Ironically, water never flowed into the bowl of the American Legion fountain. Pipes supplying the spigots on each side of the shaft had burst during the first winter after it was erected, and the water was shut off permanently.

Fig. 61

Fig. 62

When the city began a downtown redevelopment project between the Sixth Street Expressway and Ninth Street in 1958, the fountain was marked for extinction. It is to the credit of the Board of Parks Commissioners and Superintendent of Parks J.V. Lewis that a decision was made to move, rather than to destroy, the fountain. In 1960, under the supervision of Q.A. Giudici, president of a local funeral monument company, the six-ton fountain was transported to its new location at the intersection of Van Brunt Boulevard and Budd Park Esplanade (Fig. 62).

The fountain is an example of the popular pedestal type and consists of a circular base, saucer receptacle, and rectangular shaft which rises from its center to a height of approximately six feet. Four eagles are carved into the corners at the summit.

Its primary decoration is the work of Robert Merrell Gage. Two rectangular bronze plaques illustrate soldiers on one side and sailors on the other, poised in combat action. The compositions are read vertically, and Gage manipulated the height of the relief to create a spatial depth in the scenes. Gage was assisted by local architects, Wilkinson and Crans, and G.B. Franklin.

Inscriptions complete the enrichment of the other two sides of the shaft. One lists the local American Legion posts, and the other bears a quotation from Theodore Roosevelt, which reads:

All daring and courage, all iron, endurance or misfortune, all devotion to the ideal of honor and glory of the flag makes for a finer and nobler type of manhood.

Robert Merrell Gage, the distinguished sculptor of the reliefs for both of these American Legion fountains, was born in Topeka, Kansas, in 1892. He is remembered for a number of exceptional sculptures that grace the Midwest. In 1916, he completed what is perhaps his most well-known work, the Lincoln statue on the grounds of the Kansas State House in Topeka. His bronze sculpture of a police officer holding a child, which was dedicated in 1921, stands in front of the Police Headquarters Building in downtown Kansas City. It is an eloquent memorial to men who have lost their lives in the line of duty. Gage taught sculpture courses at the Fine Arts Institute in Kansas City and later moved to California, where he became a Professor of Sculpture at the University of Southern California.

Kansas City Bar Association Fountain

In 1921, the Kansas City Bar Association erected a memorial drinking fountain in the lobby of the old courthouse at Missouri and Oak streets. It was dedicated to members of the bar who gave their lives during World War I.

The memorial was another design by Robert Merrell Gage in coopera- tion with local architects Wight and Wight. It consisted of a panel of Tennessee marble, eight feet high and three and one-half feet wide,

Fig. 63

Fig. 64

affixed to the lobby wall. The names of the eight bar members were inscribed on a bronze relief panel placed above a semicircular drinking fountain basin designed as a shell. Carved in relief beside their names was a standing figure in uniform, holding a rifle in one hand and resting the other hand on a book, presumably a reference to the learned profession of the fallen soldiers (Fig. 63).

The memorial was unveiled on April 23, 1921, in ceremonies presided over by President of the Bar Association John B. Pew. After only a few years of use, the fountain of the $2,000 memorial became inoperable and was never repaired. Nevertheless, when the present courthouse was erected at Twelfth Street and Oak, the bar association planned to have the fountain moved and placed in its lobby or on the lawn. Whether or not that move ever took place is unknown; the attractive memorial is now among the missing in action.

Proposed Fountain to Masonic Veterans

In 1926, a memorial to Masonic veterans was designed by Kansas City architect Robert Peden, but it was not executed, probably because funds were never raised. The memorial fountain was to be placed in Mt. Moriah Cemetery at 105th Street and Holmes.* The planned memorial had some outward similarities to the Swope Memorial, as it was composed of a curved wall of Ionic marble columns which supported an entablature with a central pediment. In the forecourt on each side of the memorial were to be tiered fountains set in pools nine feet in diameter (Fig. 64). Six bronze tablets, three on each side of the center portion of the monument, were to list the names of persons buried in the cemetery who had served in any wars which involved the United States.

---

*Peden was the architect of the Mt. Moriah Mausoleum in 1927.

Fig. 65

Liberty Memorial Fountains

Liberty Memorial is one of this country's finest World War I monuments. The first proposals for this memorial to victory and sacrifice were made shortly before the armistice was officially signed on November 11, 1918. At the request of the city council, millionaire lumberman Robert Alexander Long served as chairman of a select committee of one hundred persons authorized to plan and develop the project. In 1920, a portion of Penn Valley Park immediately south of the Union Station was selected as the site for the memorial. Because virtually all travelers would pass through the station's doors, the site would be the most visible in the city. That same year the planning committee became the Liberty Memorial Association, a nonprofit corporation.

In June 1921, H. Van Buren Magonigle of New York City was selected as architect for the memorial project, winning a competition open to all local architects and by invitation only to other selected architects of national prominence. His concept, featuring a monumental shaft, was widely praised, but the use of that design by the Liberty Memorial Association was optional and could, by the rules of the competition, be modified by them. Several modifications, in fact, did occur so that the completed memorial only approximated the competition design. A prominent feature of the original plan submitted by Magonigle was a large circular fountain pool with a series of steps leading down from the pool to the carved north wall of the memorial below the shaft (Fig. 65). The design also included a steeper flight of steps which would lead from the base of the wall to the paved platform on which the shaft was to rest.

Almost immediately after being selected as winner, Magonigle announced that he would be assisted in his work by his wife, Edith Magonigle, a painter; George Kessler, landscape architect; and Robert Aitken, a sculptor. After years of planning, fund-raising, and anticipating, construction finally began in July 1923. When the memorial was dedicated in November 1926, the monumental shaft, towering over 217 feet into the air, and the two identical buildings flanking the shaft (a museum and Memory Hall) had been completed. Landscaping on the north side of the memorial and the treatment of the north wall beneath the shaft and adjacent buildings with a monumental relief were still to be completed. Magonigle, however, had fallen out of favor with the association. The main issue of dissatisfaction appears to have been his selection of his wife, Edith, as the sculptor and designer of the north wall frieze. From the beginning, there had been feelings about the impropriety of choosing his wife for this task. In addition, her proposed frieze, which borrowed heavily on well-known sculptural works of the past, was not well received. Her lack of experience for a project of this magnitude was also noted. In 1926, the association flatly rejected any furthe1 work by Magonigle, and they terminated their relationship with him.

In 1929, real estate developer J.C. Nichols was named to head a committee whose task was to complete the project. Because of the memorial's visibility from Union Station, the committee felt that the eight and one-half acres of land to the north, extending to Pershing Road, was one of its most important aspects.

Therefore, Nichols proceeded with great care and deliberation to see that the land development scheme was appropriate to the grand concepts already in place. Magonigle had originally suggested a large oval pathway as the approach from Union Station. Instead, landscape architect S. Herbert Hare and Superintendent of the Park Department W.H. Dunn advocated broad steps and direct walks to the center of the memorial.

Nichols then approached Massachusetts landscape architect Frederick Law Olmsted, Jr., who, after visiting the site, called it the most difficult problem he had ever encountered. Olmsted expressed reluctance to take on the project, citing the lack of support on the part of city officials and his own uncertainty as to whether any plan would ever be carried out. In 1932, Nichols' committee voted to retain Olmsted to study the problem of the north approach and also to hire the local architectural firm of Wight & Wight to work with Olmsted on plans for the terracing, walls, and steps.

In March 1933, Thomas Wight traveled east to consult with Olmsted and to locate sculptors in New York City who might be qualified to undertake the north wall frieze. A few weeks later he announced that all parties were in accord with the architectural plans and landscape development for Memorial Hill and estimated the cost at $180,000 to complete the steps, frieze, foundation, terrace walls, and fountains. Rather than the single, circular fountain envisioned by Magonigle, Wight & Wight had designed a pair of matching fountains to be integrated into the terraced north wall.

When finally constructed in 1934-35, wide staircases on both sides of the memorial buildings descended to a landing and from there to a large forecourt in front of the 488-foot north wall. Leading down from this forecourt was another flight of steps, ninety feet in width, flanked by matching fountains (Plate 6, page 17). Each fountain sits in a niche created by retaining walls and is built on two levels. The upper tier of the fountains is rectangular and contains a spray ring with the jets designed for an outside fall of water. The water flows into the lower level of the fountains through notches cut into the granite wall of the upper tier, where it falls in a miniature waterfall effect. Lining the lowermost part of the basins, which bow outward, are a series of singular jets with arcing sprays which propel the water back into the lower pools in graceful counterpoint.

The inscriptions carved over the fountains were selected by a committee who sought to find appropriate passages which would memorialize the slain war heroes. An excerpt from *America the Beautiful* by Katherine Lee Bates was selected for the east fountain and reads: "Who More Than Self Their Country Loved." The inscription over the west fountain was selected from Sir Samuel Brydge's verse on the death of Sir Walter Scott: "The Glory Dies Not and Grief is Past."

Using funds provided by the Ten-Year Plan bond program, the once rough and uneven terrain was graded, and flights of steps were constructed at the base of the hill leading to the memorial. The staircases were located at the east and west ends, framing an expansive green lawn. Because the grade is so steep, when viewed from Pershing Road at the bottom of the hill, the fountains are barely visible. Although somewhat dwarfed by the stone mass of the memorial itself, the fountains can be viewed from the Main Street approach, although their impact is greatest at close range.

The Liberty Memorial was a project that ignited the interest and imagination of the general public, which in a remarkably short period brought in the necessary funds for the completion of the project. That fund drive was a testimony to the genuine expression on the part of Kansas Citians to build a memorial not to glorify war but to stress peace. The memorial with its towering shaft, finely executed relief panels, and sparkling fountains continues to express symbolically the heartfelt gratitude of all our citizens.

American War Mothers Memorial

The cataclysm of World War I brought with it a desire on the part of American citizens to assist the war effort in ways that had not been necessary before. One organization, which experienced a phenomenal early growth, was born as a direct result of the United States' involvement in the war. The American War Mothers organization was formed to provide invaluable support and improve the morale of women and members of their families who were directly or indirectly engaged in the conflict.

The organization was chartered by a special Act of Congress in 1917 and was nationally incorporated in 1925. The group was active both in ceremonial and directly supportive roles and participated in numerous activities sponsored by the War Department. In 1923, one of their nationwide projects was to plant trees from coast to coast and from the Gulf of Mexico to the Canadian border to permanently honor the men and women who had served in the war effort.

The Kansas City Chapter of the American War Mothers was begun in 1921, and by the end of their first year they boasted a membership of almost 300. In 1931, the Park Board gave the organization a small plot of ground located at Meyer Boulevard and the east drive of The Paseo near

Brooklyn Avenue for use as a "memory garden" to honor military service. *Fig. 66*
Plans for a fountain in the small park were not completed until 1941 when
work on the project was actually begun.

The fountain memorial, although simple in form, is rich in symbolic
connotations (Fig. 66). Architect Edward Buehler Delk, who had himself
served in the armed forces, designed the eloquent monument. It reflects
the traditional, sober kind of rendition which emphasizes the memorial's
purpose more than its artistic possibilities. In its basic design, Delk
recalls the idioms displayed in heroic monuments from centuries past.

A circular pool, approximately twenty feet in diameter, surrounds an
eighteen-foot limestone obelisk. The shaft of the obelisk terminates in a
relief carving of eagles with outspread wings. Metal stars are affixed to
three of the four sides of the obelisk: one in gold, symbolizing those who
were killed in the war; one in blue, symbolizing those who were wounded; and one in white, representing those who returned from the war
uninjured. The War Mothers' insignia in colored enamel on stainless steel
was affixed to the fourth side of the shaft.

On each side of the shaft, Delk installed a single jet allowing water to
arc downward into the retaining pool, which is lined with light blue tile.
Stone benches, separated by four entrance openings, form a circle around
the fountain.

The monument was presented to the city in May 1942. Through the years and the wars that have followed, the fountain has continued to serve as a distinguished, visual epitaph describing great sacrifices.

Memorials to Individuals and Organizations

James T. Pendergast Memorial Fountain

The name of Pendergast is immediately recognizable to Kansas Citians, as the family was intricately involved in the city's politics for nearly fifty years. That involvement began in 1892 when James T. Pendergast was elected to the City Council as alderman from the First Ward. The First Ward embraced the area known as the West Bluffs, an area which attracted a great many immigrants of Irish and Italian descent in the late nineteenth century.

Pendergast, a big, jovial Irishman and proprietor of a hotel and saloon, rapidly took control of the Democratic machine in Kansas City. He was a progressive who fought for reforms and was heralded because of his concern for the poor and the working class who had elected him to office. During his eighteen years as a member of the council, James Pendergast was instrumental in the passage of major bond issues in support of public schools and construction and was a vocal supporter of the City Beautiful Movement—the catalyst for the creation of the park and boulevard system in the city.

When James Pendergast retired from the council in 1910, his brother Tom (who had earlier served as superintendent of streets) was appointed to replace him. Tom Pendergast then began his flamboyant, controversial leadership of the Democratic party in Kansas City, eventually becoming embroiled in election scandal. He was "Boss" of the city until the organization crumbled under his conviction for income tax evasion in 1940.

James T. Pendergast died of Bright's disease on November 10, 1911, at the age of fifty-five. He had established the following and loyalty of an enormous community, and his death was met with great sadness. An obituary in the *Kansas City Times* eulogized him in this way:

> Alderman Jim's political power was established by his generosity, his big-heartedness, his readiness to do favors for the "boys," to "go to the front" for one who was in trouble, get jobs and do various little acts of kindness for those who were in need. Besides, there was implicit faith in his honesty.

James T. Pendergast was to be memorialized by the people he had cared so much about. Located on the high bluffs of the West side, overlooking the city's Central Industrial District and the river beyond, the memorial bears little resemblance to the original which was dedicated on July 4, 1913, before a throng of 3,000 people.

It was during the administration of Democratic Mayor Henry Jost that the plan, funding, and erection of the memorial was accomplished. Major Jost appointed a committee to study the artistic options and develop sources of funding for an appropriate tribute.* George Van Millet, himself a distinguished Kansas City artist, headed the committee that chose

---

*It was also during Mayor Jost's term that another committee met to develop proposals for the Thomas Swope Memorial, to be located in the city's largest municipal park, donated by Col. Thomas Swope.

Frederick C. Hibbard, a Chicago sculptor, to create Pendergast's memorial. The money to pay for the monument, which was to cost $7,500, was raised through a public subscription with the friends of Mr. Pendergast, Republican and Democrat contributing alike. Hibbard, a native Missourian (born in Canton, Missouri in 1881), had studied under Lorado Taft at the Chicago Art Institute and specialized in portrait statues.* Perhaps his most popular works are found in Hannibal, Missouri, boyhood home of Samuel L. Clemens, where Hibbard modeled the figures of Mark Twain, Tom Sawyer, and Huck Finn.

Mr. Hibbard's design took the form of a tiered, bronze sculptural group. The seated figures of James Pendergast in a thronelike chair was placed in the center, elevated on a granite pedestal, with two youthful figures placed on lower flanking pedestals (Fig. 67). The figure on Pendergast's left (as one faces the sculpture) was a female youth and the figure on the right was a male youth. Both figures were seated on the pedestals, and the arms of each extended to hold a bowl from which water for the drinking fountain issued. Two animal figures, a pigeon with the

Fig. 67

*Hibbard's work can also be found in such cities as Vicksburg, Mississippi (*General Grant*); Fort Wayne, Indiana (*General H.W. Lawton*); and Winchester, Virginia (*The Virginian*).

girl and a rabbit with the boy, were placed near the bowls, as if they were being offered a drink. These flanking figures were exhibited at the Chicago Art Institute's seventeenth annual exhibition of works by artists of Chicago and the vicinity shortly before being brought to Kansas City.

From the very beginning, problems were to beset the memorial. Though the Eighteenth Amendment to the Constitution, which mandated a policy of prohibition, was not adopted until January 1918, prohibition workers were highly influential long before that. When it was announced that a statue of Pendergast was to be erected and placed in a public park, there was a vehement outcry from ardent prohibition supporters. Pendergast had owned and operated a saloon for most of his life, and the prohibitionists felt it inappropriate to honor the memory of a man who had been connected with the sale of liquor. On July 2, 1913, two days before the monument was dedicated, the *Kansas City Journal-Post* published an editorial in Pendergast's defense which summarized the general consensus:

> The *Post* makes no defense of the saloon business. It is an unnecessary business and a bad one. Pendergast made little money at it and left only a small estate. . . . The people who knew him want to erect a monument to his virtues and not his vices. It is not a bad idea to show that [a] man can run a bad business on the square— and so live that his death is mourned by thousands—so mourned that they want to remember him.

Having successfully met the first challenge to its construction, the memorial soon fell victim to another misfortune: vandalism. The monument had been erected on a recessed spot just south of Twelfth Street below the cliffs on Kersey Coates Drive. From its perch at the west edge of Mulkey Park, the sculpture of Pendergast could view much of the industrial district by the river bottoms, the area in which he had located his hotel and saloon. Because the monument was placed in a less trafficked area of the city, the location provided greater opportunity for the malicious. Only a few years after its dedication, vandals removed the two figures of the youths from their bases and carted them away. Hibbard, the sculptor, was called upon to cast new figures, which were installed around 1916.

In March 1933, the memorial was again vandalized. This time the arms of the male youth and one arm of the female figure were cut off. The police speculated that whoever had mutilated the sculpture was only interested in the value that the metal would have to a scrap dealer. Hibbard's efforts were again solicited, and the figures were repaired in April of that year. The memorial was vandalized two more times, once in November 1933 and again in July 1937.

In 1965, the Pendergast Memorial stood with its flanking figures mutilated again and the bronze relief panels which had described his contributions removed. Pendergast had now become an impediment to progress as he stood in the way of the Crosstown Freeway project. The State Highway Commission needed to use that land to link the Crosstown Freeway with the Intercity Viaduct. The sculpture was moved and placed in storage in October 1965. Sometime after August 1966 the Park Department agreed to replace the statue and committed themselves to moving

"Big Jim" to a higher elevation. The memorial was moved to Mulkey Park north of Thirteenth Street.

The flanking figures have disappeared with no trace of their whereabouts known. Speculations were made that they might have been mutilated beyond repair, stolen, or misplaced during the storage of the memorial.

A new freeway has isolated Mulkey Park, and the adjacent neighborhood is currently in a state of transition. Because of the recent construction of the freeway and the fluctuating state of the neighborhood, the park has not been well maintained. Pendergast sits in isolation on the west edge of the park, staring into a forest of overgrown weeds and trees, removed from the West Bottoms where he had risen to prominence.

Thomas Swope Memorial Fountain

On June 25, 1896, 18,000 people traveled to a heavily forested area some four miles south of the city limits. The occasion, officially declared a city holiday, was the dedication of approximately two square miles (1769 acres) of land as the city's newest and largest public park. Swope Park, a gift of Thomas Huntoon Swope, is one of the largest municipal parks in the United States, and its improvements since its dedication include an outdoor amphitheater, a zoological garden, golf course, swimming pool, lakes, trails, and acres of picnic and recreational areas.

In 1896, the park was not yet serviced by any public transportation system, causing some members of the Park Board to criticize the acceptance of the land because of its inaccessible location. That criticism proved greatly shortsighted for the city rapidly grew southward, meeting and then extending far beyond the boundaries of the park.

Col. Thomas H. Swope arrived in Kansas City in the spring of 1857. He invested heavily in real estate and became a millionaire from his land investments in the downtown area and from land that was still outside the city limits. The land that was to become Swope Park had originally been purchased by Swope as a farm. He later decided to donate this land, which ran along the Blue River to the city, stipulating that the city spend at least $5,000 a year for its maintenance (a condition that was later rescinded) and that it be named Swope Park in perpetuity. In addition to the park gift, Swope also donated land at Twenty-fourth Street and Locust on which to build a city hospital and made numerous other philanthropic gifts of direct benefit to the citizens of Kansas City.

In 1904, the Swope Park Administration Building was erected from designs by Adriance Van Brunt. The entranceway, also his design, is probably contemporary with the administration building. Two large drives lead into the park from Swope Parkway and a stone wall with tall stone pillars at each end, capped by stone spheres, runs between them. A similar, but lower, stone wall flanks the drives and is joined by a curved balustrade of stone. According to newspaper accounts, Van Brunt designed the semicircular entrance area envisioning that someday a fountain or statue as a memorial to Swope would be placed on the grassy median between the two drives. In 1904, when the Park Board first began a search for a suitable tribute to Swope in recognition of his beneficence, they considered placing an exedra inside the entranceway that would contain a bronze tablet and possibly a medallion portrait.

The Park Board approached the Commercial Club of Kansas City (which in 1916 became the Chamber of Commerce) about undertaking this project. A committee of Commercial Club members quickly expanded the original proposal. A New York sculptor, John Massey Rhind,* was brought to Kansas City to look over the proposed site, and he recommended a heroic-sized bronze statue of Swope to be placed on a pedestal just outside the entrance, with the entrance serving as a background.

In October 1904, the Commercial Club raised the $25,000 needed for the monument and also secured the consent of Colonel Swope for the project. At this point, the plan was to erect a statue of Swope in a sitting position, mounted on a pedestal. Although there was great support for the plan, nothing materialized.

Four years later, two bronze relief panels were commissioned by the Park Board to commemorate Colonel Swope's enormous benefaction, but these plans were aborted. Inexplicably, Colonel Swope had changed his mind and now expressly forbade the erection of any monuments to him before his death.

Colonel Swope died on October 3, 1909, at the age of eighty-two. His death was clouded with sinister overtones and resulted in a murder trial which attracted national attention. Swope had moved to Independence, Missouri, to live with his brother's family in a large Victorian mansion. When his niece Frances Swope married Dr. Bennet Clark Hyde and they moved into the house, unfortunate things began to happen. In 1909, Colonel Swope and two other family members died, followed shortly thereafter by the illness of nine more family members with typhoid fever. Dr. Hyde was indicted for murder and accused of administering strychnine and cyanide to Colonel Swope and introducing the typhoid virus into the food of the other family members. Since Frances Swope stood to inherit the estate of over $3 million (a most compelling motive), she was also implicated in the murder plot. After a lengthy trial, Dr. Hyde was acquitted, and the "murder" never resolved.

The unsavory circumstances surrounding the death of Thomas Swope greatly delayed the settlement of his estate and stalled all memorial projects that had been envisioned. Although it had been Swope's fervent wish to be buried in the park bearing his name, his body was placed in a receiving vault in Forest Hill Cemetery pending the resolution of these problems and the selection of a suitable memorial.

By July 1911, the relatives of Colonel Swope and the executors of his estate were becoming quite anxious to place the body in a final resting place. The Park Board asked the executors of the estate to expend the same amount of money that would be required for a monument and burial expenses as would have been expended had the body been permanently interred.

Before he died, Colonel Swope had indicated that although he had the

*By 1900, Rhind had established himself as one of the country's foremost designers of public monuments and architectural sculpture in a Beaux-Arts tradition. He was a prolific designer and among his popular works were a set of ornamental doors for Trinity Church, New York City, decorations for Princeton's Alexander Commencement Hall, and the *Corning Fountain* in Hartford, Connecticut.

financial means to erect his own memorial, he did not wish to have it built using his fortune. His sister Margaret told a newspaper reporter in 1913 that she believed he should be memorialized, but that, "I want him to have one from the hand of the people he did so much for. I do hope they will not touch Brother Tom's money. It would be humiliating for him to have to buy his own 'public' memorial." Because the executors were only being asked to provide those funds which would have been expended otherwise, they agreed to the proposal. The executors appropriated $20,000 from the estate for the memorial. In turn, the Park Board agreed to convene a committee of artists who would design the monument and pledged additional money for its completion. The executors and the Park Board would jointly select the site, although the executors preferred a secluded area away from the entrance.

The Park Board selected New York sculptor Karl Bitter to choose the location and form for the memorial.* In 1912, after inspecting the park for several days, Bitter recommended that a memorial statue to Swope be placed near the entrance to the park. He concluded that the body should be interred at a site more than a mile east of the main entrance gates on one of the highest elevations in the park. He suggested that a small obelisk, visible from the entrance, be used to mark the burial site. Bitter's proposal, however, was never executed.

By February 1914, still no action had taken place. Again, relatives approached the Park Board to ascertain what steps were being taken for a memorial. The board wanted to delay a public subscription drive until the summer.

Finally, in 1915, Mayor Henry Jost appointed a fifteen-member memorial committee to select the monument and administer the campaign for the public subscription of funds necessary for completion of the memorial. One of the proposals submitted to the committee was by landscape architect George Kessler, then serving as an advisor to the Park Board, who offered for consideration the erection of an ornamental bridge that would span the Blue River. Although there was substantial support for Kessler's proposal, it was not accepted.

Kessler also prepared another memorial design in 1915, although whether it was presented to the memorial committee is not known. The drawing indicates it was prepared for John Paxton, one of the estate executors. This design was apparently the choice of the executors for it is virtually identical to the completed work. Kessler's proposal consisted of an exedra composed of eleven Doric columns in a U-shape, which served as a backdrop for a paved court. An ornamental vase was to be placed four steps below it in the center of the court.

Work did not begin on the memorial until 1917. The location selected was the site suggested earlier by Karl Bitter, almost on a central line with the entrance and on one of the park's highest elevations. It commands a view of the lagoon, the Blue River, and beyond.

The memorial was constructed in three stages and was not completed until 1931. Kessler personally selected Kansas City architects Wight &

*Karl Bitter (1875-1915) moved to the United States in 1899 after studying at the Academy of Fine Arts in Vienna. The fact that he was in charge of the sculpture at three major expositions (Buffalo, St. Louis, and San Francisco) attests to his national reputation. At the time of his death he was serving as the president of the National Sculpture Society.

Wight to oversee the project. Kessler was at the time living in St. Louis and engaged throughout the country as a consultant and therefore could not have effectively monitored the progress. The choice was a logical one because Wight & Wight were especially adept at designs utilizing a neoclassical idiom and are perhaps best remembered for their 1930 design of the Nelson-Atkins Museum of Art, a monumental neoclassical revival building.

The first stage of the memorial, begun in 1917, was the construction of a mausoleum. The design was based on elements from classical architecture, a style especially appropriate to a funeral monument because of its timeless implications (Fig. 68). It was constructed of granite at a cost of $44,000. Twelve columns were used to create a colonnade which framed a rectangular courtyard space. The colonnade is approached by flights of stairs built on two levels of terraces. On each side of the stair rails at the highest level are two recumbent lions, also carved in granite by New York sculptor Charles Keck.* The Doric order is utilized in the treatment of the columns, capitals, and entablature.

The colonnade extends to a width of fifty feet, and the columns are fourteen feet high. The central bay of the colonnade projects and contains a bronze relief panel dedicating the monument to Colonel Swope. Inscribed into the architrave is the Latin inscription, *Lector si monumentum requiris circumspice* (Reader, if you seek his monument look about you)**Also on the bronze panel is a bas relief portrait in profile of Swope. Bronze plaques around the frieze represent the foliage of some of the

Fig. 68

*Keck, a former president of the National Sculpture Society, died in 1951. He was noted for his memorial work and for busts and medallions of famous persons. The relief panel across the facade of the Jackson County Courthouse, representing Law and Justice, was another local project by Keck.

Fig. 69

trees in the park. Charles Keck designed and executed all of the relief carving on the panels.

Swope's body was moved to its final resting place in April 1918 and is buried beneath a stone slab set into the floor of the court in front of the columns. Some of the trees in front of the memorial were removed to ensure the visibility of the site from the entrance. The landscaping around the memorial was designed by George Kessler.

The construction of a fountain and balustrade constituted the second phase of the project which began in 1922 and took approximately a year to complete (Fig. 69). The balustrade was placed eighty-four feet to the west of the mausoleum. It extends seventy-two feet and is built at the very edge where the hillside steeply drops off. The fountain and balustrade help focus the view from the mausoleum toward the entrance of the park far to the west. A grassy, open space is created between the fountain terminus and the architectural backdrop of the mausoleum itself.

The pedestal-type fountain, six feet in height, like the mausoleum derives its inspiration from classical art. It consists of a saucer bowl, carried on a slender, tapered pedestal and is set into a semicircular basin that is twenty-five feet in diameter. The walkways which flank it are of red brick.

The balustrade, which contains decorative starburst motifs, is four feet in height. Wight & Wight designed the fountain and the balustrade. They purposely used white stone to match the granite of the mausoleum, thus achieving a uniform texture in the memorial.

**The same inscription appears on Sir Christopher Wren's tomb in St. Paul's Cathedral in London. Wren, considered the greatest of English architects, was responsible for over fifty-one churches and was the designer of St. Paul's itself.

The final phase of the project began in the summer of 1930 when a special committee determined that a gate and a stairway to the memorial were necessary to afford the public access and to call attention to the rather isolated monument. The project, completed in 1931 at a cost of $3,500, included the erection of a stone portal at the base of the hill and the construction of stairs which would lead up to the mausoleum from Lakeside Drive. S. Herbert Hare, consulting landscape architect for the Park Board, also recommended the removal of some trees on the hillside to afford the monument greater visibility.

The Swope Memorial, constructed over a number of years through the dedicated work of many people, is one of the most beautiful in the city. The fountain plays an important part in the overall impact of this stunning work, which though isolated from the more active areas of the park, provides the spectator with a commanding view of Swope's gift to the city.

The George H. Lowry Memorial Fountain

One of Kansas City's most charming fountain creations now sits dry, neglected, and almost forgotten next to a vacant Presbyterian church at Linwood Boulevard and Michigan. The *George H. Lowry Memorial Fountain* was constructed in 1924 when Linwood Presbyterian Church was one of the finest and largest in the city. George Lowry was Chairman of the Building Committee which oversaw a major expansion of the church in 1922. An elder of the church for many years, Lowry was president of the Lowry Lumber Company and a successful businessman.

George Lowry died in July 1923. His wife and two children donated a fountain to the church in his honor, and it was dedicated on April 20, 1924. Appropriately, the fountain was placed at an angle where the new addition to the building joined the original, on the Linwood Boulevard side.

The architectural firm of Greenebaum, Hardy, and Schumacher, who had designed the church addition, were also selected to design the fountain. The choice of the firm was a propitious one as they achieved a harmony of design between the church and the fountain.

The fountain rests on a slightly raised octagonal stone base, nine feet in diameter (Fig. 70). The basin, elevated on a squat pedestal, is also octagonal and is four feet in diameter. A stone ornamental shaft with incised Gothic arches that echo the arches used to ornament the church building rises from the center of the basin to a height of seven and one-half feet. The body of a fish, whose head is superimposed over a shell, is carved into the base of the shaft on each of the four sides. Water originally spouted from the mouths of the fish to fall into the basin, and four other jets spouted water from the basin floor.

The fountain's general appearance is similar to ornate baptismal fonts, and the shell and the fish decorations reinforce the reference to Christianity. The shell is symbolic of pilgrims, whereas the fish is a popular symbol of Christian baptism and of Christ Himself. To complete the religious references, the fountain basin is inscribed on two sides with biblical passages that refer to water: "Jesus said come unto me and drink" and "Take the water of life freely."

This graceful fountain served as a fitting tribute to a man whose life

Fig. 70

was involved with his church. Now it stands as mute testimony to the brief passage of time in which a human life can be forgotten.

The Alfred Benjamin Memorial Fountain

Philanthropist Alfred Benjamin was described by his contemporaries as a modest man who never sought recognition for his deeds and as a man who "got as much pleasure from giving as the recipient of his gift." Benjamin died on July 18, 1923, at the age of sixty-four. Most Kansas Citians today would be hard pressed to recall who Alfred Benjamin was, much less his generous gifts to the city. Benjamin was a vice-president of the Abernathy Furniture Company and a director of the Duff and Repp Furniture Company. Half of his annual income went to charity as well as substantial amounts of his time. For many years he had devoted his

Sunday afternoons to supervising the work of the caring for immigrants at the Jewish Educational Institute. He also established a loan program for needy persons. In his will a generous sum was alloted to the United Jewish Charities and lesser amounts to several other organizations, including the Kansas City Young Men's Hebrew Association, the Young Women's Hebrew Association, and Children's Mercy Hospital. Benjamin made a sizable contribution for a medical clinic in the northern section of the city. In an unusual gesture, his friends, wishing to honor him during his lifetime, returned his contribution, underwrote the costs, and named the clinic the Alfred Benjamin Dispensary.

Following his death, a memorial fund was established with a goal of $25,000 to erect some sort of tribute to this generous man. The nature of the memorial was not specified, except that it was to be of practical value to the public, "something that will further the charitable causes to which he devoted his life." Many prominent Kansas Citians served on a memorial committee, including Chairman Frank C. Niles, William Volker, Herbert Woolf, and Ford Harvey. Money for the memorial was to be raised not through a "drive" but through voluntary contributions of citizens. Within six months, $18,000 had been raised, largely through small gifts from citizens of all walks of life. A decision was reached to memorialize Benjamin with a fountain rather than with a more "practical" memorial vehicle.

In March 1927, a site in Swope Park was selected and approved by the Municipal Art Commission, the Park Board, and the Benjamin Memorial Committee. The location was east of the Swope Park entrance on the north side of what is now called Starlight Theater Road. The sculptor selected to design the memorial was New York artist Francis H. Packer.* Construction of the memorial began in April 1927, with Kansas City architect Frederick McIlvain in charge of the project. The goal was to complete the memorial in time for its dedication on Memorial Day.

Packer chose to depict Benjamin's life and character in modern, realistic figures based on the biblical Good Samaritan parable. The interpretations of Packer's work are varied. One suggestion has been that the figures are of two exhausted workers, one of whom receives a drink of water from the hands of the other. Another view is that only one of the figures is a worker and the other figure, offering the drink, is an "intellectual" type with a kindly countenance, who is in a position to aid the less fortunate man. The latter interpretation is supported through the portrayal of one of the figures without a shirt or shoes, suggesting an impoverished laborer. Both figures are seated on a boulder with a plowshare barely visible in the background. The sculpture sits back from the road with a row of evergreen trees behind it serving as a backdrop (Fig. 71). The dark color of the trees merges with the bronze of the figural group making it difficult to distinguish any details of the work from a distance and greatly diminishing the impact of the work.

The figures are nine feet in height and rest on a five-foot-high marble

---

*Packer (1873-1957) was a graduate of Cooper Union and a member of the National Sculpture Society. He was a perfectionist who once said, "I would rather smash my work to bits than have it imperfect." Among his works was a statue of Henry Clay that was sent to Venezuela in exchange for the statue of Simon Bolivar that was placed in Central Park. He also designed the medal commemorating the Byrd Antarctic Expedition of 1930-31.

Fig. 71

base. A drinking fountain projects in a semicircle from the base directly below the figural group that portrays the slaking of thirst. Above the drinking fountain is the inscription:

In Memory of
Alfred Benjamin
Whose Noble Deeds Enshrined Him In
the Hearts of His Fellow Men.
AD. 1927

Extending on each side of the figural group, to a total length of twenty-five feet, are marble benches. On the back of one bench is carved the word, *Charity*, and *Humanity* is inscribed on the other: the two words that most succinctly describe the qualities of Alfred Benjamin. Because of the mottled coloring of the stone and the effects of years of weathering, the inscriptions are very difficult to read. The entire work rests on a stone base that projects forward, mirroring the outward curve of the drinking fountain.

The fountain was dedicated on May 29, 1927, during a ceremony attended by hundreds of Benjamin's admirers. The presentation speech was made by his lifelong friend, Frank Hall, who said, "To become very rich did not appeal to Alfred Benjamin. To make money, however, for the needy and unfortunate was to him an interesting and worthy ambition."

Mercy Hospital Century Club Memorial Drinking Fountain

Children's Mercy Hospital was constructed in 1916-17 at 1726 Independence Avenue. Behind the hospital on the north was a "curative" playground—an open air playground designed for children well enough to be able to use it. A large portion of the funds for this playground was raised through the efforts of the Mercy Hospital Century Club, a women's service organization. The club was founded in 1922, and by January 1927, the members had raised over $12,000 for the hospital, $1,000 of which was earmarked for the playground. That same year a memorial drinking fountain was erected in the playground, although reports concerning its dedication are conflicting. Newspaper accounts say the fountain was

Fig. 72

erected in honor of a past president of the club, Mrs. Harry Bixby. The inscription panel on the fountain, however, reads: "In Honor of Our Heroic Dead." Because 1927 is a late date for a World War I memorial, it might be concluded that Mrs. Bixby was referred to as "heroic dead." More likely, the fountain may have been erected to serve as both a war memorial and a monument to Mrs. Bixby.

The drinking fountain consists of a cut stone pillar that tapers to the top of the shaft (Fig. 72). Affixed on three sides of the shaft are semicircular basins that provide the water outlets.

In 1929, another $5,000 was donated by the Century Club for further improvements to the playground including rock walls, extensive shrubbery and flowers, concrete tables, and sandpits. The Children's Mercy Hospital Building is now owned by the University of Health Sciences College of Osteopathic Medicine and is used for offices. The playground area is fenced off and used only for special occasions.

The William Volker Memorial Fountain

When William Volker died in November 1947, the city swiftly resolved to provide a suitable memorial for one of its most beloved citizens. Volker, a princely benefactor of Kansas City, had done much in his lifetime to enrich the quality and cosmopolitan nature of the city. The son of German immigrants who had settled in Chicago in 1871, Volker began a career in Kansas City in 1882 wholesaling picture frames. By the end of the century, he had expanded his firm and become a millionaire.

William Volker was to bestow the city with a fortune in charity. His gifts included the establishment of a tuberculosis treatment center at Kansas City's General Hospital; a teachers' retirement fund, begun when Volker served as a member of the school board; major donations that led to the expansion of facilities at the Helping Hand Institute; and the genesis of the University of Kansas City (now the University of Missouri-Kansas City).

Volker demonstrated enormous sympathy for the plight of the less fortunate and was instrumental in the formation of a Board of Public Welfare. The ordinance which established that board, adopted by the city council in April 1910, was actually drafted by Volker and provided for the needs of the unemployed and sick on a year-round basis. Volker met his civic responsibilities with an unparalleled generosity: frequently when funds that were needed for worthwhile projects were unavailable, he provided them himself, often anonymously. Volker's gifts to the city throughout his lifetime were estimated at $10 million.

Mayor William Kemp became the catalyst for the city's tribute to Volker with the appointment of a memorial committee in 1947. The selection committee, distinct from the general and finance committees, was composed of Henry J. Haskell, editor of the *Kansas City Star*, chairman; Sigmund Stern, vice-chairman; and members Arthur Mag, Mrs. John B. Gage, Ward C. Gifford, and J.C. Nichols.

The committee first established certain criteria that they felt should be met to acknowledge Volker's legacy to Kansas City suitably. The committee decided that the monument should cost not less than $125,000; that it should be accessible to every citizen; and that it should be of a type that possessed high artistic value. The monument was to be an "object representing pure tribute to the spirit of a man whose humility almost exceeded understanding."

The public showed great interest in the campaign, expressed in monetary contributions during a public subscription and suggestions presented to the selection committee for their consideration. During a meeting of this committee in January 1948, Henry Haskell announced that thirty "very fine" suggestions had been received but that many of those suggestions that had proposed the erection of a permanent structure to house a research or charitable facility were necessarily dismissed because of soaring building costs. When the committee reached a decision Haskell summed up the rationale upon which they based that decision in this way: "A monumental and utilitarian structure worthy of Mr. Volker probably would cost $1 million at present . . . within our range it seemed to the committee that a magnificent fountain would be appropriate and representative of our affection and esteem." The committee emphasized that in addition to a building's initial cost, annual maintenance costs would be involved. Haskell noted that campaigns for large sums of money to benefit hospitals and other worthy causes were then currently in progress and that solicitation for funds for a Volker memorial would result in a competition that might severely impede those efforts. He concluded that this certainly would not be in keeping with the spirit of Volker, for whom the monument was to be erected. The committee reasoned that a fountain would not become obsolete and the public would "derive inspiration from the sight of the living water flowing in memory of a great citizen."

With the selection of a fountain as the form for the tribute, the next issues to be confronted by the committee were the location of the monument and the choice of a designer. Upon a recommendation of the American Society of Sculptors, the committee was referred to the work of the innovative Swedish sculptor, Carl Milles.

Carl Milles, Sculptor

Milles, then seventy-five years old, was generally acknowledged by art educators and critics as the greatest fountain sculptor alive. His works were already known in the Midwest, chiefly through his design for the *Meeting of the Rivers Fountain* in St. Louis, Missouri. A delegation from the committee visited Milles at the Cranbrook Academy in Michigan, where he was teaching sculpture, to offer him the commission. Although Milles first expressed a reluctancy to undertake the project, he finally agreed to visit Kansas City and eventually accepted the commission.

Born in 1875, Milles had early begun a life dedicated to the creation of sculpture. He exhibited at the Salon of 1899 in Paris, the same salon that was to ensure Auguste Rodin's importance as an innovator in the nineteenth century art world. Milles later became an assistant at Rodin's studio in Meudon, France.

Although the presence of Rodin undoubtedly influenced Milles' early work, he was soon to identify and develop a personal idiom. Many of those early works were produced while Milles was living in Sweden at his villa, appropriately named Millesgarden, on the island of Lingo overlooking the harbor of Stockholm. After several successful exhibitions of his work, in 1920 Milles was elected Professor of Modeling at the Royal Academy of Art in Stockholm. He had first visited the United States in 1929 and in 1931 took up residence after accepting an invitation to teach from the prestigious Cranbrook Academy. The first comprehensive exhibition of his work in the United States was held at the City Art Museum of St. Louis in 1931.

Meeting of the Rivers Fountain, St. Louis

In 1937, Milles was to receive the commission that secured his reputation in the Midwest—the *Meeting of the Rivers Fountain* for the Aloe Plaza in St. Louis in front of the Union Station railroad terminal (Fig. 73). Funded by the Municipal Art Commission of St. Louis and a grant from Mrs. Louis P. Aloe, the fountain was to symbolize the confluence of the Missouri and Mississippi rivers, a fact vital to the establishment of St. Louis as a major port city during the westward expansion.

For the St. Louis fountain, Milles had chosen to represent his theme allegorically as a wedding between a male figure who, representing the Missouri River, strides forth to meet his "bride," a female figure who represented the Mississippi River. A multitude of sea sprites and naiads surrounded the main figures.

The fountain created an enormous controversy as Milles chose to portray his river gods in the nude. When the figures arrived in St. Louis, Francis D. Healy, chairman of the St. Louis Municipal Art Commission remarked, "This work of art is not appropriate to St. Louis. What will

Fig. 73

people think of two nude figures being married? Why we might as well have a nudist camp on the city's plaza." Healy insisted that he would resign unless the figural scheme for the fountain was changed. He favored "something more in the Western tradition—a group of pioneers gathered around a teepee."

The fountain was ultimately installed as Milles had initially conceived it, despite the furor it created. The attention it received was on a national level and focused attention on the Midwest's rather provincial attitude toward the creation of "fine art." The fountain was to become one of that city's most popular monuments.

Milles' allegorical presentation of the merging of the Mississippi and Missouri rivers in the St. Louis fountain was compatible with the heroic concepts that the Volker committee wished to express. Haskell pointed out another reason for Milles' exceptional suitability for his role as sculptor when he remarked that although Milles was a modern "he was not extreme—you can understand what he means."

Milles' European background gave him the opportunity to study fountain masterpieces belonging to earlier centuries and that undoubtedly contributed to the conceptions for his fountains. Milles eschewed the literal, preferring a symbolic approach to his subject matter. He was especially concerned with the proper placement of the fountain in the context of its setting and insisted that all of his fountains be installed outdoors. Another major precept held by Milles was that his fountains had to be accessible to the spectator.

Fig. 74

The Cultural Mall

Milles was personally involved in selecting the site of the *Volker Memorial Fountain*, which ensured that his artistic requisites were met. The committee had already considered several possible sites for the monument, including Swope Park in the southeast part of the city and the park just north of the Municipal Auditorium (now Barney Allis Plaza) in the heart of the Central Business District. The Swope Park site was dismissed as the park had already been named as a memorial to another man. Milles himself rejected the downtown park site as unsuitable. The site selected, south of the Nelson Gallery of Art, was acceptable to all, and Milles was particularly impressed with its potentialities.

That site had long been under consideration for some form of development. As early as 1929, plans were underway for construction of the Nelson Gallery of Art, as well as for one of the most elaborate landscaping projects ever envisioned for Kansas City. The Nelson Gallery of Art opened its doors in 1933. The architects of the huge neoclassically styled building, Wight & Wight, had proposed that a large formal lake (to be named Mirror Lake) be excavated south of the gallery. The southern terminus of the lake would be 2,450 feet from the south portico of the gallery, and the lake itself would be approximately 1,035 feet long and 350 feet wide to form a large rectangle. Because the lake would be at a lower grade than the gallery building, it would reflect the mirror image of the gallery and its formally planted grounds, having an effect much like the reflecting pool in front of the *Lincoln Memorial* in Washington, D.C. The lake was also perceived as an important connecting link between the gallery and the University of Kansas City (now the University of Missouri - Kansas City) to the south.

The exact plans for the proposed lake varied from account to account. They included plans for the placement of works by American sculptors, the building of an approach from the Nelson Gallery which would feature broad stairs with water cascades 165 feet wide between them, the locating of an ornate fountain at the north end, and the building of a peristyle of Grecian columns at the southern end (Fig. 74).

The excavation for the lake would also necessitate that several streets be changed or closed and Brush Creek, which cut across the proposed site, be diverted. It was decided that the creek should be channeled under the lake through a concrete enclosure. In 1936, the diversion of Brush Creek beneath the site was made possible as a Works Progress Administration project, and work had begun by August of that year. However, the lake never materialized because of the high construction costs.

The lake concept was superseded in 1947 when the city council approved a bond improvement package. The money was to be used to acquire the land south of the Nelson Gallery. This land would constitute a "cultural center" serving as a bridge from the gallery to the university by way of a grassy mall area, uninterrupted by obstructions. In developing the mall, which was to be 600 feet wide and encompass some ten acres of land, the city would have to demolish several houses and close two streets (Houston, now Forty-seventh Terrace, and Pierce Street) that cut through the site (Fig. 75). Locust Street, the eastern boundary, would be moved 125 feet east to effect this grand scheme. The Volker Memorial Committee ruled that the best site for Milles' proposed fountain would be about 150 feet from the newly constructed Brush Creek Parkway. With the plans for the development of the grounds in mind, Milles enthusiastically accepted the commission and returned to his villa to begin work.

The William Volker Memorial Fountain

The *William Volker Memorial Fountain* portrays the equestrian figure of St. Martin of Tours, quintessential embodiment of the Good Samaritan theme. Milles' choice of subject matter seems to have come from his rejection of a specific reenactment of the biblical account of the Good Samaritan in favor of the legend of Saint Martin, who embodied those self-sacrificing ideals particularly appropriate to honor the memory of William Volker.

Saint Martin was born in Hungary during the fourth century. He converted to Christianity as a child during the reign of Constantine the Great. Martin favored a monastic life but was forced by his father, a military tribune, to become a soldier in the imperial cavalry stationed in France. He eventually left military service and founded a monastery near Poitiers, France. Later he was to be appointed Bishop of Tours. Martin is popularly remembered for a legendary incident that occurred in Amiens. During a particularly bitter winter day, he chanced to meet a beggar who, with little clothing to protect him from the ravaging cold, was suffering intensely. Martin removed his own cloak and cutting it in two with his sword, gave half to the beggar. That night Christ appeared to Martin in a vision saying, "What thou hast done for that poor man, thou hast done for me." It was after his vision that Martin devoted his life to serving Christ.

Milles' figure of Martin is centrally placed in an irregularly shaped pool, some thirty feet long. It is flanked by two larger end pools that are also irregularly shaped (Plate 14, page 33). A smaller, separate pool which contains one of the subsidiary figures is placed between the central and east basins. The interior of the flanking pools contains a raised concrete island that was originally intended for the placement of water flowers. The fountain jets are restricted to the two flanking pools with two

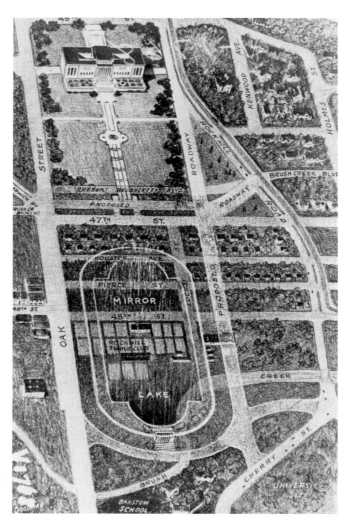

Fig. 75

placed in each. They create towers of water through three separate tiers composed of concentric circles of jets. The lowest tier raises the water five feet into the air, the second twenty feet, and the third a spectacular twenty-eight feet, creating a central "geyser." All the pools are interconnected and the water, which is discharged at approximately 1,900 gallons per minute, is recirculated by a maze of underground machinery.

The mounted figure of Martin, whose body turns in the opposite direction from the horse's head, is placed on a tiered support composed of a rectangular pedestal and the stylized vegetal motifs that bear the weight of both the horse and rider. Beneath Martin and occupying his attention is the figure of the supplicant beggar, who with his head and arms upturned reaches for the cloak that Martin has just cut in half.

The three subsidiary figures created by Milles are witnesses to the main action. They include a seated centaur who sits back on his haunches peering through upraised hands; an angel who is also seated and appears to be scratching his leg; and another angel playing a flute who appears high above Martin on a tall, slender bronze stalk. It has been suggested that the seated angel symbolically portrays divine order, and the centaur represents its antithesis: worldly indifference.

The composition that is created forms a spiral as the seated angel in the foreground leads to the centaur, who in turn regards the central group performing the action. Their interaction turns the spectator's gaze heavenward to the figure of the hovering angel on its stalk, placed to the right of the group.*

Milles, who developed the scheme for the most effective placement of the fountain, worked closely with Park Department officials in Kansas City. In a visit to Kansas City in October 1952, Milles inspected the site with members of the Park Board, architect Edward Buehler Delk, and landscape architect S. Herbert Hare. In 1952, the land was studded with trees, and there were still some houses that blocked the view to the gallery. Milles indicated that he wanted to destroy as few trees as possible in the preparation of the site for the fountain.

Milles first completed the accessory figures. His working method called for them to be executed first in plaster and then to be shipped to Florence for their casting in bronze. The angel with the flute was the first figure to be finished and arrived in Kansas City in January 1952. To complete the equestrian figure of Saint Martin, Milles took up residence at the American Academy in Rome where he could prepare the full scale model. His creation was not without incident as in 1954 Milles suffered a leg injury in a fall from the scaffolding while working on the thirteen-foot figure.

The fountain project was the victim of a great number of delays, many caused by personal tragedies. The fountain was to have been dedicated in 1953 and was already two years behind schedule when Milles died on September 19, 1955. Milles had completed his monumental equestrian figure, but problems with funding the fountain project and the acquisition of land continued to plague the efforts of the Volker Memorial Committee. Milles' bronze figures remained in storage at the Nelson Gallery of Art while these problems were resolved. Eight acres of land which had been purchased from the William Rockhill Nelson Trust remained in control of the Nelson estate through September 1956. Eighteen houses sited on that tract had yet to be demolished. There were no houses on the immediate site of the fountain but there were obstructions, such as the Rockhill Tennis Club which maintained its courts on the south edge of the mall. In October 1957, the courts were removed, and the tennis club moved its quarters east of the Nelson Gallery to occupy the former residence of Irwin and Laura Nelson Kirkwood, heirs to newspaper publisher William Rockhill Nelson.

As early as January 1955 contracts had been let for structural and mechanical engineering services, although Park Board architect Delk did

---

*At least two preparatory sketches were executed that departed from the completed concept in various ways. A sketch made in 1950, which appeared in a newspaper article, illustrated a central pool that was flanked by rectangular basins rather than the irregularly shaped basins that were actually constructed. The plan called for the central figural group to be raised on a pedestal and water to issue from spouts at the base of the figure. One of the lateral pools would contain the figure of the angel and the other the centaur. The angel perched on the slender shaft was not included. A later sketch, prepared in September 1953 by architects Edward Tanner and Edward Delk and landscaped by Hare & Hare, illustrated the sculptural group elevated on a raised platform which was approached by a flight of stairs. A circular drive was placed immediately in front of the fountain and provided a semicircular parking area.

not expect the actual work to begin until much later. When Delk died on September 4, 1956, the project was again delayed.

Delk had worked extensively with Milles in preparing the plans and specifications for the placement of the fountain. In an October 1955 meeting of the Volker Memorial Committee, Delk displayed the blueprints of the fountain and the connecting pools. He indicated that one of Milles' last instructions was that the equestrian figure of Saint Martin should be installed so that the horse faced directly south, rather than at an angle, as originally planned.

Though two of the key people in the creation of the fountain were dead, some continuity still existed as Edward W. Tanner, architect and member of the Citizens Memorial Committee, replaced Delk. Tanner had been an active participant in the project. Also, S. Herbert Hare continued in his role as landscape architect. Tanner agreed to serve on the planning of the fountain without the benefit of a commission. In preparation of the final plans, Tanner met with Peter Berthold Schiwetz, who had been Milles' chief assistant for many years and had been brought to Kansas City by the Memorial Committee to provide Tanner with information regarding the sculptor's artistic concerns.

On October 28, 1957, Tanner, Hare, and Elpidio Rocha, an architect for the Park Board, announced that the final plans had been approved by the Park Board and contracts for the installation of the basins, walks, and plumbing would be let immediately. Work was finally begun.

With the aid of a fire department truck equipped with an aerial ladder, the fountain was unveiled, and the waters loosed on September 20, 1958. In addition to the more than 2,000 people who attended the ceremony were Mayor H. Roe Bartle, some members of the original Volker Memorial Committee, and Mrs. William Volker, widow of the man for whom this impressive monument was created.

The fountain, taking some eleven years from its conception to its creation, would also memorialize Carl Milles and Edward Buehler Delk, whose artistic genius provided this deserved tribute.

Comparisons with Other Milles Works

The *Volker Memorial Fountain* was Milles' last work, and it represents a synthesis of the leitmotivs used by Milles in other fountains during his career. In a comparison of the *Volker Memorial Fountain* with other works by Milles, similarities as well as conventions become apparent. Milles, who had probably created more fountains in his lifetime than any other sculptor during the twentieth century, had a vast repertoire of motifs at his disposal. He seems to have drawn heavily from his own vast production to create the figures for the *Volker Memorial Fountain*. In fact, the *Volker Memorial Fountain* reproduces parts of fountains designed earlier in Milles' career.

In 1927, Milles created the *Fountain and Water Trough of Folke Filbyter* in Linkoping, Sweden (Fig. 76). This equestrian group illustrated the history of the Swedish dynasty of the Folkunga kings. The focus is a sculptural group placed in the center of a low, rectangular basin recreating the legend of Folke Filbyter, who is searching myopically for

Fig. 76

his lost son. Relief panels around the basin illustrate other episodes in the history of the dynasty.

The fountain is sited in the middle of a square. Throughout his long career, Milles showed a preference for the placement of his fountains in large, unobstructed spaces. In this depiction, Milles presents the horse with its turned head carrying the figure of Filbyter, who is turned on his axis in an opposite direction, creating a counterpoint in balance that is identical to the posturing of Saint Martin and his mount in the Kansas City fountain.

Milles' portrayal of the figures in this manner was not arbitrary, but integral, to his storytelling art. In the Filbyter group, the male figure leans forward to see where he is going while his horse precariously finds its way through the slippery stepping stones. In the *Volker Memorial Fountain* the horse looks backward, startled at the appearance of the angel, while Martin rends his cloak for the beggar at his feet. Milles' figures are actively engaged in the story.

The treatment of the water in the fountains is also similar in that the water jets are removed from the narrative figures. One might speculate that in both Milles was acknowledging the absence of any water-inspired motifs and in keeping with the veracity of the story related, limits the intrusion of the water spouts to the peripheral elements of his fountain. In the Volker fountain, this represents a departure from his original scheme, which had spouts of water issuing from the base of the central figure. It is not clear in the available sketch of his intended scheme what types of figures Milles intended for the sculptural base.

In 1938, Milles was commissioned to design a fountain for the National Memorial Park in Falls Church, Virginia. When complete, the fountain was to have thirty-eight figures, all in attitudes of movement. The cemetery, created by architect Walter Marlowe, features above-ground entombment and elaborate landscaping. Milles' fountain was sited at the junction of a 1,000-foot-long mall that was bisected by a 300-foot transept forming a cruciform, Milles' work, entitled the *Fountain of Faith*, depicted a joyful version of life after death and included a variety of stylized human figures: family members in prayer; children engaged in play; and the reuniting of a mother with a lost child. The figures are placed in a low, rectangular basin of dark, polished granite, and each is set upon a slender stalk so they appear to float upon the waters. Overlooking the figures, a merry angel with a flute cocks his head attentively and witnesses the activity taking place below him. Many figures Milles created between 1940 and 1955 were placed on tall, slender stalks, and by positioning the water so that it partially obscured the physical supports of the figures, Milles disguised their earthbound origin.

The comparison between the *Volker Memorial Fountain* and the *Fountain of Faith* focuses the importance of Milles' final work. In both, Milles has sited his sculpture on a broad mall concourse. One of the principal reasons that Milles accepted the Kansas City commission was its location on the Nelson Gallery mall site. Milles considered this location to be one of the "four finest sites for sculpture he knew." His desire to place his fountain in a visually unrestricted space that would both direct and focus the work is evidenced in the *Volker Memorial Fountain*, the *Fountain of Faith*, and in many others created throughout his career.

The creation of the subsidiary figures of the *Volker Memorial Fountain* demonstrated Milles' predilection for the anecdotal in his art and parallels his charming figures created for the *Fountain of Faith* and the *Meeting of the Rivers Fountain*. The similarity of the angel with the flute in the *Volker Memorial Fountain* and the angel in the *Fountain of Faith* is remarkable. It is as if he merely transported the figure from one setting to another.

Reporters were fond of asking Milles to explain his elaborate allegories and his reasons for depicting the figures as he did. Asked if the angel in the *Fountain of Faith* was listening to the children below, Milles responded, "He is listening to what the people who come down to look at the fountain are saying." His explanations regarding the *Volker Memorial Fountain* illumine the puckish humor that Milles possessed. When asked about the reason for the appearance of an angel playing a flute he responded, "Horses love music, didn't you know?" and added "Don't you think God sends His people down here to see what we are doing?" Frequently, Milles was asked about the figure of the seated angel wearing a wristwatch and scratching his leg. His explanation for the wristwatch: "I don't know why, but he has it." He explained that the figure was scratching his leg because "There are so many mosquitoes on earth." He defended the presence of the centaur by adding, "He is watching the angel. He has never seen an angel either."

While expressing intellectual and esoteric ideals, Milles' heroic art also had a quality that related immediately to the humanity present in all of us. It is his melding of heaven with earth that distinguishes the Volker monument and serves as the perfect memorial to Milles and Volker alike.

Later Events

The history of the *Volker Memorial Fountain* did not end with its dedication. Several incidents were to occur that ultimately ensured that the *Volker Memorial Fountain* would remain a permanent part of the cityscape.

In November 1958, to the horror of witnesses, the angel with the flute hovering above St. Martin began slowly, but inexorably, to sink to the ground. Architect Elpidio Rocha was immediately called in to inspect the sculpture, and speculation as to the cause of its downfall ran rampant. The angel had originally been installed by placing a two-and-one-half inch pipe into the eighteen foot bronze stem. It appears that Edward Tanner was never entirely satisfied with its placement and felt that the steel pipe anchoring the stem was never perfectly centered. Upon inspection it was found that the ankle of the right foot was damaged. It was that foot that carried the entire weight of the figure of the angel. It was then reported that during its shipment from Italy the ankle had been broken and had subsequently been repaired. The general consensus, regardless of any extenuating circumstances, was that there was simply too little support given to the figure.

Members of the Park Board responded to the incident in a rather optimistic and practical way. Indicating that things could have been much worse, J.V. Lewis, Superintendent of Parks, remarked, "It might have fallen sometime when there were persons standing around. Somebody might have got conked."

The weather conditions prevalent in Kansas City, which most probably influenced the failure of the support of the angel figure, took a toll on the figure of Saint Martin as well. In February 1959, the figure of horse and rider, which had been cast as one piece, was removed from the site to be stored in a warehouse. The strong winds that buffeted the mall seem to have caused the equestrian figure to gently rock against the brass dowels securing it, eventually causing the granite base to crack. Happily, in July 1959, the figures of Saint Martin and his horse along with the musical angel were reinstalled. Carl Milles had stipulated that only a special ebony granite available in Sweden be used for the base of the figures. Because of the great difficulty the Park Department encountered in finding a granite replacement base, a new pedestal for Saint Martin was constructed using reinforced concrete, veneered with two inches of granite. The angel was also returned to continue his floating serenade, secure on a newly reinforced base. Floodlights to illuminate the fountain were added, which aided in discouraging vandalism, as well as highlighting the fountain.

That measure was not entirely successful because on August 20, 1959, vandals tore the beggar figure from its moorings and left it adrift in the central basin. Ten youths were later convicted of the vandalism and were each fined $25, and the beggar, the seated angel, and the centaur were again placed in storage. In October, the figures were back in their places, this time with bronze plates attached to their bases and secured with one-inch anchor bolts to ensure their resistance both to the natural elements and to man-made catastrophes.

In 1960, the Park Board approved the installation of underwater lighting for the fountain. The lights were placed under the main jets and around the figures. The money necessary for the lights and their installation was made available from Cultural Center funds.

One final adjustment was necessitated because the original materials proved to be no match against the eccentricities of the Kansas City climate. Milles had specified that the decking material surrounding the pools be slate. Because of the rather high porosity of that material, it retained the water which was blown from the fountain sprays, and the surface was continuously wet. During the winter months, the expansion of the freezing water caused the slate to separate from its mortar bed. The Park Department in 1970, wishing to match the original material as closely as possible, commissioned the consulting engineering firm of Black & Veatch to prepare a study of possible choices of resurfacing materials. Although replacing the panels with the original slate material was strongly considered for aesthetic factors, granite was ultimately selected for its durability.

The area between Oak and Locust north of Volker Boulevard, which contains the fountain, was officially designated as the Frank S. Theis Memorial Mall in 1966. Theis, who died in November 1965, served thirteen of his fifteen years of Park Board service as its president. The dedication of the mall to Theis was especially appropriate as the fountain was commissioned and erected during his tenure.

In 1969, as a result of economic considerations, the Park Department turned off the water to the fountain from nine in the morning until four in the afternoon on weekdays. The public uproar at this action was loud and contagious, and the waters were soon restored.

The *Volker Memorial Fountain* has exceeded every expectation held by its original patrons. The homage which it pays to William Volker is implicit. Beyond that, it is a focal point and conversation piece, and reports of the fountain and the activities that it inspires will continue.

The J.C. Nichols Memorial Fountain

Any history or description of the *J.C. Nichols Memorial Fountain*, which was dedicated in 1960, must begin many years earlier on the "Gold Coast" of Long Island, New York. The fountain's present placement, sculpture, and basin recreate their original appearance when they were a part of a formal garden located on the estate of Clarence H. Mackay, which was destroyed many years ago.

Long Island, which inspired F. Scott Fitzgerald's novel, *The Great Gatsby*, was a favorite summer resort for the wealthy. The construction of their grand mansions spanned a period from the late 1880s until around 1929. Some of the personalities for whom these imposing structures were built included F.W. Woolworth, Alfred DuPont, Harry F. Guggenheim, and William Vanderbilt.

Clarence Mackay, whose Roslyn, Long Island, estate was called "Harbor Hill," was a leading industrialist. In 1928, he concluded an astute business deal merging his commercial cable companies with the International Telephone and Telegraph Company (ITT). A good part of his resulting fortune was devoted to support of the arts and sciences. Mackay was by nature a collector and amassed a large and particularly fine collection of tapestries and paintings. In addition, he possessed one of the world's finest collections of suits of armor.

Mackay commissioned the New York architectural firm of McKim, Mead and White to design his palatial residence where he could exhibit many of his treasures. The architects, all trained at the famed Ecole des Beaux-Arts in Paris, were affiliated in one of the leading firms of the early twentieth century. Construction of the residence began in 1902, and the architects chose a French Renaissance chateau as the inspiration for their design. The plan expressed a logical integration of parts and featured an entrance hall with two wings which emphasized the symmetry of the plan. The formal arrangement of the mansion was reflected in the design for the landscaping and gardens.

Guy Lowell (1870-1927), a European-trained architect as well as a landscape architect, began the formal landscaping of the Mackay estate in 1904. At that time the mansion was already under construction and became the pivot for his planning of roadways and the planting of the grounds. The entire Mackay estate encompassed some 530 acres, and the residence was constructed at the summit of a hill, commanding a spectacular view of Hempstead Harbor. In designing the landscaping for the mansion, Lowell capitalized on the natural topography of the site by employing strong axes and vistas, terracing, and steps which led down into a garden area.

Fountains and statuary had long been a part of the formal European landscaping tradition. The Mackay estate followed that tradition, and a monumental fountain was commissioned to become the focal point of the garden. Extant photographs reveal that the Mackay fountain was placed at the rear (south) of the mansion in a broad rectangular courtyard area framed with a marble balustrade (Fig. 77). It was sited directly opposite the grand portico of the house and was approached by a broad concourse. The fountain with its circular retaining pool was below a terraced area that contained a maze of intricately sculptured shrubbery.

The bronze group for the fountain was created by French artist Henri Greber in 1910 and consisted of four equestrian figures placed around a two-tiered basin. Smaller groups of children riding dolphins were placed between the mounted figures.

The water effects of the fountain were especially dramatic. A central vertical jet was propelled some thirty feet into the air, and the auxiliary figures spewed a stream of water toward the center. The whole functioned as a dynamic water showcase.

The Mackay estate has long since been destroyed, but a kinder fate was to befall its fountains. Fifty years later, it was to be transplanted into a similar environment in Kansas City. Jesse Clyde Nichols, the man who had applied systematic planning principles in the development of his residential and shopping districts, had done much to create a Kansas City that is famed for its profusion of sculpture and fountains. The impact

Nichols had on Kansas City was nationally recognized, and after his death *Fig. 77* in 1950, the citizens sought to create a monument to his memory that would suitably pay homage to his vision.

The *J.C. Nichols Memorial Fountain* is Kansas City's best loved, best known, and most frequently photographed fountain. In 1952, the first step toward its creation was made when the Nichols family initiated the purchase of the Mackay estate fountain. Aided by a New York art dealer, the sculptural group was purchased and brought to Kansas City.

It was not until October 1957 that the city officially took action to build the memorial to the late Nichols. Moved by the requests of the family and friends, Frank Theis, president of the Park Board, announced that the board had officially adopted a resolution favoring the construction of a Nichols fountain on Park Department lands. The ideal site recommended by the Park Board was on the north side of Forty-seventh Street between J.C. Nichols Parkway and Main Street.* Miller Nichols, son of the late developer, announced the availability of the fountain sculpture, which was appraised at a value of $250,000. It was determined that the monument was to be funded through private contributions and that no general public subscription was to be made. The board estimated that the fountain would cost some $125,000 to erect and pledged $5,000 per year for a period of five years to pay for part of the construction costs. On November 8, 1957, the city council adopted a resolution authorizing the Board of Park Commissioners to accept contributions for the construction of the *J.C. Nichols Memorial Fountain*. The resolution stated that:

> in recognition of the activities of the late J.C. Nichols in the development of the Country Club Plaza and surrounding areas, and because many citizens desire to further perpetuate the memory of the late Mr. Nichols by the erection of a memorial fountain on Park lands and to make individual contributions . . . (and that)

*The city had earlier renamed a part of Mill Creek Parkway in honor of Nichols. The J.C. Nichols Parkway is a roadway that stretches past his renowned Country Club Plaza.

the Board of Park Commissioners believes that such a memorial fountain would be an appropriate adornment of Park property . . . that the Board of Park Commissioners be . . . authorized to accept contributions from interested citizens.

Jack Henry, Barkley Meador, and Cliff Jones, Sr. were appointed to a committee that would oversee the construction of the fountain. In December 1957, the location was officially approved, and a sketch of the proposed fountain was prepared.

In March 1958, the condition of the sculptural figures which had been in storage at the J.C. Nichols Company shops was determined. After Mackay's death in 1938 the sculptural group had been vandalized; during the cataloging of the figures it was discovered that eleven parts of the group were missing and needed replacement. Among the pieces missing were the heads of two children riding dolphins and other detail pieces.

The artist chosen to fabricate the missing parts was Kansas City sculptor Herman Frederick Simon. Simon had worked extensively in Kansas City and was responsible for the bronze doors for both the Jackson County Courthouse and the city hall. Simon prepared the plaster models of the missing pieces, which were then shipped to the Bruno Bearzi foundry in Florence, Italy, for their casting in bronze.

During the time that the figural sculpture was being repaired, other events involving the construction of the fountain were taking place. Edward W. Tanner of the architectural firm of Tanner and Associates presented the final plans for the fountain to the Park Board for their approval.* Tanner told the board that the Daughters of the Confederacy Monument, which was on the site selected for the Nichols fountain, would be moved to a location at Fifty-fifth Street and Ward Parkway where it remains today.

The Miller-Stauch Construction Company was awarded the contract for the construction of the main basin in January 1959. Though numerous contributions had poured in from prominent business firms and individuals, notably from Nichols Company employees and residents of the Country Club District, more money was needed. The city, which had earlier pledged a sum of money, needed to ratify that pledge. In February 1959, a hotly debated ordinance was passed, appropriating $15,000 from the city's budget to pay for the construction of the walkways and landscaping of the grounds surrounding the fountain. The lone dissenter, Councilman Charles Shafer, agreed that Nichols had made an enormous contribution to the city, but he felt that the money would be better spent "for the prevention of tree diseases or repairs on boulevards." The ordinance was passed with a vote of five to one.

By August 1959, the basin and central tier had been erected. The fountain sculpture would not be added until the following spring, just before its dedication on May 15, 1960 (Plate 3, page 11).

The dedication ceremony was attended by nearly a thousand people who came to hear addresses by Mayor H. Roe Bartle and Laurence Sickman, Director of the Nelson Gallery of Art. On the platform listening to the tributes were members of the Nichols family, who had donated the

*Tanner's firm had designed many of the buildings on the Country Club Plaza and prepared many of the residential designs for the houses in the Nichols' Country Club residential district.

fountain group, and members of the Board of Park Commissioners and fountain committee who had done much to see that the fountain was erected.

Mayor Bartle expressed his respect for Nichols by saying that, "J.C. Nichols gave our city a heart, a mind, and a soul." Sickman declared that "Mr. Nichols was at once a visionary and a practical builder in the widest sense." A plaque installed in the concrete walkway around the fountain summarized Nichols' contributions in this way:

> J.C. Nichols was one of those rare individuals, a dreamer with a capacity for making his dreams come true. He dreamed, moreover, in terms of great practical benefit to his city; few men can have so variously and profoundly influenced the development of any American community.

In designing the scheme for the fountain, Edward Tanner kept it consistent with its original form and placement as part of the Mackay estate. The great rectangular area of ground on which it is sited approximates the courtyard of its previous garden setting. The four broad sidewalks which radiate from the circular retaining pool of the fountain establish a symmetry in the relationship of the fountain to its environment, much similar to the concept of a focusing concourse used by Lowell a half century earlier.

The pool in which the sculpture is placed is eighty feet in diameter, and the facing used around the rim is red brick. The two concentric, tiered circular bowls were recreated and placed in the center of the pool. The bronze stalky plant forms occupy the center of the highest tier as they had previously and issue a stream of water which rises to a height of almost forty feet.

The equestrian figures, each ten and one-half feet high and weighing one and one-half tons, are placed generally at the cardinal points of the fountain, and the auxiliary figures of children mounted on dolphins are placed equidistant between them. Each of the smaller figures propels a stream of water toward the center of the basin to meet the vertically rising central jet.

A great amount of speculation has surrounded the meaning of Greber's sculptural group. Some have proposed that the fountain figures portray four of the continents, whereas others have thought that the group represents an allegory of man's struggle through life. It clearly appears that the group had its specific antecedents in earlier fountain imagery, and for that reason the solution offered by Laurence Sickman, former director of the Nelson-Atkins Museum of Art seems to be the most reasonable. He concluded that the fountain represents four major rivers of the world.

It should be remembered that the fountain was the work of a French sculptor trained in a European tradition. Sickman suggests that Greber may have been drawing directly from another work of his in Beauvais, the town in which he was born, where he had depicted the four rivers.

Perhaps the most famous work using this theme in Europe was Gran Lorenzo Bernini's *Fountain of the Four Rivers* done for the Piazza Navona in Rome, completed in 1651. Though the number of authenticated Bernini fountains is small, his works had set a precedent, and his impact as a fountain designer was felt throughout Europe centuries after his death. In the *Fountain of the Four Rivers* Bernini placed four male figures on the four cardinal points of a great rocky mass that radiated from the center of a tall obelisk (Fig. 78). For each figure, Bernini depicted a major river of the world: the Nile, the Danube, the Ganges, and the Rio de la Plata. In turn each of those rivers symbolized the continents of Africa, Europe, Asia, and the Americas.

Artists have long included objects in their compositions which were popularly associated with a concept or specific subject. The use of these symbolic objects in a composition often raises a literal subject to the realm of allegory. Although any specific relationship between Greber's work and Bernini's *tour de force* is unsubstantiated, it is useful to compare the two works as both artists made use of these then widely understood symbols.

Fig. 78

In Bernini's work each male figure is given certain attributes with which it could be identified. The Nile River is depicted covering his head with a length of cloth, a reference to the lack of knowledge concerning the point of origin of the river. Beside and below him are figures of a palm tree and lion, further reference to the river. The Danube is crowned with a wreath of flowers and a horse is placed nearby. The Ganges is depicted holding an oar with a snakelike form wrapped around it. The oar made reference to the vastness of those waters. The Rio de la Plata figure is shown with an armadillo by his feet and a collection of coins nearby, indicating the riches that were to be found in the Americas. All these devices were employed so that the viewer would clearly understand the fountain's symbolic import; although it served as an artistic *tour de force*, it had a didactic meaning as well.

The *J.C. Nichols Memorial Fountain* sculpture also contains motifs that indicate a theme. Examination of the fountain's individual figures reveals that in each of the four equestrian figures Greber has provided specific attributes which offer a clue to the theme he wished to express. The equestrian figure at the south end of the fountain is a male figure who wears a feathered headdress and sits atop a rearing mount. He brandishes

Fig. 79

a spear that is aimed at an open-mouthed alligator which is placed menacingly below him. Sickman suggested that this figure represents the Mississippi River as both the alligator and the Indian might be associated with the particular locale in which the Mississippi flows.

The Rhine and Seine rivers are symbolically portrayed by the equestrians at the east and west ends of the fountain, Sickman concluded. The west figure is of a heavily muscled man who holds in his left hand a cattail, a tall reedy plant that flourishes in marshy areas. Beneath him is a scaly, half-man, half-fish figure that blows a conch shell and reaches up to hold the mane of the horse. The figure on the east is the only female figure of the four, and she is portrayed wearing a fur drape and holding a cattail. Below her is another merman figure, who holds the rein of her steed (Fig. 79).

Though all of the figures literally spill over their bases in agitated movement, the equestrian at the north end of the pool is perhaps the most dramatic. Leaning far back on his rearing steed, the figure is engaged in mortal combat with a huge bear that has fallen on his back beneath the hooves of the horse. The spear the figure holds has pierced the bear's flesh, and the moment captured is at the height of his struggle with the powerful animal. Sickman proposed that the bear is a traditional symbol for Russia, and that as such, this group represents the Volga River.

The four auxiliary figures, all facing the center of the fountain, provide a counterpoint and relief to the dramatic action that is taking place beside and above them. Each of the groups portray two children astride fish creatures, and in each the children are postured in playful attitudes.

In one group a girl figure mischievously pushes a boy back on their scaly mount. In another, the children ride contentedly carrying a garland of flowers and in another a spray of cattails. One particularly evocative piece features a chubby boy mastering his steed with reins of seaweed. Every detail of the children and their creatures has been carefully modeled, and no two are alike. One of the "fish" possesses widely bulging eyes, and another has a beaklike nose. Some of them appear to be benevolent, but others are frightening. The expressions of the children's faces range from tranquil serenity to terrified surprise. The auxiliary figures contribute more to the artistic composition than to the symbolism. Once again, Greber makes use of a long-established tradition as playful imps and water creatures had long been used as embellishments in fountains.

Colored lights illuminate the fountain at night and add a further dynamic quality to the already vital jets and streams of the fountain. The height, force, and auditory qualities of the fountain are striking. Its park-like setting with benches placed intermittently around the perimeter of the fountain basin have made it one of the most popular spaces in the city.

The *Nichols Memorial Fountain* has become an acknowledged favorite. Even more importantly, it succeeds in the very difficult task of paying suitable tribute to the man it honors. As one writer has claimed, "in his travels Nichols always kept an eye open for a handsome fountain. He found many of them. No one would have been more pleased with this new fountain than the man whose memory it will memorialize."

The Muse of the Missouri Fountain

Like many other metropolitan centers, the downtown commercial district of Kansas City has seen great changes. Older buildings have been replaced by sophisticated high-rise office structures, and parking requirements and traffic flow have been adjusted to meet the fast-changing environment. The growth of the heart of the city sometimes progresses at such a rapid pace that it eclipses the efforts spent to prepare for pedestrian amenities adequately. The erection of the *Muse of the Missouri Fountain* testifies to the successful integration of a work of art into a busy urban center.

From the middle 1950s through the late 1970s, the block between Eighth and Ninth streets on Main underwent major construction as part of a scheme envisioned by the Downtown Redevelopment Corporation. The first structure to be erected under this plan was a twelve-story office building at 811 Main Street in 1957. In 1962, construction began on the thirty-story Commerce Tower Building at 911 Main Street. This building was the first locally designed tall building constructed in Kansas City since the erection of the city hall in 1930. The project was undertaken by the Commerce Trust Company, assisted by Urban Renewal.

James M. Kemper, Sr. headed the Downtown Redevelopment Corporation and was also chairman of the board of the Commerce Trust Company. Kemper had long envisioned a monument at the Ninth and Main streets location dedicated to his son, Lieutenant David Woods Kemper, who had been killed during the closing days of the Second World War while serving as a platoon commander in the European theater. Kemper had established the David Woods Kemper Memorial Foundation to provide a suitable monument to his son and to beautify the area for the enjoyment of all Kansas Citians. The foundation paid for some of the improvements that were necessary to widen Main Street between Eighth and Ninth streets so that a wider median strip could be installed to accommodate a major fountain. The island that was created was thirty feet wide and approximately half a block long.

Kemper approached New York sculptor Wheeler Williams to create the fountain. Williams was an internationally known sculptor who had graduated magna cum laude from Yale in 1919 and received a master of architecture degree from Harvard in 1922. He studied sculpture at the Chicago Art Institute and spent eight years at the Ecole des Beaux Arts in Paris. Williams, who died in 1972, had won many honors during his lifetime, including a gold medal at the 1937 Paris Exposition International and the Mrs. Louis Bennett Prize in Sculpture from the National Sculpture Society in 1966. Williams maintained a studio in New York City for many years. Some of his best known works in the United States include the *Fountain of the Water Babies* for the Children's Orthopedic Hospital in Seattle, Washington; the *Venus of Manhattan* for the Parke-Bernet Gallery in New York City; *Steeds of the Imagination*, which was placed on the Reader's Digest Tower in Chappaqua, New York, and has since been used as the Reader's Digest logo; *Rhythm of the Waves Fountain* in Grosse Point, Michigan; and the *Wave of Life Fountain* in Houston, Texas.

The fountain design by Wheeler was to be a gift to the city from the Kemper Foundation; however, because it was to be placed on city lands and the Park Department tasked with its maintenance, the city fathers had to agree to its acceptance. In 1962, the Municipal Art Commission voted its approval of the plans and placement of the fountain, and in 1963 the City Plan Commission and the city council concurred, pledging to fund approximately $5,000 per year for its maintenance. On a bitterly cold day on December 2, 1963, the fountain was finally dedicated.

Williams had prepared several sketches for the design of the fountain for Kemper's selection. After viewing them, Kemper asked Williams to produce something "just a bit more lyrical." The result was the *Muse of the Missouri*, a bronze, nude female figure that is elevated to a height of thirty feet on a tall shaft resembling a stylized floral form (Plate 7, page 19).

Though Williams was aware of conservative attitudes toward nudity in works of art, he philosophically justified his choice in saying:

There's a difference between a beautiful nude and a figure that is just naked. Anyone can recognize it. It's the same as the difference between a charming person and a vulgar person.

Williams believed that sculpture should be a representation of living forms and incorporated a number of those forms in his conception for the *Muse of the Missouri.*

According to Williams, the female figure, weighing some 2,500 pounds, was modeled solely from his imagination. She is depicted with arms outstretched, holding a net from which spills her catch of nine fish.

Williams created the mesh of her net using a special machine that wove bronze wire.

Because the nine fish (probably a reference to the total number of muses in classical mythology) were to be water outlets, Williams was confronted with another problem. He had intended to model his fish from those that were native to the Missouri River but found that catfish were too ugly and carp had mouths too small to provide for the fountain jets. He settled on a "hybrid" which he created by crossing the body of a carp with the head of a bluefish.

In Greek mythology, a muse was any one of the nine goddesses who presided over literature, art, and sciences; more generally, they indicated a source of inspiration. By choosing the subject of the *Muse of the Missouri*, Williams personified the spirit of the goddess who guided and bestowed her interest on the mighty Missouri River. To make his intent more specific and easily recognizable, he incorporated the net of fish, as they are the subjects of her realm.

The location of the *Muse of the Missouri* demonstrates a particularly thoughtful placement of a monument on an existing site that takes into account the peculiarities of that space. The fountain, sited on the median strip between Eighth and Ninth streets on Main, has a north-south axis and is flanked by busy traffic arteries. The scheme for the fountain had to take into consideration the directional axis as well as the relationship it would have to the buildings on either side.

The total design concept for the fountain and its setting was the result of a collaboration. Hare & Hare, landscape architects, designed the pedestal as well as the pools beneath the sculpture. John Murphy, principal in the firm of Keene, Simpson & Murphy, also assisted in this phase of the fountain's construction. The result of their ideas is a narrow rectangular retaining wall that embraces the muse and the three pools of the fountain. The basins of the pools are tiered with the muse placed in the highest of the three. The two lower pools extend southward from the main basin, reaching a total length of fifty-eight feet. The form selected for the fountain beautifully reflects the conditions of its environment but gives no hint that the artists were ever limited by its restrictions.

Williams insisted that his fountain make full use of water for its artistic effect. Having remarked on his fondness for the *J.C. Nichols Memorial Fountain*, Williams assured Kemper that the muse would feature lots of water, "not just little nonsense streams of water." Williams honored his commitment, and the water effects he created are some of the most evocative to be found in the city.

The two lower pools are equipped with a circular ring of jets that propel the water toward the center, creating a "cone" of water. The main basin contains 200 jets which mirror the treatment found in the lower pools. Water pours from the shaft and out of the mouths of the fish to fall into the rim of the pedestal before falling into the main basin below. Colored lights illuminate the fountain at night, emphasizing the glittering quality of the water.

The *Muse of the Missouri* is one of Kansas City's most successful fountains. Kemper's tribute, which he lovingly dedicated to his son, provides Kansas Citians with a touch of artistic eloquence in the conscientious use of limited downtown space.

The Eagle Scout Memorial Fountain

Although not obvious, there is a connection between the massive sports arena of Madison Square Garden in New York City and the *Eagle Scout Memorial Fountain* at Thirty-ninth Street and Gillham Road. The story of their association begins in 1903 when Alexander Cassatt, president of Pennsylvania Railroad, commissioned the architectural firm of McKim, Mead & White to design a railroad terminal in New York City. That firm, established in 1878, was acknowledged as instrumental in promoting neoclassical architecture in the United States. They had earned a prestigious reputation as well as a notable place in the history of architectural design.*

The construction of New York's Pennsylvania Station was begun in 1903 and completed in 1910. The enormous Greek Revival building encompassed an area from Seventh to Eighth avenues and Thirty-first to Thirty-third streets and was comparable in size to the Capitol Building in Washington, D.C. The massive structure was built during a time when railroad transportation was the principal mode of travel, and thousands poured into the terminals daily en route to their destinations. The interior of Penn Station has been compared to a reconstruction of the Roman Baths of Caracalla and featured a huge skylighted concourse with vaulting of lacy steel ribs which provided the framework for gigantic panes of glass. In 1961, with the railroad industry in decline, an agreement was reached between the executives of the Pennsylvania Railroad and the developers who wished to erect a new Madison Square Garden to replace an older structure. To accomplish this, the grand terminal would have to be destroyed. Ironically, the old Madison Square Garden, which this proposed arena would replace, was also a design of McKim, Mead & White.

In the early 1960s New York had not yet enacted any legislation to protect its landmarks. Though the uproar and criticism of the plan to demolish the station was loud and heartfelt, there were no legal mechanisms to prevent its demolition. Civic groups beseeched the owners to stay their action, and the impending demolition received national attention. In one demonstration to save the venerable structure, a group of five hundred architects, including nationally prominent Philip Johnson and Paul Rudolf, marched to Penn Station carrying placards that read, "Don't demolish it, polish it." Even this was not enough to prevent the loss of the building. Noted architectural critic Lewis Mumford described the destruction of the building as an "act of irresponsible public vandalism."

There was for Kansas Citians, at least, one favorable consequence of that action. Penn Station had been designed with two massive porticoes that served as sheltered entrances to the building. In keeping with the classical revival flavor of the building, the entablature of the portico supported decorative sculpture that was centrally placed, composed of

---

*Among the firm's other noteworthy designs are the Villard Houses on Madison Avenue in New York City (1872); the Boston Public Library, Boston, Massachusetts (1887); and the Washington Triumphal Arch in New York City. In 1906, Stanford White was brutally murdered, and in 1909 Charles McKim died. The firm continued to exist for many years after their deaths. Charles McKim is generally credited as the principal designer of the Penn Station Terminal.

Fig. 80

two female figures almost twice life-size (Fig. 80). They flanked a huge
seven-foot laurel wreath which contained a clock face in the center. The
figures were allegorical representations of day and night, which was
appropriate to their function as timekeepers. The figure of day was
represented holding a sheaf of sunflowers. The figure of night was portrayed bare breasted and carrying a cloak above her head as if to surround
herself in darkness. An hourglass with decorative wings crowned the
laurel wreath, further alluding to the timekeeping function of the piece.

When news of the impending demolition was announced in Kansas
City, John Starr, who was then president of the Boy Scouts of America
Regional Council, decided there might be at least one element of the
building that could be saved. He wrote to the officials of the Pennsylvania
Railroad and requested that they donate one of the sculptures adorning
the porticoes to the Boy Scouts for use as a memorial to scouting. In July
1966 the chairman of the board quickly responded to Starr's request and
not only agreed to donate the sculpture but also offered to transport the
work as far west as St. Louis. Starr began to set things in motion in Kansas
City to receive the sculpture and provide a suitable setting for it and
formed the Eagle Scout Memorial Committee.

The monument was to serve as a nationwide tribute to all members of
the Boy Scouts of America that had earned the rank of Eagle Scout. The
location of such a monument in Kansas City was especially appropriate as
the Kansas City area had consistently awarded more Eagle Scout badges
than any other area council in the United States. Starr, who chaired the
committee, was instrumental in raising the funds through public donations for the erection of the memorial. The city of Kansas City agreed to
donate park land for the memorial and made several sites available. After
some discussion, the Thirty-ninth and Gillham Road site was selected.

Fig. 81

The placement of the fountain on the grounds is one of the most dramatic in Kansas City (Plate 8, page 21). It is sited on a hillside and at its base is a busy intersection of four roadways. The traffic is controlled in part by a grassy triangular island that is pleasantly landscaped by the Park Department. Gillham Park, a rectangular grassy oasis which also boasts a wading pool and fountain, is located to the south. The *Eagle Scout Memorial Fountain* serves visually as the northern terminus for this long narrow park.

Maurice D. McMullen, architect with the firm of Black & Veatch, can be credited with using the dramatic possibilities of the site to the fullest advantage. He conceived the fountain and the framing wings for the Penn Station sculpture. He designed two staircases that lead from the base of the hill to the summit. The staircases bow out in opposite directions as they ascend the hill, creating a serpentine line. The result is that the staircases frame a roughly triangular green space beneath the sculpture.

The Penn Station figures were minimally changed to serve their new purpose. The center of the wreath, which had previously contained a clock face, was replaced with a metallic Eagle Scout badge which faithfully depicts that award with its tricolored ribbon and silver eagle.

The actual fountain elements are placed in the center of the framing wings directly below the sculpture and consist of two concentric, semicircular basins. The interior contains three jets that spill over the wall to the larger collecting basin surrounding it. The pleasing combination of water sheeting over the edge with the animated splashing created by the jets has caused this fountain to become one of the most popular in the city.

McMullen described his design process and his involvement with the committee chaired by Starr. He conceived the framing walls as a stage and backdrop for the sculptural group. The most immediate problem confronting the designer was how to resolve the conflict between the obviously unrelated subject matter of the figural group with the ideals of scouting for which the memorial was created. McMullen's design, agreed upon by the committee, somewhat intentionally detracts from the female figures (one of whom is bare breasted) that have on occasion been criticized as inappropriate to the memorial's purpose of honoring scouting.

McMullen incorporated a fountain into the design not only to provide some distraction but also to "give people a reason to ascend the steps and to have something to do when they get there." His concept integrates the transplanted sculpture into a unified composition.

The allegorical nature of the figures finds its perfect complement in the symbolism achieved in McMullen's design. The stairs which lead up to the sculpture and fountain remind viewers of the levels of scouting leading to the meritorious Eagle Scout rank. The two-tiered basin also makes reference to that idea.

In an earlier design presented to the committee, McMullen had proposed a more upswept "aerodynamic" version of the side wings that frame the sculpture. (Fig. 81). The committee with the concurrence of McMullen revised the design so that the wings were geometrically square. That decision was partially based on a desire to provide an appropriate setting for the Penn Station figures, which would be more compatible with the architecture and ornament of the period rather than a more contemporary version.

The *Eagle Scout Memorial Fountain* has successfully achieved its goal in providing a noteworthy monument to scouting. The thoughtful regard for the placement of the sculpture in its new home would indeed hearten those who had protested the felling of Penn Station so many years ago.

Frank Land Memorial Fountain

The Order of DeMolay, an international youth organization, was founded in Kansas City in 1919 by Frank S. Land. Land was serving as head of a relief program at a Kansas City Scottish Rite Temple when he conceived of the organization for young men, and he incorporated many Masonic rituals into the order as well as a strict code of ethics. By the end of 1920, having spread primarily through Masonic organizations, the Order of DeMolay had grown to 3,000 young men, and by the end of 1921 there were chapters in fifty-four cities. The list of outstanding men who were once DeMolay members is impressive, including John Steinbeck, Walt Disney, John Cameron Swayze, and many members of Congress.

In 1956, after four decades of spectacular growth, an International Headquarters Building was constructed at 201 East Armour Boulevard on the site of a residence previously occupied by the order. The five-story building, designed by the Kansas City architectural firm of Neville, Sharp & Simon, was to serve as a memorial to its founder, Frank Land. Only one floor was to be used by the DeMolay organization with the other floors

Fig. 82

leased to the Phillips Petroleum Company. An unusual feature of the building was the recreation of Land's office as it had been in the old quarters.

In 1954, Land was named Imperial Shrine Potentate of North America. He remained head of the DeMolay organization until his death in 1959. Following his death, a committee was named to recommend a suitable memorial to him. In 1961, the memorial, in the form of a fountain, was erected in front of the DeMolay Headquarters Building. Funds for the $20,000 fountain were raised by DeMolay members, and Oklahoma City architect W. Dow Gumersen was the designer.

The memorial somewhat resembles a gravestone in its form (Fig. 82). The eight-foot high cenotaph of red granite is carved with the inscription, "For God—For Country—For DeMolay," and a bronze relief bust of Land is attached. A fourteen-foot rectangular pool in front of the stone was designed to contain the water activated by a single fountain jet. The fountain is currently inoperative.

The dedication of the fountain coincided with the fiftieth anniversary of the founding of the DeMolay organization, and the ceremonies were attended by 300 observers.

Nurses Memorial Fountain

Hospitals are in a seemingly constant process of change and growth, as evidenced by area hospitals which have numerous additions. One of those hospitals is Trinity Lutheran at Thirty-first and Wyandotte streets, which has evolved from a simple structure to a large complex. Trinity Lutheran Hospital had its genesis in 1910 with the construction of Penn Valley Hospital at Thirtieth and Wyandotte streets. The following year, Penn Valley Hospital was sold to the Swedish Hospital Association, and in 1921 the name was changed to Trinity Lutheran Hospital.

The hospital began operating a school to train nurses in 1906, but following the trend of closing hospital-operated nursing schools in favor of training nurses through collegiate programs, the school graduated its last class in 1972. Trinity Lutheran Hospital underwent major expansions in 1925, 1966-68, 1973, and 1982-83.

In 1973, the alumnae of the old Trinity Lutheran School of Nursing presented a fountain to the hospital as a memorial to the nurses who had graduated from the school. The fountain was placed in a landscaped garden area between the 1973 addition to the hospital and the old School of Nursing Building.

The fountain is a "dandelion hemisphere," a manufacturer's description of a fountain element composed of a cast bronze ball with a number of arms radiating from it on the upper half of the ball. Water is propelled from the ends of the arms, producing a glistening hemisphere of water. The fountain element is set into a circular, concrete, saucer-shaped basin, approximately ten feet in diameter from where the water is recirculated. The fountain is currently inoperational.

Jane Hemingway Gordon Fountain

The Garden Club of America's only area affiliate is the Westport Garden Club, which was founded in 1950. Over the years the club has been active in a number of civic projects related to gardening. By 1976, the club realized a long-standing dream by creating a garden room in the Nelson-Atkins Museum of Art. The club raised the necessary funds to create such a space, which they use occasionally for meetings, luncheons, and special events. The basement level Westport Garden Room is a light, airy space that contains garden sculpture, plantings, and a fountain. The designer of the room and the fountain was Kansas City architect Stuart Hutchison of the McCoy, Hutchison & Stone architectural firm. The fountain was donated by the George Gordon family as a memorial to Jane Hemingway Gordon, who died in 1965. Mrs. Gordon was a longtime member of the Westport Garden Club and was active in numerous other civic club organizations. A graduate of Wellesley College, Mrs. Gordon was one of the founders of the Wellesley Garden Tour in 1930. This spring tour of gardens in private homes is still a popular attraction. It began and still functions as a fund-raising project for a scholarship fund.

The semicircular fountain basin of colored cast concrete is set against the wall between two doors that lead outside to the Pierson Sculpture Garden (Fig. 83). The low, squat fountain pedestal terminates in an ovoid saucer basin. A wide cut made into the lip of the saucer allows water to sheet over the edge and fall into the retaining basin below for its recirculation. This simple fountain form is a good example of a modern fountain design.

Perhaps to some the concept seemed too simple, for sometime after 1976 a piece of sculpture was mounted on top of the fountain saucer. The bronze sculpture selected for addition to the fountain was a wise choice, for its subject, *Cranes Rising*, is complementary to the fountain and its quiet water effects.

The sculpture, approximately three feet high, is the work of Anna Hyatt Huntington.* The sculpture depicts through a spiraling composition the poses of six cranes. Vertical transition is made from a water bird at

---

*Anna Hyatt Huntington (1876-1973) was a prolific sculptor of animals. She first exhibited at the age of 24 at the Boston Arts Club, showing forty sculptured animal pieces. A

rest at the base to a crane in full flight with outspread wings at the summit. The sculpture was completed in 1934 and given to the gallery by Mrs. Huntington in 1938.

The Westport Garden Room in an intimate, quiet, reflective space and maintains its own integrity within the colossal hallways of the monumental gallery.

Kansas City Zoo Memorial Fountains

The Kansas City Zoological Gardens boasts three memorial drinking fountains that incorporate sculptural elements into their design, distinguishing them from simple utilitarian pieces. The oldest of these drinking fountains was dedicated in 1951. In November 1946, $3,000 had been given to the Park Department from the estate of Edith A. Norton to erect a memorial drinking fountain to honor Mrs. Norton's mother, Mrs. Mary A. Fraser. The only stipulation made was that the fountain be located in the children's area of the zoo.

Construction of the fountain was delayed, and the funds were held in trust pending a decision regarding a suitable location for the fountain. Although the plans were approved by the Park Board in March 1948, the location was not selected until May 1951, and construction began shortly thereafter. A seal pool was built in the zoo in 1951, and it was decided to place the fountain, framed by a semicircle of trees, just to the south of this new attraction (Fig. 84).

Fig. 84

native of Massachusetts, her interest in animals was fostered by her father's profession as a teacher of paleontology. She studied with Boston sculptor Henry Kitson and in New York City with the Art Students' League. Other castings of *Cranes Rising* were given to the Concord Free Public Library, Concord, Massachusetts, and the Dayton (Ohio) Art Institute.

Fig. 83

Fig. 85

The fountain is constructed of Indiana limestone. Two rectangular side wings, each approximately five feet high, flank a central vertical shaft that is six feet high. The central shaft is a bust of a young female with long hair and bangs, staring calmly straight forward. Her nose has been broken off and was rather awkwardly repaired. Drinking outlets and bowls are located on the lower side wings of the structure. Bronze inscription panels are placed at each end of the side wings and on the front side of the side wings are incised wreaths.

The design of the *Mary Fraser Memorial Fountain* was the work of two artists. Architect Edward Buehler Delk, working for the Park Board, designed the basic fountain structure, and Jeannette Klein* designed the bust of the girl. Although Mrs. Klein did not execute the carving of the head, she provided the plaster model from which it was made. Little is known about Mrs. Fraser or Mrs. Norton, and it is not clear whether the bust was meant to literally depict the person it memorializes.

*Jeannette Klein (ca. 1897-1980) was born in Poland and had lived in Kansas City since around 1911. During the 1940s she was an assistant instructor at the Kansas City Art Institute.

The other two fountains in the Kansas City Zoo are similar to each other in overall concept and feature animal motifs more compatible with their setting than the *Fraser Memorial Fountain*. The *Harry Evans Minty Memorial Fountain* was erected in honor of a man described as "a gentleman of the old school." While in his seventies, Minty was named president of the Park Board, a post he assumed from 1945 through 1948.

Minty, who had been a member of the insurance firm of T.H. Mastin and Company for many years, served on the Park Board from his appointment in 1942 until 1948 with an attitude of unselfish devotion that earned him the respect of many. He died in August 1955 at the age of eighty-six. Almost ten years later, a memorial drinking fountain was dedicated to him by the Park Board. Visitors to the Kansas City Zoo on a hot, summer day often pay homage to Minty, as his monument is placed near one of the most popular exhibits, the Great Cat Walk (Fig. 85).

The fountain is composed of a fluted concrete bowl engraved with the words: "Harry Evans Minty Memorial Fountain." In the center of the bowl is a seated bronze lion cub, executed by sculptor Wheeler Williams (who was also the artist of the *Muse of the Missouri Fountain*). The lion cub is a likeness of "Tike," an animal which had become Minty's favorite. Surrounding the cub at its base are several water faucets. The fountain was dedicated in October 1965 and serves as a reminder of the leadership that helped to develop Kansas City's renowned park system.

The third memorial drinking fountain at the zoo was given by Mrs. Leon Sittenfeld in July 1971 in memory of her husband who died in November 1970. Sittenfeld, an insurance underwriter, was well-known for his participation in civic affairs. He was a member of the Native Sons of Kansas City and the Friends of Art, and served on the Board of the Jewish Geriatric and Convalescent Center.

Fig. 86

The *Sittenfeld Memorial Fountain*, designed by Kansas City artist Jac Bowen, is located between the Dairy Barn exhibit and Wolf Pack Woods. The unusual fountain is constructed of cast concrete and takes the form of a tree stump complete with ridges which resemble bark and projections of tree limbs. This stump is approximately three feet high and thirty inches in diameter. The top of the stump is equipped with water outlets. A life-size bronze raccoon perches on one of the limbs, and a squirrel on the opposite side peers over the edge of the stump (Fig. 86). A bronze panel dedicated the fountain to Sittenfeld, "A friend to children, animals, and big people." The site and surrounding benches, pavement, walls, and plantings were designed by Michael Malyn, a member of the Parks and Recreation Department design staff.

8 Nature Redefined—Fountains that Imitate Natural Water Sources

Originally, the word *fountain* was used to describe the source of a spring and was not associated with any formal sculptural elements or retaining basins. Centuries later designers still intentionally mimic these natural water sources and in doing so create timeless fountain vehicles.

One of Kansas City's earliest fountains, still located on Cliff Drive, was constructed to draw attention to a natural spring set into a rustic cliffside setting. The natural spring was converted to a fountain by the addition of sculptural elements.

Kansas City possesses some other remarkable fountains which either imitate or interplay with natural water sources to achieve their primary artistic effects. The waterfall, or cascade, has become one of the principal means used by interior designers to create an outdoor ambience within an interior space as in the Westin Crown Center Hotel or to beautify an exterior wall with a shimmering curtain of water as at the Alameda Plaza Hotel (Plate 23, page 51). Though Kansas City's examples of fountains portraying nature reinterpreted are relatively few, they are extraordinary examples.

Cliff Spring/Scarritt Spring

The 1893 plan established for the park system included the development of three large scenic parks which would be connected by a network of boulevards. One of these large parks, North Terrace Park, was located on the cliffs overlooking the Missouri River and extended from The Paseo on the west to Benton Boulevard on the east. As early as 1885, the city owned some of the land but continued acquisition until 1920 through purchase, gifts, and condemnation. With its 308 acres, North Terrace Park is second in size only to Swope Park.

In 1900, a picturesque six and one-half mile roadway named Cliff Drive was cut through the wooded terrain of North Terrace Park. It rapidly became a favorite haunt of horse and buggy drivers. In fact, for a while automobiles were not permitted on the drive to avoid frightening the horses.

Originally, much of the land bordering the park on the south belonged to the Reverend Nathan Scarritt. Scarritt was a pioneer preacher, teacher, missionary to the Indians, and by the end of his life, a millionaire from his real estate investments. In 1862, Reverend Scarritt had purchased forty acres of land for a farm, then beyond the city limits and overlooking the Missouri River. He later expanded his holdings in the area.

The ancestors of Reverend Scarritt (the Scarritt-Jones-Hendrix-Simpson-Royster clan) built homes on the farm property in what is now the northeast district of the city. Between 1900 and 1940 at least fourteen homes in the Norledge/Gladstone Boulevard area were occupied by members of this family. Below the bluffs, where the original Scarritt home was located, was a spring used by the family to keep milk and butter cool. After the construction of Cliff Drive, the spring became accessible to the public and was acquired by the Park Department from the Scarritt Estate in 1899.

After its acquisition by the Park Department, a series of improvements were made. Between 1906 and 1907, a large cut stone bowl was constructed into which the spring water flowed. The bowl was fifty inches in diameter and ten inches deep. It projected perpendicularly from the wall of the cliff as a semicircular basin which was deeply carved with ridges to resemble the pattern found on a shell. A sunken relief panel mirroring the shell basin was placed above the bowl (Fig. 87). The following year a water trough for horses was constructed on Cliff Drive, opposite the drinking fountain but connected so that it too could make use of the spring water. In 1909, a retaining wall was extended east from the spring to help maintain the stone bluff in position above the spring. A wall was placed in front of the spring in 1935, probably through a Works Progress Administration project.

During the spring of 1959 the fountain was vandalized and the large stone bowl was broken into several pieces. Encouraged by support from two city council members, the Park Board renovated the spring following the unfortunate incident. Councilman Royster donated the cost of a plaque inscribed with the date of the restoration. The spring was also officially named the Scarritt Spring at this time.

Fig. 87

Fig. 88

The water from the spring was popular with residents in the area who brought jugs and filled them with the water which had a high mineral content (Fig. 88). Unfortunately, in 1962 tests revealed that the spring water was contaminated from sewer leakage. People ignored signs placed at the spring to warn of the contamination and continued to fill their water jugs with the cherished water. To combat this potential health problem, the city had the original fountain bricked over. In 1968, someone drove a pipe into the limestone rock, releasing a small stream of water, and the city once again concealed the water outlet. Today, only the plaque and the rock walls on each side of the spring are visible to remind us of this once popular natural attraction.

United Missouri Garden Bank Fountain

The United Missouri Garden Bank at 1415 Grand Avenue was built in 1962-63 from designs by the local architectural firm of Voskamp & Slezak. It was originally owned by the City National Bank and Trust Company.

The single story bank occupies a unique position in downtown Kansas City as real estate values generally have precluded the construction of small satellite banking facilities in favor of larger headquarters. The name of the bank derives from its landscaping amenities, which are also unusual for a downtown building.

A fountain resembling a small waterfall was incorporated into the landscaping. The natural stone that is used in the walls of the building is

Fig. 89

also used to line a pool. Water outlets which create a cascade appear in the front of the building, focused by a recession (Fig. 89). The water flows over the stones into a pool and then into a short channel before it is recirculated. A pedestrian bridge once was placed over the channel but has since been removed.

At the time of construction, R. Crosby Kemper, Jr., president of City National Bank, described the project as having "an emphasis on blending the building materials with the landscaping, thus enhancing the beauty of the general area." Through the use of trees, flowers, and shrubbery, in addition to the naturalistic fountain, that goal was certainly achieved.

Hilton Plaza Inn

A special atmosphere within public buildings can be created when natural water effects are imitated. The interior design of the Hilton Plaza Inn, constructed in 1967 at Main and Forty-fifth streets, illustrates the use of water to enhance a Polynesian theme.

Fig. 90

That theme is first introduced by the exterior fountain in front of the semicircular entrance drive (Fig. 90). A primitive figure carved in lava stone sits to the side of a square retaining pool. Within the retaining pool is an elevated circular concrete basin that is equipped with a spray ring with an outside fall.

Inside the hotel that motif was continued. A circular reception area that served two restaurants, the Seville and the Kona Kai, featured a low natural stone wall with artificial vines and water cascading over the rock wall. Another water cascade was featured inside the Kona Kai Room. Today, only the exterior fountain is operating.

Westin Crown Center Hotel Lobby

In one Kansas City hotel, water becomes an integral extension of the building itself. Open since 1973, the Westin Crown Center Hotel on Pershing Road between Main Street and Grand Avenue features a water display found elsewhere only in nature.

Much of a hillside site was incorporated into the hotel with a minimum attempt to "tame" the dramatic cliffside. The walls of the hotel lobby were actually constructed around the rocky cliff, allowing the rugged landscape to form the hotel's most unusual feature. To reshape the hillside into an attractive, rugged bluff, 400,000 cubic yards of rock and shale had to be removed. Architect Harry Weese of Chicago designed the hotel, and Landscape Associates, Inc. of Little Rock, Arkansas, designed the landscaping. Robert L. Shaheen was the principal designer and described the area he had to work with as "a huge planter box, just a 120 by 60 foot planter box."

Shaheen created a lavishly landscaped natural hillside and waterfall as the dramatic backdrop for the large hotel lobby (Plate 10, page 25). The tropical garden he created is one hundred feet wide and rises sixty feet (the equivalent of four stories) from the mezzanine floor at a forty-five degree angle. The hillside is landscaped with boulders, a variety of mature trees, tropical ferns, and other exotic plants. A glittering waterfall cascades down the hillside at a rate of 250 gallons per minute. The water drops in a series of four steps before finally cascading over a twelve foot ledge into a pool where it is recirculated. The pool is twelve feet at its widest point and is planted with water iris and Egyptian papyrus. Koi fish, an exotic variety cultivated in Japan since the seventh century, swim in the retaining pool. Bridges and walkways invite visitors to stroll through the lush splendor and allow the waterfall to be viewed from several vantage points, leading the spectators to feel as if they had visited a tropical paradise.

Hallmark Corporate Entrance

The Hallmark Cards headquarters building at Twenty-fifth and McGee streets has been expanded many times as the firm has grown to become America's largest producer of greeting cards and related items. The headquarters building was erected by the side of a limestone cliff in 1956. The physical peculiarities of the site necessitated that the upper floors contain greater square footage than the lower floors. In the spring of

Fig. 91   1982, a major expansion began which primarily extended the eighth and
ninth floors. To highlight the expansion and to heighten Hallmark's
visibility in the Crown Center Complex, a corporate entrance was constructed. Edward Larabee Barnes, the New York City architect who designed the *Crown Center Square Fountain*, also designed this impressive corporate entrance and its gracious water elements.

The corporate entrance is approached from Gillham Road and is
slightly above grade, so the full impact of the space is not apparent from
the street. A parklike area with plantings around a carefully landscaped
parking area extends in front of the projecting barrel-vaulted entrance to
the building. The arched entrance which features glass fanlights at each
end formalizes the entrance area. The focal point of the entire area is a
grand concourse of water treated in a naturalistic manner (Fig. 91). The
concourse consists of a 150-foot long rectangular reflecting pool which
terminates in a semicircular end pool. As the grade drops, the rectangular
pool steps down by means of six miniature cascades, which extend across
the width of the pool. The cascades are created by a metal grate with a
series of holes placed closely together. The pool is lined with small
pebbles giving it the appearance of a natural river bed. The vista from the
Gillham Road entrance terminates in front of the barrel-vaulted entrance.
Columns of aerated water are clustered on each side of the semicircular
end pool.

The interior of the building received a similar treatment. Two light
wells are formed by skylights on the roof and extend from the seventh
through the ninth floors of the building. At the base of these light wells
are rectangular reflecting pools also lined with natural pebbles.

9 Courtyard Fountains

Just as an atrium can provide interest and warmth to the interior of a building, the courtyard can add a great visual interest and variety to the exterior. The courtyard can be a way for a commercial concern to provide a public amenity as well as a pleasant area for its employees during suitable weather. Historically, the courtyard has been an uncovered space, completely or partially surrounded by walls which help to define the space. The urban open space called a plaza, a larger relative of the public square of small towns, is suitable for greater numbers of people.

Both plazas and courtyards vary in size, location, and use, but they almost always exist to provide a relief from the complexity of crowded urban areas. The fountain is frequently used in the plaza or courtyard to enliven the space both visually and acoustically. The oldest example of a courtyard space in Kansas City is Rozelle Court at the Nelson-Atkins Museum of Art.

Rozelle Court Fountain

Rozelle Court is approximately eighty-five feet square, surrounded by a two-story arcaded gallery. The spirit and ornament of the courtyard derive from the Renaissance and are consistent with the neoclassical form revival style of architecture of the museum itself. The purpose of the courtyard was explained by J.C. Nichols, a trustee of the museum:

> In designing the gallery with its acres of space on four floors, its miles of corridors, its many rooms filled with works of art, we had always in mind that unwelcome disease "museum fatigue," and everything is planned to prevent it.

The courtyard was to provide a welcome respite for gallery viewers, to refresh them, and to prevent the onset of the disease to which Nichols referred.

The court was named for Frank F. Rozelle who donated money for its construction and embellishment. Rozelle had served as an attorney for William Rockhill Nelson, for whom the museum is named. The central feature of the court, installed for the museum's opening in December 1933, is a fountain (Plate 5, page 15) consisting of a massive marble bowl, eight feet in diameter and weighing approximately four tons. It is set within a retaining basin that is approximately eighteen feet in diameter. The central bowl was not originally designed as a fountain but has been equipped with a single central outlet which propels a vertical stream of water from its center. The water falls over the beveled lip of the bowl which causes it to partially sheet over the edge. The circular retaining basin beneath the bowl contains eight nozzles that each send an arcing stream into the main basin, creating an audible, playful splashing. Nichols expressed the purpose of the court's fountain in this way: "The fountain in the center is sending up graceful sprays that fall in soft liquid splashings. Your mind is soothed."

The bowl itself is elevated on a base consisting of four lion paws designed by Thomas Wight. Wight was a principal in the architectural firm of Wight & Wight, the designers of the museum. Wight explained that the pedestal on which the bowl rests is the single ornamental detail and the collecting basin was purposefully made severe to direct the emphasis toward the marble central basin. The floor of the court was originally covered with bluegrass sod that was later replaced by stone. In the courtyard floor, surrounding the fountain are inset bronze roundels featuring the signs of the zodiac, carved in relief.

Because the bowl for which Wight created his restrained setting has an unknown origin, museum officials have not assigned it an accession number. The bowl is carved of a single piece of cipollino marine marble, tannish with moss green striations throughout. When water is added, the greenish hue becomes darker. Various suggestions have been made about the history of the bowl; however, the consensus is that it dates from around 200 A.D.

The bowl was purchased around 1930 by Harold Woodbury Parsons, art advisor for the Nelson-Atkins Museum of Art, during a one-month stay in Italy. It had been preserved by its Italian owners, and Parsons thought it to have come from one of the imperial baths in Rome. Others have been more specific, determining that the bowl was from either the Baths of Caracalla or the Baths of Diocletian. It is maintained that the bowl was used to hold oil for the athletes to cleanse themselves of the dust of the arena.

In a controversial action in 1981, Rozelle Court was enclosed with a skylighted roof. Enclosing the court had some obvious advantages: the space could be used on a year-round basis (in fact, the museum cafe has moved into the space) and the upper gallery of the court could be turned into an exhibition space. Unfortunately, the roof dramatically altered the original ambience of the space. The light, which used to vary with the weather and the time of day, became uniform, unchanging, and over-all rather dark.

The fountain was not without defects when it was purchased. Over the years as water froze in the basin each winter, it became more damaged with cracks and missing material. After Rozelle Court was protected from further incursions of weather, the fountain was restored. An epoxy filled with marble dust to match the stone was used to fill the cracks and fill in missing areas.

The fountain has been the focal point of the court since its installation. Though not fully accepted by the museum's professional staff because of its ambiguous claim to authenticity, it has continued to serve the purpose for which it was intended, the grateful relief of the visitor's fatigue.

Barney Allis Plaza

Much time and money were invested in a small downtown park that finally achieved a measure of success some thirty years after its initial creation. The park, an expensive parcel of real estate, was located in the heart of downtown on the block of ground between Twelfth, Thirteenth, Wyandotte, and Central streets. Between 1899 and 1937, that block of land had been the site of Convention Hall.* By 1930, Kansas City was beginning to feel the need for a new, modern, and larger facility to accommodate conventions, expositions, and other attractions. Thus, using funds available through the Ten-Year Plan bond program, Municipal Auditorium was built on the block south of the Convention Hall between 1933 and 1935, replacing Convention Hall which was razed in 1937.

The monumental Municipal Auditorium boasted theaters, a large arena, and convention space. Its numerous attractions drew large crowds, and by the time of its completion, the block to the north where Convention Hall formerly stood was being considered for development as an underground parking garage with a park placed on the garage roof. Although this plan was favored by City Manager H.F. McElroy, vocal private parking interests expressed opposition to the plan.

In 1946, a bond issue was passed that would enable the city government to construct the garage and park, which would be patterned after Union Square in San Francisco, a combination park/garage facility that had impressed City Manager L.P. Cookingham during a visit.

It was originally anticipated that the project would encompass the two city blocks north of the auditorium, with the southern portion constructed first and the north block developed later after the land had been acquired from private interests. The area would provide a landscaped "front lawn" for the Municipal Auditorium. The impressive Lyric Theater (originally the Ararat Shrine Temple) would be a visual anchor at the north end of the park.

Work on the project proceeded slowly. The architectural firm of Gentry & Voskamp prepared detailed plans for the garage and park in 1949, but the project continued to be delayed. Meanwhile, the need for additional parking in the downtown area was becoming more and more urgent. Registration of vehicles in Kansas City had jumped from 93,000 in 1946 to 161,000 in 1954. Even given the critical need for the garage, the plans presented by the architects were not accepted without criticism.

The grade between Twelfth and Thirteenth streets dropped sharply to the south and needed to be leveled to accommodate the underground garage. The architects planned to accomplish this by building up the south end of the block which would be supported by retaining walls. The park would be entered from this direction by staircases built into the wall. Critics of the plan felt the built-up park would obstruct a good view of Municipal Auditorium from Twelfth Street. The architects responded that in their opinion complete vistas that could be taken in at a glance were seldom satisfying anyway.

The plans for the north block never materialized, and only a scaled-down version of the project using the block immediately north of the Municipal Auditorium was completed. Construction of the three-level underground parking garage finally began in March 1954 and opened to

*Convention Hall was constructed in 1899 to accommodate the July 1900 Democratic National Convention. A disastrous fire completely destroyed the building in April 1900. One of the proudest moments in Kansas City's history was the rapid rebuilding of the hall in just ninety days, finishing the task in time to accommodate the Democrats as planned.

the public in December 1955. The roof of the garage was water-proofed for the park which would be placed on top of it, and landscaping commenced the following spring. At the dedication ceremonies held on June 21, 1956, Mayor William E. Kemp called the park, "a place of quiet beauty in the heart of the city." In more recent years, however, it has been viewed as an urban failure as the problems inherent in the design quickly became obvious.

The park had been conceived in a formal, symmetrical manner to harmonize with the formality of the Municipal Auditorium. In keeping with that formality, no diagonal walkways invited the stroller into the park, and pedestrian access to the elevated park was unclear. A sixteen-foot high retaining wall at the south end obscured the view of the park and necessitated that the park be entered from that direction by staircases. The retaining wall, faced with limestone to harmonize with the color and texture of the Municipal Auditorium, continued partially on the east and west sides of the park. Placed squarely in the middle of the park was a large fountain, but its presence was almost camouflaged (on the east and west by rows of conical evergreens placed in square, concrete boxes; on the north by a protruding concrete pedestrian entrance to the garage; and on the south by the retaining wall). Small concrete structures (housing large fans to provide ventilation for the garage) also protruded on the four corners of the park.

The fountain placed in the center of the park (Fig. 92) was intended as the focal point. It was impressive in scale and consisted of a sixty-foot   *Fig. 92*

square mirror pool with a polygonal granite basin in its center extending twelve feet above the pool. More than fifty jets expelled water from the perimeter of the basin, surrounding a central stream which could reach a height of forty feet. The fountain was equipped with automatic controls to vary the number of jets operating, their direction, and the pressure with which the water was discharged. Ingeniously, the fountain utilized water from the garage air conditioning system for part of its spray. Colored floodlights illuminated the fountain at night. Despite the beauty of its fountain, the park never became a popular gathering place for downtown workers and visitors.

A move was undertaken to have the park named in honor of Barney Allis soon after his death in April 1962. Allis, who began in the hotel business in the 1920s, had become manager of the Muehlebach Hotel in 1931. He was a tireless downtown leader and was active in promoting the development of the downtown area. Allis had been one of the principal proponents of the park and garage fronting his hotel. He had also served on the advisory board of the Municipal Auditorium and was a member of the Downtown Committee for more than twenty years. A dedication ceremony on October 15, 1963, sponsored by the Downtown Committee and the city council, formalized the naming of the "Barney Allis Plaza." The new name, however, had no effect on the park's popularity.

As early as 1974 plans were offered to improve the park so that it would be more attractive to downtown workers and visitors. New building projects in the area had made the park site increasingly important. The H. Roe Bartle Convention Center, which opened in 1976, now extends along the west side of the plaza. Both the turn-of-the-century Folly Theater to the northwest and the Aladdin Hotel (built in the 1920s and since renamed Embassy on the Park), on the east side of the park have been restored to their former grandeur. The completion of the Vista Hotel in 1985 has brought more people to the area.

The proposals for improving the park have had to appeal to both city officials and downtown business interests, who have often held conflicting opinions as to the best design adaptation for the park. The need for a consensus on the disposition of the park soon became critical as the repairs to the roof of the garage became more urgent.

In November 1982, William H. Whyte, a New York consultant on the use of urban spaces and author of *The Social Life of Small Urban Spaces*, was invited to Kansas City to study the problems of the plaza and to address the concerns of the Kansas City Redevelopment Authority and the Downtown Council. Whyte recommended that the park be converted into a place which would attract people through the addition of food services and plenty of places to sit.

After lengthy debate between the city council members concerning the design of the park and the bidding process, the final plans were approved in November 1983. Whyte's recommendations were adopted with some modifications. The final design was prepared by the California landscape architectural firm of SWA, in conjunction with the local architectural firm of Marshall & Brown. Construction of the rejuvenated park and repair of the garage began in the spring of 1984 and was completed a year later.

The newly designed park features a diagonal walkway which divides the area into two triangles. The triangle at the northwest corner of the park is planted with numerous trees, which have circular benches installed around their trunks. The opposite triangle has more of an open quality with its major design emphasis an east/west axis created by a concrete-columned pergola which is covered with wisteria vines.

In July 1984, a monumental water feature was proposed for the Twelfth Street frontage which would further enliven the atmosphere of the already dramatically changed park. This water showcase was to feature a linear arrangement of sixty-four geyser jets with three and one-half inch diameter nozzles set into a rectangular collecting pool. The geysers were to propel the water approximately four feet into the air and then fall over a series of granite steps leading into the pool to create a "white water" cascade before its recirculation. This water spectacular would include computer-assisted cycling and colored lenses to illuminate the fountain after dark. The California-based firms of CMS Collaborative and WET Enterprises were selected to provide the computer programming and design analysis for the fountain.* The water display as originally conceived was to cost between $175,000 to $300,000.

After much discussion and sometimes heated debate between city leaders and private citizens about the cost and appearance of the fountain, a consensus was reached. The water spectacular completed in the summer of 1985 was to greatly resemble the original conception with only minor modifications (Plate 24, page 53).

The fountain is composed of 112 geyser jets, each with a nozzle head one and one-half inches in diameter. The jets are spaced eighteen inches apart, a change from the original proposal, which called for an interval of every three feet. The water height was increased from four to twelve feet. Colored lenses of blue, green, red, and amber allow the creation of both primary and secondary colors which can be mixed as desired producing a color spectrum that can range from colorless to almost black. The computer-assisted cycling action can vary the height of the columns of water in predetermined sequences, and combined with the color changes created by the lenses over the lamps, the fountain is a spectacular visual display.

The water feature as built cost the city of Kansas City in excess of $1 million. The Downtown Council, an influential group of private property owners, gave $50,000 toward its completion and pledged an additional $250,000 as an endowment toward future maintenance costs, estimated at $25,000 a year. The City of Fountains Foundation assisted the fund-raising effort.

It is appropriate that Barney Allis Plaza now expresses a renewed vitality and spectacular visual interest. Its location in the heart of a cityscape surrounded by a major new hotel, newly renovated buildings, and glimmering office towers presented a unique opportunity to call attention to this "jewel" in the center of a dynamic downtown.

---

*WET Enterprise designers had previously worked on water displays and fountains for Epcot Center in Florida.

Commerce Trust Arcade Fountain   *Fig. 93*

The Commerce Trust Company at 922 Walnut (formerly the Commerce Bank of Kansas City) is distinguished by a narrow arcade along its front, with arched openings serving as an elegant "front porch" for the building. The narrow rectangular space which is formed between the arcade and the building also functions much like a courtyard.

In 1961, a majestic fountain was installed within this space. Although a beautiful work, its setting was not ideal as the fountain pool was somewhat awkwardly placed on the risers of the steps leading into the building and its support appeared precarious at best (Fig. 93).

The fountain was a design of artist and sculptor Arthur Kraft and was composed of a figural group set within a rectangular retaining basin. The life-size bronzes portrayed a family group of a man, woman, and young boy. The figures were placed in the center of the retaining pool, and a spray ring with an outside fall surrounded the perimeter of the circular base. Jets were placed elsewhere in the pool, and their arcing sprays turned the water in toward the figures.

James Kemper, Jr., the downtown leader responsible for installing this fountain, was optimistic about the effects the work might have: "Ours had long been regarded as one of the most beautiful cities in America, and this fountain shows our desire to contribute to the beauty. We hope that this fountain with its artistic sculpture might be a forerunner of similar objects of beauty at other downtown commercial buildings."

The bank originally intended to operate the fountain year-round, but, unfortunately, problems developed with a leak into a basement office.

Sometime around 1973 the fountain was removed and placed in storage. There is a strong possibility that it may find a new home and a setting that will work to its advantage in a downtown office building now under construction for Kemper's firm, Commerce Bancshares.

Business Men's Assurance Company Fountains

Towering nineteen stories above the busy intersection of Thirty-first Street and Southwest Trafficway, the B.M.A. Tower became a major addition to the city's skyline in 1963. Headquarters for an insurance firm, the Business Men's Assurance Company of America Building was sited on the second highest elevation in Kansas City.

The building and its plaza were designed by the nationally prominent Chicago firm of Skidmore, Owings & Merrill. The building sits back from Thirty-first Street, and the plaza extends between the building and the street. The 77,000 square foot plaza was originally paved with a reddish-grey brick laid in a geometric grid of eighteen foot sections. Four sections of the plaza on the west side contained reflecting pools. Each was equipped with a single fountain jet placed in the center (Fig. 94).

The fountains quickly presented a major problem. Because of the elevation, they were exposed to wind velocities among the strongest in the city. The winds blew the fountain sprays out of control, subjecting pedestrians to unwanted showers. The fountains had to be turned off for the dedication of the building and for the next two years were operated only on an irregular basis. Finally, in 1965 the water was permanently shut off.

In 1984, the plaza was renovated. Dark and light pebble aggregate paving is used to retain a grid pattern, playing off the geometric quality of the building. The original reflecting pools have been filled with earth and planted.

Fig. 94

The Kansas City Star Fountain

The impressive Italian Renaissance style building at Eighteenth Street and Grand Avenue, a landmark in the city's midtown area, is remarkable in several respects: first and perhaps most significant is its history.

The building was erected between 1910 and 1911 for William Rockhill Nelson as the base of operations for the *Kansas City Star*, the newspaper he founded. Nelson began his newspaper in 1880 and ultimately expanded its operations to include a morning edition, the *Kansas City Times*, and a weekly agricultural edition, the *Weekly Star*.

Nelson's innovative approach to reporting the news and running the newspaper business caused the *Kansas City Star* to excel over all competition. Nelson used the paper as a vehicle to expand the social consciousness of the youthful city, and he spearheaded campaigns to build an art gallery and make civic improvements as well as to promote a park and boulevard system.

A second remarkable aspect is the architecture of the Kansas City Star Building. Designed by Chicago architect Jarvis Hunt*, the building reflects the elegance of an Italian Renaissance villa while it houses the seemingly incompatible mechanized operations of a newspaper industry. The division of the building into two parts which are separated by a square tower was essential to the success of Hunt's design scheme. The west building housed the mechanical and printing department, and the east building housed the offices of the reporters and editors. This arrangement allowed Hunt to isolate the presses from the quieter aspects of the business. In keeping with the European flavor of the design, Hunt provided a paved courtyard on the south, which offered a dramatic, unobstructed view of the building from the street. That vista was to remain unchanged for some fifty years.

The third aspect of note, the Kansas City Star fountain and courtyard, came as a result of the city's emphasis on urban beautification programs in the early 1960s. The city's investment in public improvements, which included plantings and landscaping, provided a catalyst for private enterprise to follow suit. Consequently, the owners of the Kansas City Star Building converted the paved courtyard in front of the building into a lushly landscaped green space and added an ornamental fountain that would become a focal point within the midtown area.

Tom Colgrove, then an associate with the landscape architectural firm of Hare & Hare, designed the fountain and improvements for the Kansas City Star courtyard. He presented several proposals to the owners. Each of the schemes considered the existing architecture which dictated that a certain formality and symmetry be carried through to the design of the fountain and grounds. Colgrove included in the executed plan geometrically pruned hedges and paved areas which were typical of formal garden settings, and trees planted to screen the adjacent parking areas. The result was a landscaping scheme perfectly harmonious with the architecture of the building. To ensure a consistency with the formal layout of the

---

*Hunt designed Kansas City's Union Station Railroad Terminal at Pershing and Main Street. The station, completed in 1914, was the third largest railroad terminal in the United States after Penn Station (demolished) and Grand Central Station, both located in New York City.

plantings, Colgrove planned the fountain so that it would be located directly in front of the main entrance on the south, adding to the symmetry established not only by the other improvements but also by the building itself.

Constructed of sunset pink granite, the fountain is built on two levels with each level functioning in counterpoint to the other (Plate 17, page 39). A rectangular pool at the lowest level contains a series of bubbler jets around the perimeter with their sprays rising to a height of approximately eighteen inches. Elevated within this pool is another rectangular basin which contains five pedestals—a large central bowl flanked by four smaller and lower bowls. The center pedestal is equipped with a spray ring around the circumference of the saucer. The four smaller pedestal bowls each issue a single jet.

The water produced by the upper tier of the fountain spills over into the lower basin through cuts made into the wall. The resulting spillover creates animation and visual interest as well as pleasing audible effects.

The Kansas City Star fountain and courtyard were completed in October 1964. A year later the design was cited by the American Association of Nurserymen as an award winner in its Thirteenth Annual National Landscape Competition. In addition, the fountain and courtyard received the first annual award of the Federated Garden Clubs of Missouri, Incorporated, for its achievements in beautification and landscaping.

The fountain and courtyard typify the success that is possible when sensitive considerations are given to the existing characteristics of a site. The fountain's scale, color, use of water, and landscaping complemented *Fig. 95*   Jarvis Hunt's grand palazzo, the Kansas City Star Building, and, in fact,

seems to have belonged in its place in the south court from the building's inception.

The University of Missouri-Kansas City Library Fountains

The courtyard area of the University of Missouri-Kansas City Library was developed to solve the problem of situating the building on a steep grade. The construction of the $3 million library building was approved in 1966. The building had a certain symbolic importance in that it was the first new academic building to be started on the campus after the merger of the private University of Kansas City into the University of Missouri system in 1963.

The site selected for construction of the building at the northwest corner of Rockhill Road and Fifty-first Street sloped downward from Fifty-first Street. The architects, Marshall & Brown, took advantage of this downward grade to incorporate a sunken outdoor courtyard area under a bridge that leads to the main entrance on the Fifty-first Street side of the building. The courtyard, 250 feet in length, was designed to harmonize with the rough textured limestone of the library building and to provide a lounge/study area for students in warm weather. Textured concrete benches and planters surround rectangular fountain basins on either side of the bridge. The fountain basins (Fig. 95) are almost two feet deep and measure approximately ten by twenty feet. A slab of granite is elevated in a horizontal relationship at one end of each pool where three water outlets are located. The fountains are no longer operating, having been turned off in the mid-1970s when the university began looking for ways to curtail expenses.

In 1970, the library building received an urban design award from the Municipal Art Commission for solving "the problem of creating an urban academic environment without reference to the traditional approach of previous campus buildings. The bridge entrance with its planting treatment provides appropriate scale to the project."

Commerce Tower Sunken Garden—Fountain of Life

Bringing the outdoors inside to create an oasis within an urban space has long been a consideration in architectural design. Architects, planners, and even psychologists have acknowledged the beneficial aspects of bringing an outdoor ambience to a congested urban environment.

In 1964, Commerce Bancshares, Inc. completed construction of the thirty-two story, $12 million Commerce Tower Building at 911 Main Street. Designed by the architectural firm of Keene, Simpson & Murphy, the building was then the tallest in the city.

Significantly, the building was designed with some aesthetic features that added a further dimension to its already remarkable height. A sunken garden, fifty feet by seventy-two feet, was incorporated into the building's design. The garden was lavishly planted and was intended to serve a cafe and gallery area, which were situated on the basement level of the building.

The most prominent feature of the court is a fountain (installed in October 1964 and dedicated in February 1965), designed by Seattle,

Washington, painter and sculptor George Tsutakawa. During his long career Tsutakawa has designed many fountains, including the *Fountain of Wisdom* for the Seattle Public Library, Seattle, Washington (completed 1960); the *Garth Fountain* for the Washington Cathedral, Washington, D.C. (1968); and the *Phi Mu Fountain* for the Seattle Campus of the University of Washington (1967). Tsutakawa, who spent his childhood in Japan, studied for both his undergraduate and master of fine arts degrees at the University of Washington, where he later became a member of the faculty. In 1936, and again in 1952, Tsutakawa studied with innovative modernist sculptor Alexander Archipenko. Tsutakawa related that he was very much influenced by his philosophy.

Tsutakawa received the commission for the Commerce Tower fountain through a Los Angeles art agency. Because the fountain was to play a premier role in the development of the courtyard space, Tsutakawa was consulted about much of the pool, pavement, and landscape design. The sculpture was fabricated in the sculptor's Seattle studio and installed on the site by Tsutakawa who employed his own engineer to handle all of the hydraulic and mechanical details.

The artist has developed his own personal design philosophy with regard to fountains. In an interview conducted in 1979, Tsutakawa remarked, "A piece of sculpture with water flowing relates to the material world . . . skyscrapers to concrete." Tsutakawa placed heavy emphasis on the dynamics of water in its ability not only to produce movement but also to produce sound. He noted that, "Rhythm and sound contribute to the totality of the fountain." He added, in reference to the fountain's relationship to the cityscape: "The sound, aside from being delightful, neutralizes the sounds of the city. The screeching of cars, the noise—it is almost drowned out."

The Fountain of Life, a name given Tsutakawa's work by a Commerce Bank executive, is an abstracted form which rises thirteen feet in the center of a circular basin set into an elevated rectangular platform (Plate 18, page 41). The courtyard surrounding the fountain is paved and incorporates grassy areas along the south side of the court which is landscaped with rows of trees and other plantings.

Tsutakawa's design for the fountain is unmistakably a twentieth-century interpretation. Abandoning the traditional spray rings and vertical jets, Tsutakawa has constructed his sculpture with bladelike projections which "bend" the water to produce the desired effects.

In the notes accompanying a recent catalogue, the sculptor remarked: "Over the past twenty years I have endeavored to create new fountain designs based on forms and rhythms found in nature." The *Fountain of Life* derives its form from a lotus blossom and consists of a petaled bloom rising from a vertical stalk in the center, surrounded by protecting leaves. The tubing which carries the water through the fountain is ingeniously integrated into the sculptural form so that it appears as stems of the flower. Vertical jets of water issue from the center of the lotus blossom which is surrounded by fans of sheeting water, created by the water breaking against the outer leaves.

The fountain composition demonstrates Tsutakawa's predilection for sound and movement. Although the sculpture is "self-contained" without its water effects, it only truly achieves its fullest dimension with the addition of the life-giving waters.

Tsutakawa's work is one of the lesser known fountains in Kansas City, partially because of its relative newness but primarily because of its lack of visibility as the courtyard where it is located cannot be seen from the street. A flight of steps leads from the sidewalk into the courtyard, but the staircase seems somehow foreboding. The sun rarely floods the court because of the tall buildings that surround the Commerce Tower Building and because the courtyard faces the west, allowing only late afternoon rays to penetrate the space.

James M. Kemper, Jr., chairman of the board and chief executive officer of Commerce Bancshares, Inc., indicated that in the future he would only consider the creation of a courtyard on an elevated level which would invite pedestrian access. In the meantime, those who do venture into the courtyard are treated to a sensitive, artistic expression that is seldom found in the heart of a city.

The Civic Plaza Attempt

The proposals for the development of a civic plaza in Kansas City have a long, complicated, and intriguing history. The impetus for the creation of a civic plaza was the construction of three buildings at Twelfth Street and Locust: the Jackson County Courthouse, completed in 1934; the City Hall, completed late in 1937; and the Municipal Courts/Police Headquarters Building, erected in 1938. The construction of these structures was facilitated by the passage of a $50 million bond issue in 1931 to support a "Ten-Year Plan." This massive public works program was jointly sponsored by the city and Jackson County to upgrade roads and government facilities and to make improvements to the parks and the airport. Federal money was added to the program to help pay construction costs.

A concerted attempt was made to relate the siting of the government buildings to each other and to use compatible construction materials, style, and ornament. When construction was completed, a rectangular courtyard space was formed running north-south with the Police Headquarters on the east, City Hall on the north, and the courthouse on the south.

City Hall Fountains

City Manager H.F. McElroy had tried to interest the county in jointly purchasing a square block of land on which both the City Hall and the courthouse could be built. The county declined this proposal and used an entire block for the courthouse alone.

The site for the City Hall on the block directly north of the courthouse was selected in August 1934 and was originally planned to encompass only the north half of the block bounded by Eleventh and Twelfth streets, Oak to Locust. However, by December of that year, efforts were underway to purchase the south half for use as an underground parking garage and plaza.

In August 1936, the Swenson Construction Company was awarded the contract for the construction of an underground parking garage for the City Hall on the south half of the block. Plans included a plaza on the roof of the garage that gradually sloped down to Twelfth Street. The central part of the plaza, fifty-four feet wide, was paved with a russet concrete and was framed by a series of fountain pools. Landscaped lawns extended beyond the fountains on each side to Oak and Locust streets.

The City Hall fountains are arranged in parallel rows on either side of the plaza, each row consisting of four rectangular basins, approximately ten feet by twenty feet, which were originally lined with blue and green tile. Each basin contains sculptures which derive their motifs from the sea (Plate 2, page 9). The northernmost fountain pool on each side contains a winged bronze mythological sea horse, flanked by smaller dolphins. The horses spout a stream of water into the basins. The remaining three fountains on each side contain upright concave bronze shells from which emerge the head of a dolphin that functions as the water outlet to the basins beneath. The basins follow the grade of the plaza so that each is set slightly lower than the one to the north, creating a terraced effect (Fig. 96). Originally, hedges surrounded each pool and framed the fountains behind green walls.

The fountains, designed by Carl Paul Jennewein, were installed in the spring of 1938. All but forgotten today, Jennewein (1890-1978) was one of America's foremost sculptors between 1920 and 1940. Jennewein came to the United States from Germany in 1907 and studied at the Art Students League. He was the recipient of numerous awards and prizes,

Fig. 96

and for several years served as the president of the National Sculpture Society. His neoclassical style has been described by sculptor critic and historian Wayne Craven as a merging of antiquity with an art nouveau decorative quality. The polished surfaces and strong graceful lines of the Kansas City works are typical of Jennewein's sculpture.*

The erection of these fountains as part of a plaza connecting two government buildings (City Hall and the courthouse) is especially note-worthy since this expenditure of money that some might have perceived as superfluous took place during the depression years. In fact, city employees nicknamed the fountains "Cut" and "Lug," in reference to the days of political machine campaign lugs and cuts in salaries of city employees.

The fountains did not exist without problems and controversy. In May 1942, the fountains were turned off as a way to support the war effort—thus saving the city $1.50 each day in electricity used to operate the recirculating pumps. The fountains were turned off from 1946 until 1948 because extensive leaks had developed and repairs needed to be made. Engineers said the entire piping and plumbing system needed rehabilitation as the system had not been installed in accordance with the original plans. Finances were still a consideration in August 1952, when signs were posted noting that the water was "recirculated and not wasted" to alleviate criticism of their operation. Late in the 1950s the fountains were turned off once again. They had begun leaking into the basement garage and had also been damaged by young boys frolicking in the waters, splashing out so much water that the recirculating controls were put out of commission, necessitating costly repairs.

The Linscott Plan

The plaza began to steadily decline. The tiles in the fountain basins became loose, and the paved area between the fountains started to crumble and was described as "not unlike strolling down a dusty gravel road in the Ozarks." What had been intended as one of the city's most beautiful assets had turned into a civic disgrace. Finally, in the spring of 1964, Kansas City architect Mayol Linscott was hired by the city to furnish designs for a renovated entrance plaza to City Hall. Linscott presented a plan which reflected his belief that the broad sidewalk area between the fountains was an eyesore that could be made more visually interesting.

Linscott suggested removing the three lower pairs of fountains, leaving only the two sea horse fountains in place. He concluded that this elimination of the lower tiers would save on maintenance and repair as well as solve the problem of leakage into the garage. He suggested that the four shell/dolphin head fountains could be better used in a fountain placed in the center of the plaza, surrounded by planting beds. The areas

---

*The south frieze of the City Hall building was also executed by Jennewein and provides an example of his relief work to compare with his free-standing fountains. Other important works by Jennewein include the *Darlington Memorial Fountain*, Washington, D.C.; war memorials in Providence, Rhode Island, and Worcester, Massachusetts; a polychromed pediment for the Philadelphia Museum of Art; four pylons for the 1939 New York World's Fair; and the Harry S. Truman inaugural medal.

Fig. 97

previously occupied by the fountains would be covered with grass (Fig. 97).

The *Kansas City Star* editorialized against this rather drastic change to the City Hall Plaza, noting that: "A community with the resources of Kansas City ought to be able to afford a few decorative effects at City Hall. . . . The appearance of City Hall would be drastically altered by any new design for the south approach. A full public discussion of any modification is in order."

Linscott's controversial proposal stimulated a beneficial public dialogue. Henry Scott, a member of the Municipal Art Commission and chairman of the Art Department at the University of Missouri-Kansas City, was interested in a suggestion that had been made earlier by architect Elpidio Rocha. Although acknowledging that parking would pose a problem, Scott suggested closing off Twelfth Street between City Hall and the courthouse (between Oak and Locust streets) and using that space to create a civic center which would unite the two buildings more cohesively.

Shortly thereafter, architect William R. Bovard responded to Scott's suggestion with an alternative idea. Instead of closing off Twelfth Street, a major east-west traffic artery, he proposed it be bridged by an "elevated" park. Bovard's suggestion was not adopted.

The need to reach a decision regarding the treatment of the City Hall Plaza soon became more immediate because of adjacent construction projects. In 1958-60, a new public library building had been erected just west of the courthouse at Twelfth and Oak streets. In addition, in April 1963 construction had begun on a new federal office building, just east of the courthouse. Further, in 1959 plans had been announced for the construction of a state office building at the southeast corner of Twelfth and Locust streets. That site was eventually appropriated for the federal office building. The state then selected its current site at Thirteenth and

Cherry streets, planning to place the building close to Thirteenth Street. It was not until 1965 that the decision was made to use the entire block and place the building far back from the street. Actual construction of the Missouri State Office Building did not begin until late in 1966.

These important civic structures had been or were in the process of being constructed within a few blocks of each other without benefit of any centralized planning. In June 1964, in response to this spurt of activity, representatives of the Municipal Art Commission, City Hall, the public library, courthouse, federal building, and police headquarters building finally convened to explore the possibility of a landscape design which would unify all of these major public buildings. Because construction had already begun on the federal office building, immediate action was needed. As the landscape architectural firm of Hare & Hare was already involved in the federal project, it was suggested that they undertake a study to explore a unification project.

Linscott's earlier proposal to alter the City Hall fountains was the departure point that stimulated planning for all of the civic buildings. In July 1964, it was decided that the City Hall fountain should be repaired rather than altered. The repair project involved the removal of $5,000 worth of mosaic tile. The tile had been intended to appear as water when the fountains were drained for the winter. The tile was replaced with concrete painted blue. For the first time since 1957, the fountains were returned to full operation.

The Halprin Plan

Evidently, Hare & Hare did not elect to work on developing a civic center master plan, as in October 1964 a group of Kansas City architects, who volunteered at the request of the Municipal Art Commission, presented a proposal to beautify and develop the civic center area. However, in August 1965, after this consortium of local architects began their planning, the city council placed Lawrence Halprin in charge of the beautification project for the civic center. The council stipulated that Twelfth Street had to remain open to traffic although it could perhaps be ramped over for pedestrian traffic. Halprin, a noted San Francisco landscape architect, had been the principal designer of a number of important urban projects in Chicago, Seattle, and Tel Aviv and was most noted for San Francisco's Ghirardelli Square. In 1963, he wrote the book, *Cities*, which reflected his belief in the need for a variety of experiences in the urban world. His involvement in the Kansas City project caused some disgruntlement as the local chapter of the American Institute of Architects felt that their talent had been overlooked. They approached the council with a proposal to appoint a local architect as project supervisor with Halprin to serve as a consultant but were unsuccessful in their efforts.

Before Halprin could complete his proposal, the federal government proceeded with the construction of a 150-foot diameter, dish-shaped, sunken plaza which would contain a fountain and be installed in front of the new federal building. City officials were shocked, believing that all interested parties were holding back on the landscaping and improvements until a final, integrated plan could be agreed upon. The federal officials explained to the art commission that the plaza was part of the original plan for the building and that it would be completed independently of a civic center master plan. Those officials knew that if construction were interrupted they would be liable to the building contractor for the construction costs. There was also some concern that the Municipal Art Commission was slow in finalizing plans, and representatives of the government pointed out that their building was scheduled for completion in November, just a few months away.

Halprin, noting that the federal building was the single largest tract of land in the proposed civic plaza area, felt that its plaza was disruptive and said: "It will have to be torn out. . . . It has no relationship to any of the buildings except the federal building. I doubt that it could fit into any major scheme to unify the buildings." Halprin felt that the large circular configuration of the plaza, a dominant shape, would only disassociate the huge federal building from other buildings in the area. In reply, Donald W. Bush, a landscape designer for the federal building, explained that the design was meant to separate the more contemporary federal building from the older city and county buildings.

In April 1966, Halprin completed his proposal for the Civic Center, a plan *Progressive Architecture* magazine touted as one of the most exciting recent open space plans. According to the magazine, Halprin's plan was based entirely on pedestrians and "how they might be entertained, amused, refreshed, and generally given a little respite from the hectic atmosphere of downtown." Halprin proposed that a wide ramp be built which would bridge over the traffic on both Twelfth and Locust streets. The ramp would tie together the major civic buildings and would also create three connected plazas: one in front of City Hall, a commercial plaza east of the police building, and a plaza in front of the federal office building. Trees, fountains, and sculpture were an integral part of the plan (Fig. 98). His proposal would have cost the city an estimated $2 million. The Municipal Art Commission tried to generate local civic support and urged the city to submit an application to the Federal Housing and Urban Development Department for funds so that the Halprin plan could be carried out. However, by December 1967, the city still had not submitted the federal grant application for funding assistance. The delay was due to the City Plan Commission's consideration of an urban beautification plan. Despite continued interest and support by the Municipal Art Commission, funds for the project never materialized, and the exciting proposal died a quiet death. The buildings in the civic center area did utilize fountains: a large rectangular fountain pool was placed in front of the Missouri State Building plaza and a small curved fountain basin was placed at the edge of the circular federal building plaza. Neither of these fountains is currently operational. The fountain pool in front of the state building was shut off in 1981 because the thirty-horsepower motor used to recirculate the water was requiring too much electricity to operate. The motor is currently being redesigned to operate more efficiently so that it may again be used. The federal building fountain has not operated since the late 1970s as trash thrown into the fountain basin had damaged the pumps. That damage, coupled with new federal guidelines calling for the conservation of water by all of its agencies, caused the fountain to be turned off. Repairing and restoring the fountain to operate again have not

Fig. 98   been ruled out but are not priorities for managers of the federal building.

In the spring of 1970 the City Hall fountains were cleaned, underwater lights were added, and the deteriorated surface of the plaza was replaced. The sea horses and dolphins continue to beautify the City Hall, oblivious of the fate that once almost befell them. Although the $125,000 necessary to clean the fountains and to replace the plaza surface was a considerable savings over the $2 million Halprin plan, the city lost an opportunity to create a truly unique and exciting unified civic area.

The E.F. Pierson Sculpture Garden Fountain

An outdoor sculpture garden, an important addition to the Nelson-Atkins Museum of Art, was made possible through the generosity of Elmer F. Pierson, a Kansas City philanthropist who had served as chairman of the board of the Vendo Company. For many years Pierson had been interested in providing an outdoor setting for monumental sculpture, which was finally realized in 1972 with the construction of the E.F. Pierson Sculpture Garden on the terrace at the southeast corner of the museum building.

The garden was designed by Thomas Colgrove, then associated with the landscape architectural firm of Hare & Hare. Colgrove's design consisted of a walled space, entered from the Westport Garden Room in the basement of the museum. The garden overlooks the expansive front lawn of the gallery toward the *Volker Memorial Fountain* to the south. The garden is graded in two levels with paved floor areas for the sculpture, which is surrounded by planters and ample foliage. An interesting fountain construction on the western side of the garden is composed of five tiers of rectangular concrete slabs. The cantilevered slabs have a depression in the center, much like a splash block used under gutters. Water slowly trickles from the highest centered slab and drops onto the lower slabs to each side of it (Fig. 99). Water trickles from level to level, to fall into a rectangular basin at the base where it is recirculated. Although the garden is not symmetrically arranged, it does convey an element of formality in its contained planters and walls—a conscious attempt to achieve harmony with the existing classical-styled museum building. Although the fountain is modern in its elements and design, it is not unlike certain Renaissance fountains which were characterized by their minimal water effects.

Fig. 99

The garden was dedicated in the spring of 1972 and has proved to be an ideal setting for large, modern works of sculpture which can be viewed under conditions of changing light and atmosphere. The fountain functions as an integral part of that garden space.

Pierson died in 1982 and in his will provided a trust fund for the maintenance of the sculpture garden and the establishment of an annual lecture on sculpture or a related topic. His generous gift should ensure that the sculpture garden and its quiet fountain remain beautiful for future generations of museum visitors.

Grace and Holy Trinity Cathedral Courtyard Fountain

The beautiful courtyard and fountain that are part of the Grace and Holy Trinity Episcopal Cathedral are yet another unique attraction in the downtown area of Kansas City. An appreciation of this fountain requires an understanding of the complexities surrounding its construction. The courtyard and fountain evolved through a systematic planning process begun in 1976. The architectural firm of Abend, Singleton & Associates was employed to develop a master plan for expansion of the block of land owned by the cathedral, bound by Thirteenth and Fourteenth streets,

Broadway and Washington. The goal of the plan was to identify suitable locations to build a diocesan office building, a chapel for the cathedral, a columbarium (area for the placement of urns containing ashes of the deceased), and additional parking areas.

This proved to be a challenging commission for the Abend, Singleton firm, principally because the cathedral and the diocese functioned independently of each other. Stephen Abend, acting as principal designer, was faced with the difficult task of simultaneously pleasing two different clients—the administrators of the diocese and of the cathedral. Each wanted their project (an office for the diocese and a chapel for the cathedral) to maintain individual identities, yet still maintain a harmonious relationship with the existing cathedral and educational building, called Hadden Hall. The master plan first examined the axes and vistas to and from the church, and an interesting discovery was made.

The cathedral members had a long-standing image of their church as a "church in a park." That was an accurate perception if one viewed the church from the north and east sides for it sat back on the lot, surrounded by lush, green lawns. However, if viewed from the south or west, a vantage point that the general public usually had by entering the downtown area from the Fourteenth Street freeway exit, the view was much different. The reason for this difference was a result of former developments in the immediate vicinity.

The Benjamin Franklin public school had been located south of the church property at Fourteenth Street and Washington since the turn of the century. The playground for the school was north across Fourteenth Street on the block that is now solely occupied by the cathedral. An under-the-street tunnel connected the school and the playground with a concrete "bunkerlike" structure serving as an entrance to the tunnel from the playground. Although the school was demolished in 1976 and the playground was purchased by the church, the unsightly concrete structure remained, obstructing the view of the cathedral when approached from the southwest.

The developing master plan revealed that the visual image of the south side needed great improvement. Rather than interfere with the parklike north and east sides of the property, the new buildings were located on the southern portion of the property and arranged so that they would not block the view of the cathedral but enhance it. As the plan evolved, the office and the chapel were envisioned as two elongated ovoids. Their placement would frame a view of the cathedral for downtown-bound motorists. A courtyard became a logical device for linking the new buildings with the church and educational building already on the grounds and for providing an entry area for both the diocesan building and the chapel. Placing the diocesan office at the southern edge of the property with its own entrance ensured its separate identity.

After agreeing upon the placement and design of the new buildings, attention was focused on creating a courtyard that was beautiful as well as functional. The courtyard, which became the heart of the entire project, was built slightly below grade to protect it from street noise, to give a sense of privacy, and to provide the handicapped with an entrance to the cathedral. The courtyard was planned to be used for public gatherings—

Fig. 100

outdoor religious services, weddings, receptions, and other activities. The office and the courtyard were completed in 1978, while the construction of a chapel and columbarium was delayed by a lack of funding.

The office structure serves as the rear wall for the courtyard. The ground to the west is landscaped and terraced and will eventually become the columbarium space. The chapel was designed to function as the east wall of the courtyard, but in lieu of its construction, a covered walkway was built that leads to the cathedral and extends around three sides of the courtyard. Low, rounded arches of concrete provide openings into the courtyard. The piers of the arches project into wings which function as benches.

The design and materials of the office and the courtyard blend in with the older church structures, and the elliptical shape chosen for the courtyard is echoed by the shape of the office building. The red tile roof of the new building matches the existing tile roof of the cathedral, and the wall surfaces of hammered concrete containing a stone aggregate harmonize with the rough limestone walls of the cathedral.

The courtyard has two entrances. The entrance on the south is next to the office building and leads directly into the open court. The other entrance is from the north through a glass-walled connecting hallway that joins the cathedral with Hadden Hall. The northern entrance opens onto a flat, narrow space that gradually widens and steps down into the courtyard. The courtyard fountain begins there.

The water of the complex fountain first flows from a basin resembling a baptismal font supported by a concrete pedestal approximately three feet high. Each of the four sides of the pedestal is incised with a cross. A water outlet is in the center of the font. Openings on the four corners recreate the design of the rainspouts of the office building and allow the water to flow over into a surrounding pool. One edge of the pool is open, permitting the water to flow down a brick wall set at approximately a thirty degree angle (Fig. 100). The brick wall is constructed in horizontal bands with each band recessed approximately one-quarter inch behind the band above it, which causes the water to break into patterns as it flows down the wall. The water is then channeled into a long, narrow trough (approximately eight inches wide and fifty feet long) alongside the walkway. Paralleling the descent created by the steps that lead down into the courtyard, the water then falls a series of eight small cascades and enters a triangular pool in the floor of the courtyard.

The triangular pool is approximately one and one-half feet deep, and the sides are approximately sixteen feet long. At the south end of the pool, the water falls over the edge into a one-foot wide collecting basin where it is recirculated back to the font (Fig. 101).

The original plans for the fountain called for a further diversion of the water through a long narrow trough from the triangular basin across the courtyard floor to the entrance by the office building. Here the water would enter a circular reflecting pool with a work of sculpture placed in the center. That final path of the water had not been undertaken because the sculpture for the pool has not been acquired.

The Grace and Holy Trinity Cathedral courtyard fountain is one of the most unique in Kansas City. It is rich in symbolism expressed by the baptismal font and incised crosses. The religious import of the fountain is enhanced by the placement of an altar on the wall above the triangular pool. This carved, red sandstone altar was preserved from the Trinity Episcopal Church that once stood at Tenth and Tracy streets and was restored after many years in storage.

This unique fountain has the capacity to create a great variety of water and auditory effects. Its quiet reflecting pool dramatically contrasts with its more active water effects. The fountain provides a fascinating visual element in a space that functions equally well as a quiet, contemplative area or as a public gathering place.

Fig. 101

Fig. 102

H & R Block Fountain

The H & R Block Company was founded in Kansas City in 1955. In 1962, the firm moved to a building at Forty-fourth and Main streets, which was later expanded as the company experienced rapid growth. In the spring of 1983, an addition and remodeling of the building more than tripled its previous space and provided the company with impressive corporate headquarters.

The addition is set back from the street, providing space for a rectangular fountain, approximately eight feet wide and forty feet long. The fountain is quite simple, consisting merely of a rectangular retaining basin with seven evenly spaced, centered jets that send vertical aerated columns of water into the air (Fig. 102). The height of the columns can be adjusted, or they can be programmed to cycle at alternating heights. The fountain and the building addition were designed by Marshall & Brown, a Kansas City architectural firm.

Unfortunately, at least for the general public, the fountain is almost concealed behind a long rectangular planter with foliage that is tall enough to nearly mask the presence of the fountain. However, in conjunction with the noise of the falling waters, the planter does muffle the traffic noise for those enjoying the courtyard space.

10 Atrium Fountains

The use of the atrium, one of the most popular current architectural trends, is simply the adaptation of a very old idea. Atriums made feasible by a temperate climate were common features of ancient Roman domestic architecture: it was a central court, enclosed by the four walls of the house and open to the sky. Angled roofs diverted rain water into a collecting pool in the center of the court. The atrium brought light into the center of the building and was regarded as the most interesting and essential room of the Roman dwelling. The atrium also became a feature of early Christian churches. In an adaptation of a residential atrium, a walled enclosure in the front of the church contained a fountain used for ritual bathing.

Hundreds of years later the basic concept of an atrium was still being used. It became especially popular in nineteenth-century commercial buildings.* Tall buildings became possible through the use of the steel frame, but advances in illumination lagged behind. One way of providing light to the inner portions of a tall office building was to design the building with a "light court" or recession in the wall plane. Thus, buildings with U- or H-shaped floor plans became common. Another solution was to leave an open core through the center of the building roofed with a skylight to provide light to the center of the building in addition to the light entering through exterior windows. As electricity improved, this need to bring natural light into a building became less pressing and the interior, skylit court was no longer constructed.

When interest in atriumlike interiors began to revive (starting perhaps with Frank Lloyd Wright's Guggenheim Museum in New York City, 1956-59), the primary objective was to create a dramatic space rather than to provide light. Although not strictly an atrium, the Plaza branch of the Kansas City Public Library was an important precursor to the new atrium structures that developed in Kansas City.

Kansas City Public Library, Plaza Branch, Fountain

The Plaza branch of the Kansas City Public Library at 4801 Main Street was designed by Tanner, Linscott & Associates and dedicated in October 1967. A narrow, two-story light court on the interior of the north side runs the length of the building. The court extends from the ground floor level to the ceiling of the first floor and is treated as an interior, but inaccessible, patio. The development of this light court seems to have evolved for several reasons. The only windows in the building were incorporated

*Examples of buildings with these features include the Providence Arcade in Providence, Rhode Island (1828-29), a market building with a glass roofed interior court; the Rookery in Chicago (1885-86) with a light court extending down to a skylighted two-story lobby; the Guaranty Loan Building in Minneapolis (1888-89) with a skylit interior court of

Fig. 103

into the north side to allow more wall space for the shelving of books and storage. Combining the light from these windows with a gardenlike patio helps to create a quiet, reflective atmosphere especially appropriate for a library. Immediately adjacent to the court on the first floor is a large reading area. A reciprocal benefit of the area is that the high humidity that needs to be maintained for the benefit of the books also makes an excellent atmosphere for tropical plants which thrive in this patio area.

The court area contains granite stepping stones, hanging baskets of plants, and huge planters resting on the floor of white and green marble chips. At one end of the court is a fountain consisting of a clear plastic tube, about fifteen feet high and approximately five inches in diameter. Water constantly bubbles up through the tube, only occasionally spilling over to trickle into a pool of water below (Fig. 103).

It was John Portman's use of the atrium in his designs for the Hyatt Regency Hotels (starting with Atlanta in 1967, Chicago in 1971, and San Francisco in 1974) that really sparked the current widespread popularity and treatment of this design feature. Today the atrium is in fashion for all types of buildings, especially hotels, office buildings, and shopping malls. Reasons for the popularity of the atrium are diverse. Linked to the "return to nature" philosophy of the 1960s, the atrium was a way to humanize an interior and at the same time create a dramatic, visually exciting space. The multi-story atrium can become the equivalent of an

twelve stories; the Brown Palace Hotel in Denver (1892); the Bradbury Building in Los Angeles (1893); and Frank Lloyd Wright's Larkin Company Administration Building in Buffalo, New York (1903), also with a skylit interior court.

outdoor street, which is oriented vertically rather than horizontally. Plants and fountains can further accent the outdoor quality that begins with the flooding of the space with natural light.

Kansas City has benefited from the atrium boom and has several fine examples, many of which incorporate fountains into their design. Unfortunately, in some cases the fountains have failed to achieve their maximum impact.

City Center Square Fountains

One of the first of the city's "new" atriums was in City Center Square, a towering thirty-story structure in the heart of the downtown commercial area at Eleventh and Main streets. Ground was broken for the building in August 1974, and construction was completed three years later. The building was designed by Skidmore, Owings & Merrill of Chicago and was the first multi-use structure to be erected in the downtown area, combining substantial retail space with office space. The retail area, taking up the first four floors, is the equivalent of four square blocks arranged vertically in tiers. The small shops and restaurants are primarily oriented toward the noontime shopping/dining needs of downtown workers. Entrances to the retail spaces are from both Main Street and Baltimore Avenue. Because of the grade of the streets, the Baltimore entrance is on the second floor of the building.

The irregular interior space of the atrium is lighted through the skylight above. Escalators in the center of the area provide access to all four of the retail floors. Wrapped around the base of the escalators is an irregularly shaped fountain pool. The fountain is composed of two   *Fig. 104*

bronze-finished concentric metal circles, one mounted inside the other. Both circles generate shimmering sheets of water, which then fall into the pool below (Fig. 104). The atrium of the City Center Square is not a particularly dramatic interior space, primarily because the first floor is overly crowded. The openness of the space is lost by the escalator placement and further complicated by graphics on the escalator walls. The area is crowded at noon, and most of the floor space is used as a dining area, further diminishing the sense of openness, although it provides real advantages for people-watching. Although the fountain design is interesting, it is not of sufficient size or effect to become the focal point of this busy interior space.

Boatman's Bank Fountain

One of the major tenants of the City Center Square Building is Boatman's Bank and Trust Company. The Baltimore Avenue entrance to the bank is from the second floor. The bank interior is not an atrium in itself, but large windows provide the interior with natural light. The fountain here, similar in design and placement to the City Center Square atrium fountain, functions much more effectively. Just as the atrium fountain wraps around the escalator, this fountain encircles the base of a stairway leading to a mezzanine level. The irregularly shaped basin of the fountain is of glazed brick with a beveled top (probably to discourage its use as a seating area). Thin streams of water are propelled from the outside walls of the basin into the pool of water.

Penntower Building Fountain

A different atrium treatment is seen in the Penntower Building at 3100 Broadway (constructed in 1973-74). The atrium of this thirteen-story office tower is U-shaped with tropical plants, seating, and fountains in the court at the corners provided by the U-shape. The designers have created a quiet, restful area in the space as a counterpoint to the activities of businesses that encircle the atrium space. The two identical fountains in the atrium consist of a circular basin lined with tile that rests on a conical brick base (Fig. 105). The brick of the fountain bases matches the brick used for the nearby planters. The fountain jets are set within a smaller circular receptacle within the basin and consist of a spray ring with jets designed to produce an inside fall, meeting in the center to form a column. Cuts made into the spray ring element on four sides allow the water to fall into the retaining basin, but the water effect is minimal.

Granada Royale Hometel Atrium Fountain

Another dramatic use of an atrium fountain can be found within the Granada Royale Hometel (now the Embassy Suites) at 220 West Forty-third Street just north of the Country Club Plaza. The hotel, constructed in 1976, was designed with a Spanish flavor on the exterior and interior. The 265 hotel suites encircle an enclosed atrium, twelve stories high. Walkways surround the central core from the second through twelfth floors and feature wrought iron railings. A green tile shed roof supported by

Fig. 105

columns accents the second floor meeting room level. Natural light floods through the five skylights in the roof and provides the lobby/atrium with a distinctive sunlit ambience.

The focal point of the atrium/lobby is a large fountain approximately fifteen feet tall, which is placed in the center of the space. The fountain, a four-tiered pedestal set within a circular retaining basin, reflects the interior perfectly. Its reddish-colored stone blends with the warm hues of the paving stones and stands out amidst the greenery of tropical plants (Fig. 106). The saucer at the base of the fountain is approximately six feet in diameter, and the saucers above it gradually diminish in size to create a tapered effect. The pedestal stem and the saucers are deeply carved with a foliate motif, assuming an organic character much like the growing plants surrounding it. Four upended dolphins terminate the pedestal stem. Water issues from the top of the stem and from the mouths of the dolphins ultimately to fall into the retaining basin.

Identical fountains were installed by the Granada Royale Hometel chain in other parts of the country, including San Antonio, Texas, and Covina, California. All the fountains were the design of architect Jerome D. Jackson of Jerome D. Jackson & Associates, Phoenix, Arizona.

Jackson's design is inspired by a composite of elements from fountains that he had seen elsewhere, infused with a strong Mexican flavor to correspond with the Spanish architecture of the Hometel buildings. The material of the fountains, a pink Mexican stone called Cantera Rose, is quarried in Mexico, then cut and carved by craftsmen in Guadalajara. The fountains are then shipped to the hotels where they are assembled by local masons.

Fig. 106

The use of the fountain in the Kansas City hometel is the success its designer intended, as it creates the impression of a sunlit Mediterranean Plaza, an effect particularly noteworthy in the heart of the Midwest.

Fountain of the Animals

One Ward Parkway, an office building constructed in 1979 by the J.C. Nichols Company, exhibits an entirely different atrium treatment. The three-story atrium space is forty feet wide, ninety feet long, and forty-seven feet high. Three pyramidal skylights flood the interior with light and in the center of the atrium, surrounded by lush foliage, is the large *Fountain of the Animals*, designed by Italian sculptor Sirio Tofanari* in

*Tofanari (1886-ca. 1969) was a specialist in the sculpture of animals. He reached his prominence in the late 1920s and early 1930s. During that time he exhibited some of his bronze animals at the Venice Biennial Exhibition.

Fig. 107

1951 (Fig. 107). The fountain is contained within a sixteen-foot square basin turned so that the walls of the basin are diagonal with the walls of the building, creating a diamond pattern.

As the name of the fountain indicates, animal figures are the focus of the work, but the collection of animals the artist has chosen to portray is indeed unusual. At first glance the work may appear as an idyllic grouping of animals around a body of water; further examination reveals a menacing quality. Tofanari has chosen to depict the animals in attitudes of movement, animals who appear threatening, and animals attacking each other. He has revealed the violence and activity of the animal world rather than a peaceful, romanticized version.

Bronze birds are placed at each end of the four corners of the basin. Water issues from the mouths of the birds in a single stream and falls into the pool. At one corner is a pelican, at another an eagle, at another a swan sheltering two baby swans, and at the fourth corner is a duck, wings drawn back in anger.

The marble basin that is the reflecting pool for the fountain is approximately two feet deep, and the marble is a white and brown variegation. Numerous Koi fish swim in the basin. A truncated pedestal, approximately five feet high with four extensions that provide supports for the bronze animals placed upon them, is centered in the basin. On two opposite sides, are crouching panthers. Water streams from their mouths to fall into the basin. Panthers who have been successful in the hunt are placed on the other two sides. One panther has captured a bird, which hangs upside down from its mouth. Water falls from the mouth of the bird into the basin. The other has attacked an alligator, whose tail is wrapped around the panther's neck. Water issues from the alligator's mouth into the basin. Placed at the summit of the central pedestal is the figure of a gazelle peacefully nursing her young, oblivious to the struggles going on below her.

The fountain is provided with a dramatic setting. Most of the north wall of the building is of glass, which supplements the light provided by the skylights. Three stories of office space are arranged in a U-shape around the atrium on the east, west, and south. Bridge walkways at the north and south ends of the atrium link the east and west sides of the building and provide a perfect vantage for viewing the fountain.

Brick planters and wooden benches surround the fountain. The brick of the planters continues up the east and west walls of the atrium as piers that terminate in arched window openings on the third floor. Red carpeting is used on the walkways around the fountain, providing a visual contrast to the dark green foliage and white marble.

In 1961 during a trip to Florence, Miller Nichols visited the Marinelli Studio to observe the bronze casting process. He saw the *Fountain of the Animals*, which was fully assembled although unconnected to any water. Nichols learned that the sculptor Tofanari had been commissioned to create the work for a wealthy Bolivian, who had never furnished payment after its completion.

Nichols purchased the piece even though at the time he did not have a site in mind for its placement. The piece was stored until a suitable environment was found. Miller Nichols' foresight ensured a dramatic addition to Kansas City's collection of beautiful fountains.

11 The Fountain's Role in Planned Development

Country Club Residential District

Many Kansas City fountains have been erected to commemorate events or people or to decorate individual buildings and parks. Even those that were erected as part of the park system sprouted up without benefit of a forward-looking, comprehensive plan. However, there are two areas in the city where fountains and other art objects have been utilized as an integral component of a development plan. Those two areas, the Country Club residential district and the Country Club Plaza, a retail shopping center, were both projects of the J.C. Nichols Company, and both set precedents that were emulated by scores of later ventures. It was J.C. Nichols' control over the use and development of the land within these areas that gave a uniformity which would have otherwise been impossible.

Jesse Clyde Nichols, the genius behind both projects, was a native of Olathe, Kansas (Fig. 108). After graduation from the University of Kansas in 1902 and a brief period of study at Harvard, he came to Kansas City. His first venture in Kansas City real estate was in 1905-06 when he purchased ten acres of land in the vicinity of Fifty-first Street and Grand, then outside of the city limits. He continued to acquire land and in 1908 announced plans for a large development of 1,000 acres located between Holmes Street and State Line Road, from Fifty-first to Fifty-ninth streets. At the time the tract was covered with hog lots, rubbish dumps, pastures, and stone quarries.

Nichols' master plan for the development of this land was influenced by his knowledge of William Rockhill Nelson's accomplishments in the Rockhill district just east of the Nelson-Atkins Museum of Art. Many of Nichols' ideas for his developments were clearly based on Nelson's prototypes, such as the use of winding roads, stone walls, and rustic bridges to define and embellish the grounds.

However, in many ways the development of his residential district was unique. He avoided the grid plan of rectangular blocks, using instead irregular lots with shapes defined by curving streets that followed the terrain. Landscape architect George Kessler was employed to provide a street plan for the entire Nichols development that incorporated small parks and triangles. Kessler also recommended a parkway through the district, a suggestion that led to the development of Ward Parkway, which originally ran from Wornall Road to Fifty-third Street. By 1925, it was extended to Meyer Circle, and it currently runs to Ninety-second Street. The majority of the land for the parkway was deeded to the city by J.C. Nichols and Hugh Ward (heir to the Seth Ward estate near Fifty-fifth Street and Pennsylvania).

Houses within a wide range of prices were allowed in the district, but

Fig. 108

all building plans had to be approved by the J.C. Nichols Company to ensure their compatibility with the lot and its surroundings. Neighborhoods often contained houses grouped by a particular architectural style, for example, all Old English, Italianate, or colonial. Even outbuildings and garages were regulated; in fact, this is said to be the first residential development to recognize the presence of the automobile. Because people walked less, Nichols favored large blocks and narrow sidewalks, choices which also were more economical.

A major feature of the district was the use of protective covenants, which united a very large area of land (1,000 acres that later was expanded to 2,000) into a common protection and destiny. In addition to deed restrictions, the Nichols Company continued its considerable influence by establishing several homeowners' associations, which were responsible for supplying neighborhood conveniences (such as trash removal), maintaining property values, and enforcing restrictions. The Country Club district became one of the most fashionable places to live in the entire city, largely as a result of these controls. By 1917, the district, made up of numerous additions, including Rockhill Park, Country Side, and Rockhill Place, had grown south to Sixty-fifth Street and west into Kansas.

Mission Hills, Kansas, just west of the Kansas-Missouri state line, was developed from land Nichols purchased in 1908. The first house in Mission Hills was constructed by his company in 1912. By 1917, there were approximately twenty-five homes there. Eventually, the city encompassed three subdivisions: Mission Hills, Sagamore Hills, and Indian Hills.

One of the most noteworthy features of the Country Club district is the placement of fountains and art objects throughout the development. Although Nichols very likely had the idea for beautifying the district from its earliest beginnings (as grassy circles, triangles and parklets were a part of the overall plan), he did not actually begin the placement of art objects or the installation of fountains until around 1923, at least fifteen years after his first development. In fact, Nichols did not recommend the use of outdoor art until after a development was well founded. He suggested that, "A developer who started to sink money into them at the very outset would go broke fast. It is always advisable to wait until the district can afford them."

The inspiration for the use of outdoor art undoubtedly came from Nichols' visits to Europe. While still a sophomore at the University of Kansas in 1900, he toured Europe on a bicycle and found that his interest was "aroused by the stability, beauty, charm, and orderliness of the villages and cities as compared with our American communities." In 1922, Nichols and his family traveled to Europe where as vice-president of the American Civic Association he attended an international housing conference in Rome. He also represented the National City Planning Conference of the United States at an English town-planning conference. This was Nichols' most extensive visit to Europe and included lengthy visits in Spain and England.

Nichols returned to Kansas City from the 1922 trip with fresh ideas to begin the beautification of the Country Club district.

Still remembering the beauty of foreign plazas and little squares,
we endeavored to make our property sort of an outdoor museum
and installed in some 200 locations garden ornaments comprising
fountains, vases, statues, wellheads, and other objects of art.

Nichols believed these embellishments would also stimulate the home-owners to beautify their own property. Many years later, Nichols' son Clyde remembered his father's fondness for fountain art: "Of all art forms, Dad loved fountains best. Wherever we travelled, a fountain always made him stop the car and take plenty of time to enjoy it. A beautiful fountain took lots of time!" Jessie Eleanor Nichols, wife of J.C. Nichols, also travelled abroad many times, and the choice of much of the fountain and garden ornaments probably reflects her taste as well as Nichols'.

Nichols felt that if he could foster an appreciation of art and have it perceived as a community asset, it would increase the standard of living for the homeowners. For that reason he sponsored free lectures on landscape art, architecture, and interior decorating. The homes associations began to sponsor lawn and garden contests. When he was ready to introduce outdoor art into his district, Nichols had already developed a responsive and appreciative audience.

Nichols regarded the placement of his newly purchased *objets d'art* as carefully as he had considered the planning of the streets, parks, and services throughout his developments. The company accumulated a vast collection of sculptural ornaments of a wide variety of types. Each piece that was to be installed was chosen for its own unique qualities and its suitability to a specific location. The art objects placed in Nichols Company subdivisions on both sides of the state line were primarily used to accent traffic triangles in the curved street patterns, to decorate small parks, and to add a pleasing visual image. The result was that each subdivision assumed a character of its own, and its embellishments did much to provide each neighborhood with a unique identity.

It is unfortunate that many of the original pieces have become victims of accidents and vandalism. Some of the damaged monuments were never replaced, and others were repaired or replaced with different works. The homes associations were ultimately responsible for providing security for the artworks, and that effort tended to form another bonding agent for the neighbors within each subdivision.

Unfortunately, little information is available surrounding the placement, execution, and disposition of many of the monuments that once graced the Country Club district. Documentation of the origin of the works is sparse, and records concerning any changes which may have occurred are virtually nonexistent. Many art works were probably imported from Europe, not necessarily as superb examples of a particular sculptor's artistry, but nevertheless old and aesthetically pleasing. It is more useful to consider their placement as important from a historic perspective, for the site, regardless of the work placed there, tells us most about the desire of J.C. Nichols to beautify his developments and best suggest his truly noble vision.

Sixty-seventh and Wornall Road Fountain

In 1923, the J.C. Nichols Company installed a fountain on a small traffic triangle on the west side of Wornall Road at Sixty-seventh Street. It was the first fountain known to have been placed by the company in one of its subdivisions.

Originally, the fountain consisted of a Y-shaped retaining basin with a six-foot high pedestal fountain placed in its center (Fig. 109). The pedestal supported two saucers.

The history of the fountain since its placement is unknown, but presumably it fell prey to vandalism or accidental destruction. A more modern fountain, unlike any of the traditional forms of others in the Country Club district, has replaced the original fountain. The pedestal has been replaced by a truncated square brick projection, approximately three feet high, with a bifurcated water outlet at the top (Fig. 110). The water runs down over the bricks into the Y-shaped retaining basin, a design element suggesting the original.

Fig. 109

Fig. 110

Meyer Circle "Sea Horse" Fountain

The fountain at Meyer Circle and Ward Parkway is in many ways the most characteristic of Kansas City's fountains. It is sited on a circular plot of ground between the junction of two major traffic arteries from which six streets radiate. Long a favorite of both natives and tourists, the fountain's history is like that of many others with a record of travails and successes. The fountain's enduring qualities have saved it from neglect and proposed changes perceived by some as progress. The *Meyer Circle Fountain* has served as a statement which publicly acknowledges the import placed by the citizens of Kansas City on its works of art. It is a triumph to its benefactors, planners, and designers who initially conceived its dramatic plan.

Considered a masterstroke in thoughtful urban planning, Ward Parkway is a north-south boulevard that begins at the Country Club Plaza and extends to Ninety-second Street. Traffic runs in a one-way thoroughfare on each side of an expansive green medial strip which not only features plantings of every form and variety but also contains mirror pools, balustrades, gateways, art objects, and fountains. Many houses lining the parkway are elegant structures tastefully designed in a variety of architectural styles.

Ward Parkway was developed by the city upon the recommendation of the Board of Park Commissioners, who had as early as 1911 established a plan for the creation of parkways and boulevards in the Westport and Southwest Park districts of the city. The land on which to construct the parkway was acquired largely through the major gifts of several private donors. Large tracts of land were deeded to the city by the Ward Investment Company, the Wolcott and Wornall families, and the J.C. Nichols Company. The remaining land necessary for the construction of Ward Parkway was acquired through purchase or condemnation.

In April 1914, the City Council of Kansas City adopted an ordinance which accepted certain deeds "to be used forever for parkway purposes" and that the specified parcels would be known hereafter as Meyer Boulevard and Ward Parkway. The construction of Ward Parkway proceeded gradually with the costs repaid through the assessment of special real estate taxes. It was not completed south to Meyer Circle until 1925.

Both Meyer Circle and Meyer Boulevard were named for the first Park Board president, August R. Meyer.* He served in that capacity from 1892 until 1901 and was instrumental in developing the city's park and boulevard system. The major elements of that system—Penn Valley Park and The Paseo Boulevard—were his own suggestions.

J.C. Nichols continued to expand his residential developments south and west from their germination at Fiftieth Street and Grand at a phenomenal rate. The new subdivisions of the Nichols Company generally followed the progress of the continually growing Ward Parkway.

In keeping with his beautification theories for his subdivisions, Nichols approached the Park Board in 1924 with a proposal for the donation of a major art object. At that time, a circular traffic island was being developed by the Park Board at Meyer and Ward Parkway, to be called Meyer Circle. Nichols planned to donate a fountain and pay for its installation on the circle, asking the city to pay only the costs of the landscaping.

At a meeting of the Municipal Art Commission on October 19, 1924, architect and planner Edward Buehler Delk, who had been commissioned for the project by Nichols, presented his plans for a majestic Italian fountain. The commission, composed of architects Henry F. Hoit and William Drewin Wight and landscape architect S. Herbert Hare, overwhelmingly supported the project. The plans illustrated a sculpture equipped with water outlets placed in a circular pool one hundred feet in diameter. The fountain was surrounded by a flagstone terrace, which had five walkways radiating from it. A circular planting of poplar trees was to surround the wide basin.

To execute the dramatic overall scheme envisioned by Delk, the Nichols Company had already built a low rock wall circling the perimeter of the property that was connected by wrought iron gates. A marble balustrade which also featured wrought iron panels was installed north of the fountain pool. A marble bench was added to enable visitors to pause longer and enjoy the spectacular fountain.

The fountain Delk proposed survives virtually intact today (Plate 15, page 35). Delk's drawings illustrated three sea horses elevated on a triangular natural stone pyramid. The sea horses, perched at the truncated extensions of the pyramid, were odd mythological beasts with scaly fishlike tails, feathery wings, horse heads, and webbed feet. They formed the base for a fluted saucer which composed the second tier of the fountain. The saucer had a carved lion head spigot at each side, from which spouted a jet of water. The third tier of the fountain consisted of another pedestal supporting an identical saucer equipped with lion head spigots and two small cherubs clinging to the pedestal stem. At the summit of the fountain was another sculptural group depicting a child astride a dolphin.

Delk indicated that sixteen jets of water would play on the fountain from the basin and water would also issue from the nostrils of the sea horses and from the mouth of the dolphin that terminated the upper

*Meyer, born in St. Louis in 1851, was European-educated in mining and engineering. Upon his return to the United States, he began to build a fortune in his mining interests in Colorado. He moved to Kansas City in 1881 and established a smelting plant, which became known as the U. S. Zinc and Chemical Company.

portion of the sculpture. The fountain is virtually identical to this original conception with the exception of the water treatment and the loss of the original summit figure of the child and dolphin.

J.C. Nichols had purchased the sculptural decoration for the *Meyer Circle Fountain* in the early 1920s on one of his European visits. The sculpture, which dates from the seventeenth century, came from Venice, where it had once adorned a piazza.* The cost of the sculpture, pedestal, pool, and landscaping totalled $18,000, an enormous sum of money for the time.

The *Meyer Circle Fountain*, or the *Sea Horse Fountain* as it became commonly known, gained an unprecedented popularity quickly, especially among neighborhood residents, who in the years to come were to witness a surprising amount of activity around the fountain.

The fountain operated without major difficulties until 1960. When the fountain was turned on in the spring, it leaked badly and could not be continuously operated. That summer, after some delays, work to repair the fountain commenced. New plumbing and spray nozzles which could be removed were installed, and six "underground" lights were added to illuminate the fountain from beneath the water.

In 1961, the ancient figure of the child and the dolphin perched at the summit of the fountain was stolen. A fragment of the sculpture was found in the basin, leading Park Superintendent J.V. Lewis to speculate that vandals had tied a rope around the figure and pulled until it eventually fell. The Park Board offered a $500 reward for anyone with information that would lead to the recovery of the damaged piece. At the same time, the board offered a $100 reward for information leading to the conviction of persons placing detergent in the fountain, as that act sometimes caused irreparable damage to the pumps supplying the water to the fountain. The missing sculpture was never located and was soon replaced with a similar figure of a child with a dolphin. In 1966, the piece was again toppled by vandals and was once again replaced by the Park Department.

The water treatment in the fountain had originally consisted of sixteen jets arranged in a circle, pointed inward to spray over the central sculptural ornament. The water scheme as it appears today is quite different. In a 1966 project, the direction and size of the water outlets were changed, resulting in water effects that are much more dramatic. They now consist of three nozzles mounted together which expel a steady stream of water at each of the four quadrants of the pool toward the center of the fountain. Four vertical columns of water are set closer in toward the center to contrast with the arcing sprays. In each multiple arrangement, the water is expelled with greater pressure than before, which creates agitated patterns in the reflecting pool. The smaller jets of water tend to create a mist when the slightest wind is blowing, creating an atmospheric softening of the edges of the sculpture.

Ward Parkway is one of the busier traffic arteries in the city during rush hours. When the volume of traffic lessens, the parkway becomes tempting for those who sometimes use it as a speedway. At Meyer Circle, a triangular yellow sign graphically illustrates the approach of the circular island, which must be approached with caution. Still, the wide thorough-

---

*A conflicting report ascribes the origin of the fountain to a private Venetian villa.

fare leading to it has caused some motorists to approach it at excessive speeds, resulting in accidents, property damage, and even the loss of life. At least one person in city government has perceived the number of accidents occurring at Meyer Circle as disproportionately high. In the late 1960s, Transportation Director O.J. Falin made traffic safety a major priority of his department. He instituted or recommended many changes to the city's network of streets to make intersections more visible and to reduce the number of hazardous curves. In 1968, Falin told the city council that he considered the *Meyer Circle Fountain* to be a traffic hazard. He presented approximately twenty proposals for the redesign of some "geographically inadequate" intersections, one of which was Meyer Circle. One of his proposals entailed moving the fountain to the north of its present location. The reaction to this proposal was immediate and loud. A newspaper editorial accused Falin of going systematically "from one section of the city to another, re-engineering intersections and boulevards and ripping out beauty spots in an attempt to speed traffic movement and remove what he calls 'hazards'."

Mayor Ilus Davis pointed out that Falin had an unlisted telephone number and remarked, "If you're going to make proposals like that, why don't you give the press your silent telephone number at the same time so people can call you with complaints instead of calling me." Mayor Davis' ultimate suggestion was, "Let's table that until 1982."

Interestingly, some of the most ardent critics of the proposal were residents of the houses around the perimeter of the circle, who would have been disturbed when another car failed to complete the circuit. One of these residents, Earl Tranin of 6400 Ward Parkway, had the rock wall in front of his property knocked down by automobiles five times. He pointed out that the fountain was not the cause of those accidents, but rather the motorists themselves who tried to navigate the circle at high speeds. Another resident, A.H. Meyers of 6335 Ward Parkway, insisted that "It would be terrible to move the fountain. We've lived here 22 years, and the beauty of the fountain was part of the reason that we bought our home."

In March 1972, a fatal traffic accident at the circle once again revived the plan to move the fountain. Sentiments as to its removal were, as in the past, overwhelmingly against the idea.

The late Carl Migliazzo, former park commissioner, was particularly scathing in his criticism of the plan. He said that if the transportation department "wants to continue turning boulevards into trafficways, they should melt down the *Pioneer Mother* sculpture in Penn Valley Park and recast it as a monument to the automobile."

The citizens of Kansas City are far from passive in their regard for the works of art that grace this city and seem to recognize them as an integral part of the qualities that make Kansas City a unique urban environment. Each time a proposal was made to somehow alter Meyer Circle it was met with enormous resistance, and ultimately those concepts were indefinitely tabled. The sculpture of *Meyer Circle Fountain* endured for centuries before its move to Kansas City, and it would seem that because of the collective passions of the citizens of this city, it will endure for many more. A *Kansas City Star* editorial summed up the issues and meaning of the fountain to Kansas City in this way:

For many motorists, Meyer Circle is not a roadblock they try to get around with their hearts in their mouths, but one of those rare beauty spots that heightens the pleasure of driving to and from work each day. When the fountain, with its soaring jets of water, is illuminated on a summer night, the circle does not scare away motorists. Instead, it lures people from all over Greater Kansas City.

Romanelli Park Fountain

The subdivision located on the west side of Wornall Road between Sixty-seventh Street and Sixty-ninth Street was developed by the Nichols Company in the 1920s. Nichols chose to call the subdivision "Romanelli Gardens" after the Italian sculptor, Romano Romanelli. J.C. Nichols was especially fond of art works produced by the Romanelli Studio and had become personally acquainted with the sculptor during his visits to Italy. Romano was the third generation to head the Florentine Romanelli Studio, which was founded around 1860 by Pasquale Romanelli (1812-1887). Romano (1882-1958) became a member of the Royal Academy of Italy, had exhibited in Paris in the Salon d'Automne of 1913, and had worked in Paris with some of the followers of sculptor Auguste Rodin.*

The entrance to Romanelli Gardens is on the west side of Wornall Road at Sixty-ninth Street. The focal point of the entrance is a long, rectangular grassy island that is flanked with homes. That area, named Romanelli Park, contains a fountain by Romanelli that was purchased in Florence by landscape architect and consultant for the J.C. Nichols Company Herbert Hare. The firm of Hare & Hare designed the distinctive landscaping that surrounded the fountain.

The fountain, installed in 1925 shortly after the first homes in the subdivision were sold, is a classic pedestal type (Fig. 111). The scalloped bowl, raised on a stem, is reminiscent of an inverted turtle's shell. The edges of the bowl are beveled so that the water falling from it tends to sheet as it falls into the collecting basin. The overflow from the bowl is directed toward two indentations at either end that feature ram heads. The figural sculpture created by Romanelli for the summit of the pedestal is composed of a group of children surrounding a goose, with an upraised neck providing the column for the single jet of water. The *Romanelli Park Fountain* is one of only a few remaining original pieces that were placed by the Nichols Company.

Today the fountain appears much the same as it did in 1925. The most obvious difference is the wear resulting from inhospitable weather conditions. The fountain was constructed of travertine, a limestone material which tends to be less resistant to weather than a harder stone. The most

*Romano's father, Raffaello (1856-1928), achieved the greatest fame and success of the family of sculptors. His works include the equestrian statue of Garibaldi that stands in the People's Park in Siena; the portrait of Benvenuto Cellini on the Ponte Vecchio, Florence; and the monument to sculptor Donatello on Donatello's tomb in Florence.

The Romanelli Studios almost closed during the difficult period following the Second World War. The present head of the studio, Raffaello (named after his grandfather), became the fourth generation to operate the family firm at the urging of John C. Taylor of the Nichols Company who visited the studios around 1950. Raffaello revived the business and in 1972 became the first member of the Romanelli family to visit Kansas City and see first-hand how their works added to the beauty of the city.

Fig. 111

damage has been suffered by the goose, which has become almost un-
identifiable. Though the fountain has been scarred by the elements, it
seems appropriate that the sculpture not be replaced as it is through its
identification with the fountain's creator that the subdivision derives its
own unique character.

Pelican Fountain

Another fountain that was placed in Romanelli Gardens was to suffer a
less kind fate. The *Pelican Fountain*, which once graced a parklet at
Sixty-eighth Street and Pennsylvania, was lost to thievery and man-made
disasters. The fountain was composed of an antique rectangular lead
basin, originally from an English garden, that was crafted in 1701. At the
four corners of the basin were wooden shafts. Perched at the summit of
each was a lead pelican, fourteen inches in height (Fig. 112). Each served
as an outlet for a single jet of water that issued from their beaks in an
arcing curve. The water effects were completed by a single jet of water
that rose from the center of the basin. The fountain was surrounded by
barberry bushes, selected by the firm of Hare & Hare.

In 1928, just three years after its placement, a motorist skidded across
the parklet, uprooting the pedestals and tearing the basin loose. Less than

a month later, one of the four pelicans and the lead basin were stolen. The Nichols Company offered a $50 reward for the return of the basin as they considered it the most irreplaceable component of the fountain. The pelicans had been created at the time the fountain was placed and could have been created anew. The basin was never returned, and ultimately efforts to reconstruct the fountain were abandoned.

Fig. 112

Armour Center Fountain

Armour Hills, once the site of pastureland for the grazing herds kept by the Armour meat packing dynasty, was a subdivision opened by the Nichols Company in 1924. Nichols entrusted some of the finest pieces in his collection to the embellishments of its many green spaces, placed amidst its gently rolling hills.

The *Armour Center Fountain* is located at the gateway to the subdivision on the west. It is placed within a triangular park area bound by

Edgevale, Brookside Boulevard, Sixty-ninth Street, and Winthrope Road. The fountain, which was unveiled on April 24, 1924, was a companion-piece to the *Romanelli Park Fountain* and is related on an east-west axis, separated by the wide expanse of Wornall Road, the trolley car tracks, and a viaduct constructed for the transportation requirements of the citizens of the subdivisions. The two fountains shared similar landscaping treatments as well as similar sculptural themes.

Over 1,000 people came to watch J.C. Nichols dedicate the *Armour Center Fountain*, which was a gift of the company to the Armour Hills Homes Association. The fountain included as its center piece a sculpture of Carrara marble purchased in Venice (Fig. 113). The shape of the basin was a quatrefoil, with the sculptural group elevated on a pedestal in the center of the pool. The sculpture was composed of two children placed around an American eagle with outstretched wings. A newspaper caption describing the fountain noted that it embodied "patriotism and child life as the foundation of the American home." The fountain was destroyed in April 1954 by vandalism. The Nichols Company estimated the cost of its replacement at over $1,000. A decision was made to place a new ornament in the center of the pool.

The original sculpture was replaced by another group that represented a similar theme—a child with a goose, reportedly a reproduction of an old Pisan fountain. The bronze child figure stands on a pedestal supporting a small bird on his shoulders with a goose placed beneath him spouting the single jet of water (Fig. 114).

The original basin of the fountain has been retained along with the first tier of the pedestal. The landscaping has also been preserved as a circular flagstone courtyard surrounds the pool and four walkways radiate from the cardinal points of the basin.

Fig. 113

Fig. 114

Armour Green Fountain

A second fountain located in the Armour Hills neighborhood was originally called the *Armour Green Fountain* and was placed in a triangular traffic island specially created for its placement at Sixty-ninth Street, Grand, and Rockhill Road. The fountain, purchased in 1922 by J.C. Nichols in Italy, was installed in 1925.

Armour Green was a section of Armour Hills featuring houses of moderate cost, many of which were designed as bungalows. The scale and design of the fountain, which was described by the Nichols Company as "simple" and "unpretentious," was intended to be harmonious with the small parklet and modest dwellings surrounding it.

Originally, the fountain was placed in a pool twelve feet in diameter. The marble fountain consisted of a pedestal resembling a rock formation, supporting a saucer carved as a scalloped shell (Fig. 115). A youth and an

Fig. 115

infant were placed in the center of the saucer. Water issued from the summit of the rock formation. Two-foot stone walls surrounded the park at a height suitable for sitting.

The original work was vandalized in 1953 and was replaced by a lead statue of a boy holding a vase, obtained from the Nichols Company. That work was also vandalized.

The park has been recently restored by the Armour Hills Neighborhood Association. The fountain that is presently gracing the parklet is composed of a series of three tiers consisting of gradually diminishing scalloped basins. The pedestal base is rather squat and bears relief carving (Fig. 116).

A single jet of water is propelled through the center of the pedestal to the summit through a pinnacle shaped something like a pinecone. The water falls back catching the edges of the basins to fall into a circular retaining pool.

Stratford Garden Park Fountain

A small triangular parklet in the Country Club residential district is located where Sixty-second and Sixty-third streets converge just east of State Line Road.

In 1927, a fountain was placed at the east end of this parklet by the Nichols Company. The fountain is a hybrid of sorts, as it consists of a rectangular horse trough basin affixed to an upright wall surface, typifying the classical wall fountain character (Fig. 117). This antique Carrara marble horse trough was reportedly first used in a public square in Rome.

A smaller rectangular basin placed above it was originally used to

Fig. 116

refresh humans waiting on their animals to drink. Two openings in this upper basin allow water to stream into the larger trough. Both basins are carved with ornamental fluting.

The fountain is sited on an elevation. As the water issues from a spout in the center of the horse trough, it is carried through a stone-lined channel approximately thirty feet to terminate in a circular reflecting pool six feet in diameter.

Fig. 117

Fig. 118

Fifty-second and Brookside Fountain

In 1929, as a way to recognize the area that constituted the initial step in his residential development, J.C. Nichols presented a fountain to the Country Side Homes Association. The fountain was placed on the east side of Brookside near Fifty-second Street. The fountain was unveiled on September 12, 1928, and accepted at the presentation ceremony by the president of the Country Side Homes Association, John M. Guild.

The marble fountain had been purchased in Europe by Nichols in the summer of 1928. The pedestal fountain (Fig. 118) was placed in an eight-foot square pool, which in turn was surrounded by a flagstone walk. The pedestal of the fountain was incised with floral reliefs, and a figure of a boy astride a dolphin was in the center of the basin supported by the pedestal. Water from the mouth of the dolphin arced up to fall over the body.

The fountain remained as a decorative element in the neighborhood approximately until the 1950s. When and why it was removed is unknown. Most likely it fell prey to vandalism. Although the pedestal and basin located on the Ward Parkway median strip at Sixty-ninth Street are virtually identical to the pedestal and basin of the original *Fifty-second Street and Brookside Fountain,* the relationship between these two fountains is unknown.

The fountain's stone retaining basin at Fifty-second Street and Brookside remained, often covered with weeds. In the spring of 1983, the Country Side Homes Association investigated the possibility of returning a fountain to the basin but were advised that the cost of its maintenance would become prohibitive. They elected instead to cover over the top of the basin and place a figural sculpture upon it.

Ward Parkway Pedestal Fountains

In the spring of 1930, the Nichols Company added two small pedestal fountains to the embellishments already completed for Ward Parkway.

The pedestal fountain on the Ward Parkway median strip between Sixty-eighth Terrace and Sixty-ninth Street features a solitary saucer on a two and one-half foot bulbous pedestal mounted on a stone base (Fig. 119). It is placed within a rectangular concrete pool measuring thirty by thirty-six feet. A relief carving in a leaf motif decorates the base of the pedestal, and extant photographs reveal that this pedestal and saucer are

Fig. 119

Fig. 120

identical in appearance to those of the fountain that was formerly located at Fifty-second Street and Brookside.

The second pedestal fountain, the *Romany Road Fountain*, is just three blocks south of the first on Ward Parkway and is also placed within the median strip. This fountain was planned to serve as the focal point of a sunken garden, as indicated by the coursed stone walls at the north and south ends which have steps leading down into the garden area. Originally, lion figures were placed at the north end, and a balustrade capped with antique stone baskets which had been imported from Budapest was at the south end. The fountain was originally composed of a rectangular pool measuring sixteen by thirty-six feet with a pedestal fountain supporting two saucers in its center (Fig. 120). The lower saucer was supported by a fluted, bulbous pedestal. Above it, another pedestal supported a smaller

Fig. 121

saucer with the graceful figure of a girl playing a double flute in its center.

Vandalism destroyed this original work, and the fountain was replaced. The present pedestal fountain is even more sculptural as the shaft carrying the fountain's bowl is composed of a child who, displaying Herculean effort, lifts the basin onto his shoulders (Fig. 121). The bowl at the summit has a scalloped edge around its perimeter. A single jet of water issues from the center of the bowl.

Mission Hills Fountains

Mission Hills, Kansas, developed by the Nichols Company beginning in 1912, is noted for its spacious, elegant mansions and a street plan that takes maximum advantage of its forested, rugged terrain. The portion of Mission Hills north of Sixty-third Street was developed first and is bordered on its west edge by the golf fairways of the Kansas City Country Club and the Mission Hills Country Club. The portion south of Sixty-third Street was developed after 1919, following three years of planning and design studies by Kansas City landscape architects George Kessler and Hare & Hare, and John Nolen of Cambridge, Massachusetts.

As with other Nichols residential developments, a number of small park areas are incorporated into the subdivision and are ornamented with statuary and fountains.

Colonial Court Fountain

Colonial Court is an area of Mission Hills located on Fifty-ninth Street, running west between Oakwood Road and Overhill Road. The prominent feature of this area is the landscaped median strip over 600

Fig. 122

Fig. 123

feet long and 120 feet wide. A fountain was placed at the east end of this median sometime after 1920.

The Colonial Court pedestal fountain is delicately proportioned and evidences a wealth of artistic detail (Fig. 122). Volutes at the base provide a short stem which carries the circular bowl. That bowl is fluted and maintains the upward sweep begun by the volutes. A second tier is created by a smaller bowl which bears a scalloped relief around the edges. Water is propelled from the top of the smaller bowl, then trickles down into the larger and lower bowl, ultimately reaching the circular retaining basin.

Brookwood Fountain

During a sunset ceremony on June 24, 1923, a fountain was dedicated at the southern gateway to Mission Hills on a median green space between Drury Lane and Brookwood, just west of the state line. The fountain was a gift of the Nichols Company, which reported that the fountain dated from the seventeenth century and had been first placed at an Italian villa near Siena. However, for the eighty years prior to its placement in Kansas City, it had been in an English estate garden and was purchased by the Nichols Company from a London art dealer.

The fountain consists of a rectangular stone pool with a marble pedestal placed in the center (Fig. 123). Three children are grouped around the shaft of the pedestal and support a saucer. They stand on a square marble base decorated with swags and an egg-and-dart molding. A single jet of water rises from the center of the saucer, then gently spills over the edge into the pool below. A child figure embracing a fish whose mouth served as a water outlet was originally centered in the saucer but has been lost.

Swan Fountain/Verona Columns

The firm of Hare & Hare was responsible for much of the planning of Mission Hills. In 1913, S. Herbert Hare began working with the J.C.

Nichols Company in subdivision planning. After studying at Harvard University under noted landscape architect Frederick Law Olmsted, Hare joined his father Sidney in 1910 to form the firm of Hare & Hare, which became nationally recognized in areas of civic planning and landscape design.

In 1927, S. Herbert traveled to Europe to purchase ornaments, fountains, and vases for the company. Hare carried with him topographical maps of the Mission Hills area and a letter of credit from J.C. Nichols. Eight columns of pinkish-hued Verona marble with bases and capitals of white marble were among his purchases. A result of Hare's buying trip was the creation of a lovely park in Mission Hills. The setting for this unique park is an intersection of several streets: Ensley Lane, Overhill Road, and Mission Drive. A creek had flowed through this area, but it was channeled underground through a concrete box and then covered over to provide this park setting.

The marble columns purchased by Hare are twelve-feet high and twist in a graceful spiral design. They form the visual terminus of the small sunken park, where they rest on a raised terrace of weathered stone. The columns are arranged in a slight curve, as though forming the backdrop for a stage. In the center of this curve is a white Carrara marble urn resting on an ornamental stone base. The urn was purchased in Italy by Hare and is reportedly a copy of a vase from Versailles. Four columns are placed to each side, spaced an equal distance from each other.

A flight of stone steps, sixty feet in width, leads down from the columns to an oval fountain pool (Fig. 124). In the center of this pool is a large pedestal of Carrara marble. The fountain was purchased in Rome

Fig. 124

and consists of a base around which are four swans. Unfortunately, the swans have been severely damaged. A stem rises from the base to support a saucer. Above this is another grouping of three swans and a smaller saucer. A single jet of water issues from the summit.

Leading north from the fountain toward the street is a narrow fifty-foot long, rectangular reflecting pool. Surrounded by elegant homes, this fountain contributes to the creation of one of the most picturesque spots in Mission Hills.

Fig. 125

Belinder Court Fountain

The *Belinder Court Fountain*, installed in the center of a traffic island between 1925 and 1927, is the Mission Hills equivalent of the *Meyer Circle Fountain* in its placement and effect. Belinder is a divided street with a long median lined with cedar trees. As with Meyer Circle, several streets lead into Belinder Court, focusing its prominence within the traffic pattern.

The fountain was purchased by Nichols in the early 1920s during a visit to Rio de Janerio. Sources indicate that the three-hundred-year-old fountain had been imported to South America from France.*

The fountain is composed of three marble child figures, their arms intertwined, clustered around a pedestal which supports a saucer, all within the center of a circular retaining basin approximately ten feet in diameter (Fig. 125). The figures, two boys and a girl, are elevated to a

---

*Other sources indicate the group had come from Florence.

height of six feet by a squared stone base. Wet clothing clings to their chubby bodies, and they each hold clusters of grapes in their hands. The saucer above them is equipped with a spray ring with an inside fall. The water produced falls over the edge of the saucer, splashing over the children before falling into the retaining basin below for recirculation.

At sometime, a terminal figure of a boy with a bird had been placed in the fountain. That piece was an addition that was unrelated to the figural group below it. Some years ago the piece was stolen, and the fountain now appears as it had originally.

Tomahawk/Wenonga Road Fountain

Between 1925 and 1927, the Nichols Company installed a fountain on the traffic island bordered by Tomahawk Road, Sixty-seventh Street, and Wenonga Road in Mission Hills. The fountain was said to be three hundred years old and had been imported from Venice.

This pedestal fountain was especially ornate in its sculptural decoration (Fig. 126). Three small, mythological sea horse figures were entwined to provide the base and stem for the scallop shell which surmounted it. Three figures, a dolphin and two children, were atop the shell and were depicted in attitudes of movement. A standing child was placed on top of the dolphin's back, with his arms upraised to blow a conch shell from which issued a single stream of water. Another youth knelt on the shell and was depicted stroking the head of the animal.

In 1960, the fountain was damaged by vandals and was restored by the Kansas City Monument Company. Evidently, sometime thereafter, the fountain again suffered acts of vandalism which completely destroyed it.

Fig. 126

Fig. 127

The original sculpture has been replaced with a much simpler fountain sculpture (Fig. 127). It is set in the center of a circular retaining basin some ten feet in diameter and is composed of a bulbous, voluted stem that carries a single saucer. Three gradually diminishing plantlike forms rise from its center and provide the channel for a single stream of water which falls over the edge of the saucer before reaching the retaining basin beneath.

Pompeiian Urn

The Baltimore Hotel, once located at West Eleventh Street and Baltimore Avenue, had a long reign as Kansas City's most elegant hotel. Designed by Louis Curtiss, who was sent to Europe for three months to research the project, the hotel opened in 1899. Many of the public rooms in the hotel were based on a theme and were decorated appropriately: the Italian Room, the Elizabethan Parlor, the Heidelberg Room, and the Egyptian Room.

The Pompeiian Room was described as one of the finest examples of Pompeiian architecture in the United States. Even the furniture in the room duplicated pieces found in Pompeii. The floor was of marble and the ceiling was gilded. Placed at one end of the room was a marble replica of a vase, approximately six feet tall, whose fragments were excavated at Herculaneum. A ring of water jets was placed inside the vase which, as a hotel advertising publication described it, rested "on a pedestal rising from a large water basin, the whole forming a fountain of great purity of design and grace."

A photograph (Fig. 128) shows the fountain serving as a backdrop for a musical revue presented in the Pompeiian Room, the E. George Woods' "Merry Go Round Revue."

In 1939, the hotel was demolished. The owners of the property, the Corrigan Realty Company, presented the fountain from the Pompeiian

Room to J.C. Nichols. In 1940, Nichols had it placed in Mission Hills on a large oval traffic island on Wenonga Terrace, just north of Sixty-seventh Street (Fig. 129). The fountain is surrounded by cedars and shrubs, but the water elements were never installed at its Mission Hills location. The *Pompeiian Urn*, a large and impressive work, provides tangible testimony to the splendor that was the Baltimore Hotel.

Fig. 128

Fig. 129

The Nymph

One of the most recent additions to the Nichols residential district ornamentation is the figure of a nymph, placed just west of State Line Road at Sixty-ninth Street in 1963 (Fig. 130). The triangular park at that location had been given to the city of Mission Hills by the Nichols Company. The *Nymph* was purchased by Miller Nichols during a visit to Florence in 1962, the year before the fountain was placed. The marble work by Raffaello Romanelli was originally intended as a fountain, although currently it is employed as a sculptural work without any water elements.

The eloquent sculpture consists of a seated female nude, elevated to a height of approximately six feet by a marble pier resting on a tiered pedestal base. Carved on the pier is a masklike face that once served as a water outlet. The water fell into a circular basin which curves into wavelike forms where it joins the pier. Another bearded mask is carved on the inside of the basin, and its mouth served as an additional water outlet. The female figure clasps her hands together beneath her chin and leans forward slightly, as though looking at her reflection in the basin below.

The Country Club Plaza Fountains

In addition to his residential developments, J.C. Nichols was also a pioneer in the development of planned neighborhood shopping centers. They were first introduced to provide convenient shopping areas for his residential developments and were designed to be compatible in scale and style with the adjacent neighborhoods.

In 1912, the Nichols Company began assembling a tract of nearly sixty acres just north of Brush Creek and west of Mill Creek Parkway (now Nichols Parkway). Here the Brush Creek valley widened into a broad level plain which, when first considered for purchase by Nichols, was nothing more than a swamp and city dump. Tributary valleys also entered the plain from the north and south, providing in landscape architect George Kessler's view, depressions that could serve as natural travel routes.

J.C. Nichols did not turn his attention to this area until the Country Club district was fully developed. His plan called for a "dignified, stately and monumental gateway" to the residential area. Although land acquisition had begun in 1912, it was not until 1922 that a comprehensive plan was diagrammed, the result of five years of coordinated planning by the Nichols Company; Kessler, who served as planning advisor; architect Edward Buehler Delk; and the firm of Hare & Hare. The result was a shopping center known as the Country Club Plaza.

The theme for the Country Club Plaza was derived from Spanish design motifs, using colorful stucco, balconies, decorative tile, open courtyards, ornamental ironwork, ornate bell towers, and tile roofs. Ten thousand front feet of property, designed to serve 1,000 commercial establishments, were included in the original plan. A feature of the plan was a diagonal, tree-lined street called the Alameda running through the center of the complex. At a central point, the street was to open into a　*Fig. 130* large plaza featuring a fountain. The Alameda is now known as Nichols Road, but the plaza and fountain did not become part of the realized center.

The shopping center was also distinguished as one of the first to recognize the importance of the automobile to its trade. It was developed away from public transportation and catered to customers with private transportation. Ample parking facilities were an important part of the 1922 development plan, and care was taken to ensure a compatible integration of the parking lots into the total decorative scheme. The lots were paved, lighted, and tastefully concealed behind four-foot decorative walls.

The projected cost of the development of the Country Club Plaza was $5 million, and the land had already cost $1 million. A further investment was made when adjoining land was acquired for the construction of apartments to house a population of 5,000 to 10,000 people, a move to provide a constant market for the shopping center.

Construction of the first building on the Country Club Plaza, the Suydam Building (presently the Mill Creek Building), began in October 1922, and by 1925 the Plaza had grown to five completed buildings. The Suydam Building set the tone for the structures that followed. Its tile roof was of apricot and Indian red tones; arches on the building were decorated with mosaic tiles set into the stucco walls; and polychromed terra cotta formed a decorative band around the building. According to his son Miller, it was J.C. Nichols' visits to Seville that inspired the use of Spanish architecture on the Country Club Plaza. J.C. Nichols expressed his fondness for the style this way: "It has humor and sparkle and color. It's a lot of fun."

Just as he did in the Country Club residential district, Nichols began incorporating sculpture and fountains into the Plaza. The Plaza is noted today for its fountains, most of fairly recent vintage. Only six fountains were erected by 1930 and of those six only four remain. Two more fountains were erected in the 1950s, and the remainder have been placed since 1962. Several of the Country Club Plaza fountains illustrate a blending of traditions with their Gothic-inspired quatrefoil basins constructed of red stone and figural sculpture based on Greek and Roman mythology.

Though public relations people tout the Country Club Plaza's special attractions (the famous Christmas lights and annual art fair), it is the gradual changes on the Plaza that have received the most attention. The traditions of the Plaza have evolved with the shopping center's growth and change. Although the street layout remains close to the original plan and many of the earlier buildings remain, the tenants have changed many times. High-rise apartments and hotels have been erected around the perimeter of the Plaza, and several "veteran" buildings have been demolished to make room for buildings that deviate from the Spanish architectural theme.

For many Kansas Citians the Plaza and its traditions have created special memories. As a result, any changes that have occurred have required adjustment and in some instances have met with unfavorable public response. Tracing the evolution of the Plaza from its inception to its current status demonstrates that those changes are reflected not only by

Fig. 131

new buildings but also in the Plaza's fountain art. To study the Plaza's fountains is to witness the dynamic history of the shopping district itself.

Boy and Fish Fountain

The first fountain on the Country Club Plaza was given to the city in 1923 by J.C. Nichols. It was placed on park property, a traffic island at the busy intersection of Forty-seventh Street and J.C. Nichols Parkway. Purchased by Nichols in 1922 in Venice, it reportedly once graced the grounds of a villa near Lake Como.

The fountain consisted of two tiered basins supported on a pedestal (Fig. 131). Resting on the top basin was the figure of a child holding a fish whose mouth spouted water. Water also streamed from the mouths of three animal heads (probably dolphins) on the pedestal between the upper and lower basins.

Although the fountain was an attractive addition to the Country Club Plaza shopping area for many years, in 1968 it was removed to accommodate the *Seville Light Fountain*. The fountain was relocated by the Park Department to the median strip of The Paseo at Seventy-ninth Street, becoming one of the most recent decorative elements to be added to this long boulevard. The fountain now only approximates its original form.

Fig. 132

Both basins and the lower pedestal appear to be original, but the terminal figures of the boy and the fish are gone, as is the upper pedestal featuring the animal heads (Fig. 132).

Plaza Wall Fountains

The Balcony Building at 300-16 West Forty-seventh Street, constructed in 1925, is one of the oldest of the Plaza's buildings and is reportedly a replica of a building in Seville. A small, recessed, walled court in front of the building served as the visual focal point, and an exterior brick staircase provided access to the second floor. The court remained unnamed until May 1947, when it was dedicated by Mexican President Miguel Aleman, in whose honor it was named.

The *Aleman Court Fountain*, a relatively unknown piece, adds a decorative element to the court. The lack of public awareness of the fountain has been in part due to its position far back from the street.

The court was altered in 1983, making the fountain even less visible. The floor was lowered below street level so that the court must now be entered by a flight of steps. The wall fountain was moved from the north to the west wall. The fountain sculpture (Fig. 133), composed of a dolphin, shell, pedestal and reflecting pool, is set within a shallow niche featuring a shell motif. The dolphin, carved of white marble, appears rather awkwardly upended; that is, his head rests flatly on the scalloped shell basin, while his body is affixed perpendicularly to the wall surface. The head of the dolphin, as it makes the junction from a horizontal to vertical plane, is crudely executed. However, the scales of his body are carved with geometric precision. A single jet of water trickles from an outlet placed in the dolphin's mouth and falls into the scalloped basin. The shell is supported by a tapered rectangular pedestal, which is fluted

Fig. 133

Fig. 134

and bears a carved foliate relief on the base. The water is recycled to the dolphin's mouth from the semicircular concrete retaining pool at the base. While the delicacy of the fountain is now overshadowed by a large wrought iron decorative fixture suspended over the court, it continues to provide a touch of beauty and restrained vitality to this small space.

The placement of a second Plaza wall fountain on the exterior of the Medical Office Building at 4706 Broadway is much less effective. The sculpture was originally executed by an Italian sculptor, Cipriani, in 1965 at the Romanelli Studio in Florence, Italy. Shortly after its carving the sculpture was purchased by the Nichols Company. The studio owns a plaster model of the work but since 1929 has not made over five replicas of the piece. The fountain is approximately five feet high and is composed of a figural group, a pedestal, and a semicircular basin, all affixed to the wall surface (Fig. 134). In this fanciful work, the focal point of the piece is the head of a bearded man and three child figures, much smaller in scale, that surround him. Two children are placed above his head and are depicted tipping over a vase, as if to shower him with water. The third child is placed to the side and reaches over to cover the man's nostrils. The jets for the water are placed in the vase and in the man's mouth. Water cascaded from the vase over the man's head and fell into the semicircular basin.

Although the activity of this sculpture demands the use of water to complete its whimsical storytelling, it is no longer operating. It is less effective than the *Aleman Court Fountain* because it lacks animation which would have been created by the water and its installation on the side of a door jamb faced with light-colored marble disguises its existence.

Boy and Frog Fountain

One of the most picturesque fountains on the Country Club Plaza and a work that has inspired much good-natured chiding is the *Boy and Frog*. Located at the northwest corner of Nichols Road and Central Avenue, the fountain is a classic pedestal type and abounds in puckish humor. The focal point of the work is a nude, bronze boy standing in a shallow marble saucer (Fig. 135). He is responding with arms outstretched in gleeful surprise, as a bronze frog, perched at the lip of the saucer, sprays a stream of water at his body. The pedestal itself is composed of a bronze faun who crouches over the figure of a dolphin. The base on which the pedestal rests and the saucer itself are of a rose colored marble. The collecting basin, approximately one foot deep, has broken colored tiles inset in the floor.

The *Boy and Frog Fountain* was purchased in Florence, Italy, by John C. Taylor, chairman of the board of the Nichols Company. The purchase was made in 1929, when Taylor was making one of his frequent trips to Italy to acquire works of art to embellish the Nichols Company developments. The bronze boy was executed by Raffaello Romanelli. Taylor dubbed the figure "the Bronze Baby," a name which is frequently used to describe the piece.

Originally, the work was located at the southwest corner of Forty-seventh Street and Pennsylvania and was placed in front of a stand of

Fig. 135

evergreen trees which provided a natural backdrop. With the construction of the Plaza Central Park, a parking area, the fountain was moved one block south to its present location. In January 1960, shortly after the fountain was moved, vandals carted away the figure of the bronze baby. The Nichols Company swiftly issued a reward for its return, and a few days later the figure was found abandoned in some bushes not far from the Plaza. Fortunately, it had suffered little damage, and after some minor repairs the bronze baby was quickly reinstalled.

The playful nature of the work seems to inspire some equally playful responses from the public, as occasionally the "Baby" has been found more suitably attired in sweaters or hats. Though small in scale, it is undoubtedly one of the most popular works on the Plaza.

Four Fauns Fountain

In 1928, John C. Taylor purchased four bronze pieces in Brindisi, Italy, that were reportedly over two hundred years old. Later that year they were incorporated into a fountain pool at the southwest corner of Forty-seventh Street and Broadway near the entrance to a Country Club Plaza parking facility.

The bronze pieces depict fauns, which are the Roman equivalents of the Greek satyrs. These half-human, half-goat creatures with small horns on their heads, hairy legs, and cloven hoofs are approximately fifteen inches tall.

In 1958, the figures were moved to their present location on the north side of Nichols Road just east of Broadway. Only one of the playful fauns now sitting at the corner of a rectangular pool is an original piece, as the original fauns were the victims of thievery. The first piece was abducted in April 1964. To have a duplicate made, one of the remaining three was

Fig. 136   sent to Italy for a casting model. Meanwhile, in January 1965 the two remaining fauns were also stolen. Thus, it was necessary to duplicate three. Although each of the original fauns was distinctive in its pose, all are now identical.

The fauns are arranged at the corners of a rectangular pool (Fig. 136). Inset into the floor of the pool are broken pieces of colored tile. Red stone lines the top of the concrete pool. The water effects of this fountain are minimal, as only a single stream of water issues from the outstretched hand of each faun to arc into the pool.

The Plaza Theater

The Plaza Theater was erected in 1928 by the Nichols Company at the southwest corner of Forty-seventh and Wyandotte. This building, which provided popular cinematic entertainment for patrons of the Country Club Plaza, was designed to be in harmony with the Spanish flavor of the other buildings of the shopping center. The theater went a step further in that it was an "atmospheric" design. Atmospheric theaters, popular in the 1920s, were designed to create a total environment, which in this case was to reproduce a Spanish courtyard.

The Spanish influence of the Plaza Theater Building comes from Mexico as its tower is almost an exact copy of the tower from the eighteenth century church of San Martin in Tepotzotlan near Mexico City. Immediately north of the prominent tower was the entrance to the theater lobby that carried the Spanish spirit of the exterior to the interior, which resembled a courtyard. In the center of the lobby/courtyard was a fountain (Fig. 137), which J.C. Nichols had reportedly bought from the town square of a small Spanish village. The blue-tile, quatrefoil basin of the fountain had a jet placed at each of the four lobes as well as a central water jet. The fountain was surrounded by curved tile benches.

Wall fountains and balconies were embellishments that further heightened the Spanish atmosphere. The treatment of the ceiling and the indirect lighting of wall niches further provided the illusion of open sky and distant landscape.

In 1923, the architects of the theater, Edward Tanner and the Boller Brothers (specialists in theater design), were presented with an award from the Architectural League for the finest commercial structure of the year. While the building still remains, the lobby has unfortunately been modernized, and all traces of the fountain obliterated.

Fig. 137

The Mermaid and The Pomona Fountains

Woolf Brothers, a clothing store that is one of Kansas City's oldest firms, has been a Country Club Plaza tenant since 1957. Between 1957 and 1975, the firm enlarged and remodeled its space four times. A major addition in 1968 tripled the square footage. During this activity, a new courtyard was created at the northeast corner of Broadway and Ward Parkway, and a smaller courtyard was restyled at the southeast corner of Broadway and Nichols Road. Each incorporated fountain works.

Fig. 138   The *Mermaid Fountain* had been installed in the smaller courtyard at Broadway and Nichols Road in 1930. Originally, two mermaid figures graced a rectangular pool measuring twenty-three feet by ten feet. Sources indicate that the figures are more than three hundred years old and were imported by the Nichols Company from Italy. In 1968, with the enlargement of the Woolf Brothers Building, the courtyard was restyled and the fountain altered.

In the restyled fountain, a white marble mermaid is placed at each end of a trefoil-shaped pool (Fig. 138). The mermaids are semireclining, supporting themselves by resting on an outstretched arm. Each mermaid blows into a shell, held by the other extended arm, sending a single stream of water into the pool. The marble is skillfully carved, vividly depicting the scales of the mermaid's lower body and the gentle waves of water curling up in front of her. The white marble of the mermaids markedly contrasts with the red stone used to form the curvilinear retaining basin.

Although the figures of the marble mermaids themselves are among the most interesting works of sculpture on the Country Club Plaza, the total effect of the fountain is rather disturbing. The most jarring aspect of the conception is the addition of a small bronze figure of a kneeling, praying child placed in the center of the basin and elevated on a metal grill. A circular spray ring with an inside fall surrounds the maudlin child figure, which has no discernible relationship to the mermaid sculpture that provides the fountain with its identity. However, the child does function to attract donations for the Children's Mercy Hospital.

A service station was removed to provide space for the new, larger courtyard at the northeast corner of Wornall Road and Ward Parkway. The courtyard was designed by McArthur, Jarchow & Associates primarily to provide visual relief from the congestion of the busy intersection. The floor of the court is paved with brick, and a wrought iron decorative fence, extending between brick posts, surrounds the perimeter of the courtyard. The *Pomona Fountain*, installed in November 1969, serves as its focal point. The fountain was imported from Italy and is the work of Donatello Gabrielli.* It is composed of a life-size bronze figure of Pomona elevated on a shallow saucer, which rests upon a shaped, polished marble pedestal (Fig. 139). Pomona is the Roman goddess and protector of gardens, orchards, and the ripening of fruit. In this work she is depicted with classical beauty as her lithe proportions and posturing are reminiscent of Greek figural forms. One arm gathers a cloth to drape her lower body, and the other hand, bent at the elbow, supports a cluster of fruit. The pedestal on which Pomona stands is placed in the center of a quatrefoil reflecting basin constructed of red stone. Water issues from the center of the saucer and creates a curtain which partially obscures the beautiful pedestal. The

Fig. 139

* Donatello Gabrielli was born in Florence in 1884 and taught sculpture at the Academy of Art and Design in Florence.

retaining basin which surrounds the pedestal is equipped with a spray ring that features an inside fall. The fountain is illuminated at night by underwater lights.

Neptune Fountain

It was the discovery of the *Neptune Fountain* that led Miller Nichols to the Bromsgrove Guild of Worchestershire, England, an atelier that was to provide him with a number of other remarkable Plaza art works. Nichols acquired the *Neptune Fountain* from a Kansas City scrap metal dealer who had stored the fountain in his warehouse. Nichols was able to purchase the marvelous fountain for its weight as scrap metal.

In 1953, when the *Neptune Fountain* was being installed in front of a new Plaza building on the north side of Forty-seventh Street just west of Wornall Road, the signature of the Bromsgrove Guild was discovered on the base of the piece. In tracing the work, Nichols ultimately located G.H. Whewell, the business manager of the guild, who supplied Nichols with its history.

In 1911, the Bromsgrove Guild had been commissioned by Alba Johnson, president of the Baldwin Locomotive Company, to execute the fountain for his home in Philadelphia. When he died in 1946, his estate was sold to the New Sharon Convent of the Holy Child Jesus of Rosemont, Pennsylvania. After the convent closed several years later, the fountain was sold and passed through several dealers before it was acquired by Nichols in 1952. Eventually, Miller Nichols traveled to England and visited Whewell, who was aged and ailing at the time, and purchased many of the works in his possession.

The 8,000 pound cast lead fountain is placed in an oval pool (Plate 20, page 45). Neptune, god of the sea, is depicted in an attitude of movement as three mythological sea horses, residents of his realm, move his chariot through the waters. Bearded Neptune, trident in hand, leans forward urging the horses on. Two dolphins, sacred to Neptune, appear in the water between the horses. Water outlets are ingeniously placed in the nostrils of the dolphins and horses, and additional streams issue from the horses' mouths. The imagery expressed in this fountain captures the salt-sprayed essence of the oceans dominated by the sea god.

The *Neptune Fountain* has had an interesting sidelight to its history. In 1969, the horses' heads were used as models for special horse costumes for the Missouri Repertory Theater's production of *The Taming of the Shrew*.

The fountain is one of the Plaza favorites. In winter, the oval basin is planted with greenery, as freezing water could damage the sculptural components, and Neptune patiently awaits the return of his watery realm.

Pegasus/Flame Fountain

The dynamic growth of the Country Club Plaza is reflected in the changes made to the fountain located at the northeast corner of Ward Parkway and Pennsylvania Avenue. In July 1954, True Milliman opened his new restaurant, Milliman's, at 4747 Pennsylvania to a waiting crowd that had come to experience not only his food but also his unusual decor.

The interior included a dining area called the Web Room, which featured a jeweled spider and a fly entwined in a large black web. Other dining areas were the Fountain Room, which had tables surrounding a central, interior fountain, and the Pegasus Room, which derived its theme from the fountain located outside the entrance.

The Pegasus Fountain had a small, winged horse as the focal point of the work. The sculpture was placed atop a pedestal in the center of a basin. The water elements were restricted to a circular spray ring surrounding the perimeter of the pool. The Pegasus was the work of sculptor Wheeler Williams who had also designed the *Muse of the Missouri Fountain.*

In 1963, restauranteurs Joe and Bill Gilbert and Paul Robinson announced plans to remodel the restaurant, then named the Embassy. They enlisted the architectural firm of Linscott, Kiene & Haylett to design the decor of their new restaurant to be called Plaza III, relying heavily on Spanish motifs.

The plans for the renewal of the building also called for a radical change to the *Pegasus Fountain.* Linscott, Kiene & Haylett determined that while they would retain the existing pool, they would remove the sculptural decoration long associated with the previous restaurants. The Pegasus was removed from its pylon and placed at a new location on West Forty-seventh Street near Broadway.

The bold and seemingly incongruous design for their new fountain disproved the adage "You can't mix fire with water." The fountain consisted of a bronze bowl mounted atop the pedestal, equipped with a gas jet to produce flames (Fig. 140). The water elements of the fountain were not changed and still consisted of the circular arcing jets that spray toward the center of the pool. The *Flame Fountain*, as it has now been dubbed, enjoys a popularity resulting from its mixture of fire and water.

Fig. 140

Fig. 141

Boar Fountain

Once upon a time, Danish storyteller Hans Christian Anderson was inspired to write a story entitled "The Metal Pig." The source of his inspiration was a small bronze fountain which still stands at the south end of the Loggia of the Mercato Nuovo in Florence, Italy. The bronze, a figure of a boar mounted atop a rectangular pedestal carved with the figures of myriad living creatures, issues a single stream of water into a collecting receptacle. A coin collection box is built into the sculpture, and the monies collected are given to a Florentine orphanage.

The Florentine boar was a work by the seventeenth century sculptor Pietro Tacca, who created it for Fernando II de Medici. That boar, which graces the Florentine Straw Market, is itself a copy of a Greek Hellenistic sculpture which was executed in marble and is now housed in the Uffizi Gallery's east corridor. In Florence, the fountain has become a local favorite and has been affectionately dubbed *Il Porcellino* ("piglet") by the local residents.

The Country Club boar, located on Forty-seventh near Wornall Road, is one of three reproductions that were cast in 1857 by the Italian sculptor Benelli. It too functions as a coin-collecting bank, and the monies that are received are given to the Children's Mercy Hospital.

On April 28, 1962, Mayor H. Roe Bartle dropped the first coin into the newly dedicated boar. On hand for its inauguration were Frank A. Theis, president of the Kansas City Park Board, and Miller Nichols, who had brought the boar back from a trip to Italy in the summer of 1961.

The boar, approximately life-size, is seated with its head turned at a slight angle from his body (Fig. 141). The bronze is intricately detailed and gives the appearance of bristling hairs covering the beast. Jac Bowen, a local artist, designed the base which elevates the boar from the sidewalk. It is composed of coursed stone and is roughly circular in shape.

Bowen also designed the reflecting pool and coin-collecting area. Originally, water spouted from the mouth of the boar to fall over the base into the reflecting pool.

The swarming creatures at the base require a long look before one can grasp the infinite variety and number of aquatic figures present. They include snakes, frogs, and lizards.

The boar, whose snout has been rubbed bare of its patina for its promise of good luck, no longer spouts water but has provided rather sizeable contributions to Children's Mercy Hospital through the years. It is indeed a worthy addition to the Plaza's variety of fountain figures.

Three other reproductions of the boar are located in Kansas City. Two were gifts of the Nichols Company. One was placed at the TWA Terminal at the Kansas City International Airport in 1973, and the other was given to Children's Mercy Hospital. A smaller boar figure is in the collection of the Nelson-Atkins Museum of Art. It was cast from a model by seventeenth century Italian sculptor Gianfrancesco Susini.

Allen Memorial Fountain

A short distance from the heroic fountain memorial to J.C. Nichols is a smaller, more intimate fountain dedicated to two other members of the Nichols family: Earl Wilson Allen and his wife, Eleanor Nichols Allen.

On February 28, 1961, the Allens were killed in a fire which destroyed their Mission Hills home, which Allen had himself designed. Allen was formerly an architect with the firm of Tanner, Linscott & Associates, the group that designed many of the homes in the Country Club district as well as some of the Spanish-influenced commercial buildings of the Plaza. Allen had retired from active practice in 1960.

Eleanor Nichols Allen was the daughter of J.C. Nichols. She was active in many of the Plaza's promotional activities and was an avid gardener with memberships in the Westport Garden Club and the Kansas City Art Institute Garden Club.

The fountain memorial to the Allens was a project of their daughters, Suzanne Allen Weber and Molly Allen Kennedy, along with Mrs. Allen's brothers, Clyde and Miller Nichols. Miller Nichols had selected the bronze sculptural group for the fountain while on a visit to Italy. The bronzes were executed by a Florentine sculptor named S. Gemignani and were cast by the Marinelli Studio of Florence.

The fountain group, which was unveiled without fanfare in 1962, consists of a bathing female figure, seated with one knee drawn up. She is elevated on a square pedestal (Fig. 142). Beneath her, in a retaining basin of a quatrefoil shape, is the figure of a child standing on the back of a small turtle. The child reaches up to the female figure as if to engage her in play. At three points along the rim of the basin are ducks, which not only take part in the action but also conveniently provide the outlets for the water streams. A stream of water is also propelled from the mouth of the turtle. A single jet of water gracefully arcs from the base of the female figure (perhaps from her bathing sponge) to fall gently onto the child.

The group is framed by three panels of white aggregate stone which function as stagewings in focusing the action as well as forming the

Fig. 142

boundaries for the figural group. A bronze plaque installed west of the fountain gives the only indication that the fountain is intended as a memorial. The result is a lyrical, sentimental tribute to motherhood.

The Pan (Bacchus) Fountain and The Seville Light

Seville, Spain, was a prosperous city during its five centuries of Moorish domination between the eighth and thirteenth centuries, resulting in an architecture that reflected both its Spanish and Moorish heritage. In the early 1920s, J.C. Nichols returned from a visit to Seville with a deep admiration for that city's architecture.

During that visit, Nichols purchased a three-foot square ceramic tile mural which he later used to decorate his penthouse office on the Country Club Plaza. The mural by Spanish artist, Ramas Rejano, included a view of the Giralda Tower which is sited next to the Cathedral of Seville. Nichols also brought back photographs of the tower, the most conspicuous landmark in Seville. The tower was completed in the late twelfth century as the minaret of Seville's main mosque. Although the mosque was eventually destroyed, the minaret remained as an excellent example of Arabic-inspired art. The five-story upper belfry section of the tower was added by the Spaniards around 1568, and a small dome on which stood a bronze figure representing Faith was at the top. The figure serves as a weathervane, or *Giradillo*, which gives the tower its name. Nichols' fascination with the tower was such that in 1929 plans were drawn incorporating a replica of the tower as part of a building which was to be constructed at the northwest corner of Broadway and Nichols Road (now the site of Helzberg's). Before the building was constructed, however, it was decided that the tall tower would be unsuitable for that location, and it was not built.

In 1966, Miller Nichols, Davis K. Jackson, a vice-president of the

Nichols Company, and architect Ralph Myers traveled to Seville to acquire works of art for the firm and to study the architecture. They had in mind the upcoming construction of a new building being planned for the Country Club Plaza. When plans for Swansons, a clothing store, were announced later in 1966, they included a reduced scale duplication of the Giralda Tower and two fountains. The site for the new building was at the corner of Forty-seventh and Wyandotte streets, the former site of a business operated by Clarence A. Chandler*.

Construction of the Swansons Building commenced in 1966. The Plaza version of the Giralda Tower was incorporated into the northeast corner of the building. The tower is 130 feet in height, about half the height of the Spanish original, and the figure of Faith is seven feet tall.

Pan (Bacchus) Fountain/Chandler Court

The fountain that was to be a part of the Swansons Building project was located in a courtyard at the southwest corner of Forty-seventh and Wyandotte streets. This rectangular space, measuring eighty by fifty feet, was named Chandler Court in memory of Clarence Chandler, the Plaza's earliest businessman. The court is enclosed on the south and east by the walls of the Swansons Building and is paved with colored stone and surrounded by a custom crafted, wrought iron fence.

The focal point for the court is a fountain that has a sculptural group set within a quatrefoil basin carved of red Mexican stone. A male bust surrounded by four female figures is at first glance disconcerting as its obvious classical antecedents appear out of context with the powerful Spanish motifs and red stone quatrefoil basin.

The central figural bust is classified as a "term" or "terminal pedestal." The form, which is defined as a tapering rectangular shaft which carries the bust of a person or mythological creature, derives from the Greeks and Romans, who often used it to mark boundaries or as a small decorative sculpture for use in gardens.

Indeed, the original setting for the piece was far removed from the Mediterranean ambience of Chandler Court. The sculpture had been located on the English country estate known as Moreton Morrell in Warwickshire and was cast by the Bromsgrove Guild of England around 1912-14. The sculpture was raised on a concrete base forming an island in the middle of a large reflecting pool on the estate (Fig. 143). The embellishment of lakes or man-made bodies of water in this manner had been popular in Europe for centuries, particularly during the eighteenth century. Sometimes a grotto fountain was used, a reference to the cavelike grouping of rocks which supported or framed the fountain group.

Since its installation in 1969, the fountain has been referred to as the

---

*Chandler had been superintendent of the grounds at the St. Louis World's Fair of 1904. Impressed with his work, Park Board landscape architect George Kessler brought Chandler to Kansas City, where from 1905 to 1909 he served as superintendent of Swope Park. In 1910, Chandler opened his own business, the Elmhurst Landscape and Nursery Company (which later became the Chandler Landscape and Floral Company) at Thirty-fifth and Main streets. In 1916, he relocated to the Forty-seventh and Wyandotte site. His business activity at this location predated construction of any of the Country Club Plaza buildings by six years. In 1928, the Nichols Company bought the property, although the Chandler Nursery continued to operate at that location until 1958.

Fig. 143   *Pan Fountain.* When Miller Nichols began negotiations for the purchase of the work in the late 1950s, G.H. Whewell recalled the title of the work as *The Nymphs of the Forest, Fields, Rivers, Fruits, and Flowers of the Earth Paying Homage to Pan.* Although there is no doubt that the figures portray a mythological group, the specific subject matter illustrated is open to other interpretations.

In ancient Greek mythology, Pan was the god of the woods and fields, flocks and shepherds. He was fond of music and merrymaking and is credited with the invention of the shepherd's pipe. Edith Hamilton, a scholar of mythology, described Pan as a noisy, merry god who often joined with wood nymphs in dancing with abandon. Pan is characteristically depicted with a goatlike face with a pointed beard and horns (Fig. 144). Along with wood nymphs and satyrs, he composed the retinue of Bacchus, who is also associated with physical abandonment. Bacchus, popularly remembered as the god of wine, was generally portrayed in classical literature and art wearing a crown of vine leaves and grapes, holding a thyrsus (a wand tipped with a pinecone) and surrounded by ivy, which was sacred to him.

Upon examination of the Chandler Court sculptural group of the fountain, it becomes clear that the figures represent Bacchus holding court, surrounded by his female nymphs and male satyrs, rather than a representation of Pan. The male bust that serves as the focus for the group which radiates around it depicts a youthful head with rather long, flowing locks of hair. There are no horns or beard on the figure to indicate Pan, but rather there are grapevines which curl around the pedestal, a specific attribute of Bacchus. Oak leaves and acorns form a wreath in his hair, further referencing attributes associated with Bacchus.

The female figure to the left of Bacchus on the north elevation is portrayed kneeling and looking backward with an upraised arm that supports multiple folds of drapery. The representation of a female figure with a flowing drape is again characteristic of an associate of Bacchus, the Maenad or Bacchante. Her backward gaze is directed toward a cloven-hoofed satyr figure who is reaching up to touch her with a branch of a pine tree, another symbol associated not only with Bacchus but also with his attendant satyrs. Another satyr, placed in front of the female figure, leans against the backdrop of her cloak.

The figural group to the right of Bacchus on the north side of the sculpture consists of a female figure looking up at the bust of Bacchus and a child figure holding a garland of flowers and leaning back against her. A child figure with insectlike wings appears on the west elevation.

The south elevation of the sculpture contains a female figure who gazes outward, portrayed with sheaves of wheat beside her and sprigs of wheat in her hair. She holds a cornucopia, an attribute commonly associated with fertility spirits, another reference to Bacchus and his agents.

The adjacent figure on the south side has a cat-o'-nine-tails in her hair and is depicted holding a scallop shell. The child figure in front of and beneath her is perhaps the oddest figure of the group. He is shown on his hands and knees in pursuit of a frog. His legs, crafted somewhat awkwardly, terminate in a webbed taillike form suggesting a merman figure, a complimentary reference to the sea as depicted in the accompanying female figure.*

All the figures are intricately detailed, and the cast lead in its weathering process gives the impression of stone rather than metal. The base for

Fig. 144

*The figure might portray Vulcan, the god of fire. Both Bacchus and Vulcan were the sons of Jupiter. Vulcan was crippled from birth, having been thrown down to earth in a fit of anger. This may explain the rather awkward pose of the figure.

the sculpture itself is carved in a series of small rises, giving the appearance of a natural topographical feature.

The sculpture was purchased by the Nichols Company in 1960 and was placed in storage until a suitable location could be found. To move it from the Moreton estate, the ten-thousand-pound sculpture had to be cut into sections and the lake drained. Because it is located above the basement of the Swansons Building, special footings had to be designed to support the excessive weight. Recirculating pumps were also located in the basement. The water treatment of the fountain consists of two spray rings placed at the east and west ends. The rings are equipped with fifty-two water jets, arranged to produce an inside fall. Four bubbler jets are evenly spaced in a line across the north and south sides of the fountain. The water from the bubblers reaches a height of approximately eight inches. Underwater floodlights placed around the perimeter of the fountain not only provide for nighttime illumination but also provide enough heat to keep the fountain operational on a year-round basis. Today Chandler Court is set up with colorful umbrellas and tables, resembling a European outdoor cafe. The figure of Bacchus holds court appropriately as cocktails are served in the elegant atmosphere of the Plaza.

The Seville Light Fountain

In May 1966, the Nichols Company offered to give the city a replica of the fountain in the Plaza de Los Reyes in Seville, Spain. The company proposed to duplicate the relationship between the fountain and the Giralda Tower as it appeared in Seville. The fountain, which they named the *Seville Light*, was to be placed on a triangular traffic island belonging to the Park Department at the northwest corner of Forty-seventh Street and Nichols Parkway. A modest, tiered pedestal fountain, constructed of Carrara marble, was already on the site, and it was proposed to move it to another location. The Nichols Company offered to spend $32,000 in the fabrication and erection of the *Seville Light*. Because of its location on city property, the gift had to be approved by the Municipal Art Commission. At first, the commission failed to approve the conception of the fountain and was critical of the fact that the fountain would be a reproduction rather than an original art work and that it would be out of scale and too big for its surroundings. Commission member Henry Scott noted that most open spaces on the Country Club Plaza were being taken over by parking lots and that the construction of the new Swansons Building and this large fountain would further diminish the "plaza" effect. It was decided to poll the entire membership of the commission before making a final decision. The commission then approved the gift by a 4-3 vote.

The Nichols Company commissioned New York City sculptor-designer Bernhard Zuckerman to make an exact replica of the Plaza de Los Reyes fountain, which he produced in his Italian studio. The fountain is composed of a central shaft, thirty feet tall, that was carved from several kinds of marble (Plate 9, page 23). The shaft is six feet square at the base and is contained within a reflecting pool, approximately twenty feet square and two feet deep.

Four masked faces are carved on each side of the shaft, and water flows from their mouths into scalloped basins to overflow into the pool below.

The masks are carved from white Ravaccione marble from Carrara. The walls of the pools are of Tuscan travertine marble, quarried near Siena. The scalloped basins are made of red travertine marble from Pakistan. At the top of the shaft is a cast and hand-forged bronze chandelier that supports four lamps. Underwater floodlights provide enough heat to allow the fountain to operate year-round.

Both the Giralda Tower and the *Seville Light Fountain*, which function as a formal eastern gateway to the Country Club Plaza, were dedicated on October 12, 1967, to "the spirit of friendship and goodwill which unites our Sister Cities: Seville, Spain, and Kansas City, Missouri." That festive occasion featured the participation of the mayor of Seville, Felix Moreno de la Cova, who along with a throng of dignitaries and citizens witnessed the tangible expression of J.C. Nichols' goal conceived so many years ago.

Community Federal Savings and Loan Fountain

In 1932, the Safeway Company built a grocery store on the Country Club Plaza at 608 Ward Parkway. In 1971, the PBNA architectural firm remodeled and modernized the building for the Plaza Savings Association (now the Community Federal Savings and Loan).

The remodeling resulted in a building which appeared more modern than most of the other Plaza buildings. PBNA wanted to add a fountain to the building but did not wish to imitate other Plaza fountains. Thus, the fountain they designed was modern in character, in keeping with the lines of the remodeled building.

The architects selected free-lance sculptor Norman Brunelli, who was then teaching at the Kansas City Art Institute, to design what would

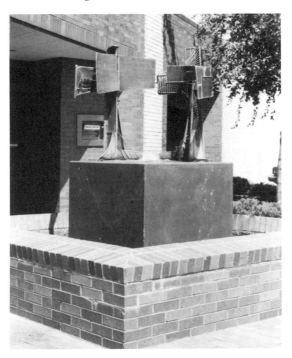

Fig. 145

become the focal point of the fountain. Robert Berkebile of PBNA designed the fountain's base.

The abstract sculpture by Brunelli was inspired by armature, the skeletal construction that a sculptor uses as support when building up his work in clay or plaster. Brunelli conceived of an artist's armature as a metaphor for the banking industry itself. Armature provides a base which enable other things to be built.

The fountain is composed of a rectangular brick block, approximately three feet high and six feet square. Submerged in the center of the block is a large cube of concrete which resembles stone when covered by water. A large bubbler jet emerges from an indentation in the center of the concrete. The water that issues from it sheets over the top of the cube (Fig. 145). Underwater lights inside the concrete cube illuminate the fountain at night. The abstract welded metal sculpture by Brunelli is mounted along two sides of the brick block at the top.

The fountain is carefully integrated into the total design of the building. The brick of the fountain basin matches that of the floor and appears to merge into the brick of the building itself.

Alameda Plaza Hotel Fountains

Although the Alameda Plaza Hotel is now an integral and permanent part of the Country Club Plaza serving as its southern focal point, a long and bitter fight preceded its construction. When the plans to build the hotel were announced by the Nichols Company in June 1963, eleven duplexes and two single-family residences occupied the proposed construction site at the southwest corner of Wornall Road and Ward Parkway. To enable the construction of the hotel, a zoning change was required, which was approved by the city government in October 1963.

Homeowners in the neighborhood immediately filed suit protesting the city's action, and a long, vitriolic legal battle followed. The issue was finally resolved by the Missouri Supreme Court in June 1967 which ruled in favor of the zoning change. Construction of the hotel began in early 1969, and after several delays created by labor disputes, the hotel was finally opened in the spring of 1972.

The fourteen-story hotel was designed by the prestigious architectural firm of Kivett & Myers and was planned to accommodate the needs of both general hotel guests and conference participants. To accomplish this efficiently, separate entrances were designed.

The grade changes abruptly from the frontage of the hotel on Ward Parkway, which actually forms the base of a hill, to the steeply rising pitch of Wornall Road. The entrance for conferees is on Ward Parkway and leads directly into a basement garage. Because of the grade change, this garage entrance is approximately one story below the main entrance off Wornall Road. This entrance was planned for use by hotel guests and visitors to the restaurants and lounges.

The architects ingeniously utilized the eccentricities of the site to create a fascinating water display. They created a fountain for each of the two entrances, one directly above the other. Although physically separate, they actually function in tandem.

The uppermost fountain component, located in front of the visitor's

Fig. 146

entrance on the Wornall Road side, is formed in a circle described by a concrete retaining wall (Fig. 146). The circle is equipped with a series of jets arranged around the perimeter, producing an inside fall. The water effect is regulated so as not to produce any great height, and because there is no floor on this level, the jets meet in the center to form a dramatic "column of water" which falls to the basin located in the garage below.

The lower fountain pool placed in the garage is also circular and not only serves as a receptacle for the water produced above but is also equipped with a series of jets to add to its visual interest. Six vertical bubbler jets are placed within its circumference. When the water from the upper tier meets the pool below, it creates a deafening roar. The spectacle is enhanced by the light which floods in from above, reminiscent of the gigantic oculus of Rome's Pantheon.

The fountain is extremely sensitive to gusts of winds and as a result has not frequently been in operation. When both levels of the fountain are operating, it becomes one of the most unusual and fascinating water displays in the city.

Two other smaller fountains are located adjacent to the sidewalk on the Wornall Road side of the hotel. They are composed of square basins, each equipped with an aerating bubbler jet. Because of the steeply rising grade, the fountains are tiered, with one actually placed above the other.

Alameda Waterfall

The concave facade of the hotel is angled and faces northeast toward the Plaza. It overlooks an elevated garden terrace which contains two swimming pools. The focal point of this elevation is a curved, man-made waterfall which is placed below the terraced garden area. The waterfall is seventeen feet tall and fifty-six feet wide. Two thousand gallons of water circulate over the edge every minute, creating a shimmering wall of water which produces a din as it falls to the base. The waterfall serves as a backdrop for a sculpture entitled *Diana of Alameda Plaza*, which at one time was also equipped with a water display (Plate 23, page 51).

The sculptural group for the Alameda Plaza Hotel is a replica of a sculpture that was originally created in 1912. The Bromsgrove Guild executed the piece for the Moreton estate in Warwickshire, England. The estate is now a part of the Warwickshire Institute of Agriculture where the original Diana is still located.

The Alameda Diana was commissioned by the Nichols Company and executed in 1970 by New York sculptor Bernhard Zuckerman, who used both copper and bronze to create the piece which gives it a verd antiqued patina with golden brown highlights.

The group, which portrays Diana, the goddess of the hunt, surrounded by three children, is supported by an eight-foot base placed within a twenty-foot reflecting pool. The pool is now filled with plants, presumably because of difficulties that have occurred with the plumbing of the fountain.

When the waterfall is illuminated at night, a dramatic effect is created as light plays off the glistening beads of water produced by the etched lines of the waterfall's surface. Diana and her agents are softly backlit, a memorable vision for the many who tour the Plaza to view its panoply of noteworthy art works.

Fig. 147

Seville Square Fountains

One of the most remarkable transformations to take place on the Country Club Plaza was the 1976 refurbishing of the Sears, Roebuck and Company Building at 500 Nichols Road. The building, which had been erected between 1946 and 1947, was converted from a conventional department store into Seville Square, a five-story enclosed market space containing forty-two shops and facilities. Two years after its completion, the Nichols Company and its architects, Kivett & Myers, were honored for their accomplishment by receiving an Innovative Development Award from the International Council of Shopping Centers.

The award was well deserved as the modernization involved much more than mere cosmetic treatment. The concrete and masonry at the southeast corner of the building were removed to create a tempered-glass atrium-entrance. Parts of the second, third, fourth, and roof level floors were removed to create the main feature of the building: an impressive central atrium. Light panels installed on the roof provide sunlight and add an outdoor ambience to a building once entirely artificially lighted.

The Nichols Company employed the New York firm of Norwood Oliver Design Associates to create the interior design. In keeping with the Spanish theme of the Plaza itself, the firm relied heavily on Spanish art objects and architectural motifs. In fact, Norwood Oliver and architect Ralph Myers traveled to Mexico specifically to find suitable embellishments for the newly created atrium space.

Some of their discoveries are among the most notable features of the Seville Square shopping complex. Two identical pedestal fountains which were presumably imported from Mexico are located on the first floor (Fig. 147). Three saucers of gradually diminishing size are arranged around the pedestal of the fountains which are set into the center of tile-lined retaining basins. The edges of the saucers and the pedestal stem are carved with an intricate foliate motif. The fountains and their setting within the court create an impression of a Spanish Plaza, an effect intended by its designers.

Diane: Sitting

In 1976, the Columbia Union National Bank and Trust Company remodeled an 8,000-square-foot building that had formerly been used as the Sears, Roebuck and Company lawn and garden department. This building at 4720 Jefferson was redesigned to be compatible with the Spanish theme of the Country Club Plaza and to replace a temporary drive-in banking facility. A new drive-in banking area was included as an integral part of the design. The local architectural firm of Kiene & Bradley worked closely with Gordon Jarchow, architect with the Nichols Company, to coordinate the bank design with the remodeling of the Sears Building into Seville Square just east of this building. The bank exterior featured brick trim, wrought iron lanterns mounted on the facade, and wrought iron gates to close the drive-in lanes at night. The interior of the bank building was also designed with a Spanish theme, using tiles, paintings, and wall hangings.

A fountain was designed for installation south of the drive-in banking

Fig. 148

lanes (Fig. 148). The fountain does not carry through the Spanish theme. A seated, bronze female figure, six and one-half feet tall, is mounted on a slender pedestal in the middle of a triangular basin which is trimmed with brick. The minimal circumference of her seat requires that one leg extend off to rest on the slender support of the pedestal itself. Entitled *Diane: Sitting*, the figure slowly rotates in a complete circle while a large spray ring around the elevating stalk sprays water up to her waist. Small bubbler jets, placed at each corner of the triangle, add another water effect to the work. The artist for this realistic sculptural work was Richard McDermott Miller.*

Obviously, the fountain was placed here to continue the tradition established by other fountain works on the Plaza. Unfortunately, the setting for the work is not ideal. It is placed back from the street, is usually in shadows, and bears no relationship with banking or with the Spanish character of the building it adjoins.

Court of the Penguins Fountains

In 1978, the Sears, Roebuck and Company automotive and catalog store (located on Nichols Road between Pennsylvania and Jefferson avenues) was purchased by the Nichols Company, which began an extensive remodeling of the property for its conversion into a group of retail outlet stores. The focal point for the new group of shops was a courtyard, erected in place of the old waiting area that had been in front of the service bays.

*Miller is a native of Ohio. He studied at the Cleveland Institute of Art from 1940-42 and 1949-52. His primary interest has been "the return of the human form to contemporary art," especially the female nude.

The courtyard is paved with brick and contains two free-standing pedestal fountains which co-exist with three penguin sculptures designed by the late Kansas City artist, Arthur Kraft. The five-foot penguins, for which the court was named, were cast in bronze from models three inches high that had been made by Kraft before his death in 1977.* Hand-wrought wooden benches that were inspired by a Spanish design are placed around the courtyard, and replicas of Spanish lamps of the nineteenth century were installed along three sides of the courtyard.

The fountains, which mirror each other across the courtyard, are placed in the center of quatrefoil basins of red stone, twelve feet in diameter and eighteen inches high. The fountains are constructed of cast iron and stand approximately five feet tall (Fig. 149). Three griffins, or winged lions, are placed back to back, forming the pedestal for the lower saucer which has a scalloped edge. Dolphins appear between each of the griffin figures. The smaller upper basin is also scalloped. The water issues from a single outlet at the top which resembles a stylized floral form. The water falls back into the fluted bowl of the pedestal to collect and recirculate from the reflecting pool below.

The Court of the Penguins, which was dedicated on October 10, 1979, was one of eleven recipients of a 1980 Urban Design Award from the   *Fig. 149*

---

*Arthur Kraft lived most of his life in Kansas City except for a short period which he spent at Yale University and in New York City. Kraft was renowned for his quizzical good-natured menagerie of sculpture. Some of his best known works in Kansas City were the mosaic for the children's section of the Kansas City Public Library and a fountain for the arcade of the Commerce Towers. Outside of the city, he created a penguin group for an Indianapolis shopping center, a ten-foot laughing elephant for a Detroit shopping center, and a group of three walruses for a Cleveland shopping mall.

Municipal Art Commission of Kansas City. In the estimation of the judges, the court provided a low-lying, open air relief to the tall building that is located to the north (Seville Square) and served to repeat the Spanish motifs that give the Country Club Plaza its Mediterranean flavor. The judges noted that the benches, "playable" penguins, and fountains offered many "small-scale distractions" to the attractive store facades. The designer of the court was Ed Wimmer of the architectural firm of Linscott, Haylett, Wimmer & Wheat.

The special problems related to the maintenance of fountains were spotlighted when in December 1980 the stone used for the fountain basins began to break off. The damage was caused by water freezing in the pores of the stone. Miller Nichols replaced the damaged stone quickly, after seeking advice on a more permanent kind of material that could withstand the harshness of the climate. That, in addition to new methods of waterproofing, ensured that the fountains would not fall prey to winter again.

Other Shopping Centers

The Country Club Plaza was only the beginning of a seemingly endless number of shopping centers in Kansas City that developed like ripples in a pond, further and further away from the center of the city. By 1966, more than seventy self-contained centers had been erected away from the downtown business district, twelve of which were owned, developed, and managed by the J.C. Nichols Company. The peak year for shopping center construction was 1963, when nine centers were built. Since that time, the use of fountains in shopping centers has become *de rigueur*.

Prairie Village Shopping Center

In 1954, the Prairie Village Shopping Center at Tomahawk and Mission roads at the west edge of Mission Hills was developed by the Nichols Company. The center is typical of shopping centers constructed in the 1950s in that it is an outlying grouping of shops with plenty of free parking but is not an enclosed mall. A fountain stands near the north end of the shopping center, gracing a mall between two rows of shops (Fig. 150).

The fountain consists of a pedestal of colorful variegated marble, carrying a shallow, circular basin in which rests the bronze figure of a child. The child provides the water outlets as he holds to his mouth a double flute from which water issues. The water falls back into the shallow basin and is recirculated. The pedestal stands within a circular, brick-walled planter.

Ward Parkway Shopping Center

In 1958, ground was broken for the Ward Parkway Shopping Center, the first large, enclosed, all-weather shopping mall in the area. Developed by Kroh Brothers, it was opened to the public in 1961 and was

Fig. 150

designed with shops that lined each side of an indoor "street," 44 feet wide and 312 feet long. The interior was originally lighted with gas lamps.

Ward Parkway Shopping Center has been altered and enlarged over the years with the addition of many new stores. An entrance near the northwest corner of the building originally featured a rock wall designed to resemble a waterfall. Although it had not operated for a number of years, it was not completely removed until one of the most recent remodeling projects.

The Landing Shopping Center

In 1957, the Nichols Company announced plans for a new forty-unit shopping center at Sixty-third Street and Troost Avenue. A Macy's Department Store was to be the hub of the center, and a 2,500-car parking lot would surround the south, east, and west sides of the buildings. The center, designed by Edward Tanner & Associates, opened in March 1961.

Fountains played a great role in the decoration of this center and provided both its theme and its unique qualities. At the main entrance to Macy's was a large exterior "waterfall," operational year-round through the use of heated water (Fig. 151). It took the form of a three-dimensional wall mural which depicted a seascape created by space-defining "ribbons" of granite and aggregate stone. Stylized sea birds stood out in relief against the backdrop of the "sky." The water effects were especially unique, as cascades of sheeting water fell over the lips of the bands of

Fig. 151

stone. The "waterfall" was designed by Macy executive and artist Mary Wiedenmann of Kansas City.

The Landing was not originally an enclosed mall but consisted of two levels with the lower group of shops arranged in two rows on each side of a thirty-foot wide pedestrian mall. The mall was to be landscaped with trees and decorated with a variety of life-size fabricated animals. Jac Bowen, a Kansas City artist, was commissioned by the Nichols Company to produce the animals.* Bowen created the whimsical animal creatures and appropriate backgrounds using steel and concrete forms covered with a fiberglass material. The animals were painted with a polyester resin resistant to weather and wear.

On the lower level entrance patio near the center of the mall was "Noah's Ark," symbolic of the "landing" which gave the shopping center its name. The choice of the name also had a further connotation as it reflects the importance of Kansas City as a major riverfront landing for steamboats on their way west. The ark was modeled to resemble a Missouri River steamboat, and the fifteen-foot-long ark was placed in a retaining basin which simulated a small lake (Fig. 152).

Bowen's animal creations peered out of windows or posed on the deck. The Noah's Ark story was carried one step further with the ingenious addition of water jets placed underneath the ark, appearing as the waves of the sea, which sheeted into the retaining basin below.

A variety of creatures decorated the pedestrian mall area, including two giraffes with their necks intertwined, a large turtle with a jackrabbit on its back, an iceberg complete with walrus and penguin, and a mother bear and cub. Steps and rails encouraged children to climb on the animals, and they remained a favorite part of the shopping center until 1978

*Bowen graduated from Kansas City Junior College and the Kansas City Art Institute. He also created similar animal figures for the Cris-Town Shopping Center in Phoenix; the relief panel depicting sheaves of wheat for the Board of Trade Building, 4800 Main; and a fountain for the Swope Park Zoological Garden.

when they were donated to the zoo. The mall was enclosed in 1968 and underwent a major remodeling in 1978, at which time the ark and other animals were given to the Park Department.

Fig. 152

Bannister Mall

When Bannister Mall at Interstate 435 and Bannister Road opened in August 1980, it was thought to be the last regional shopping center needed in the Kansas City area for some time. The huge complex was designed by The Ramos Group, a Kansas City architectural firm, for developers Copaken, White & Blitt. It is the largest shopping mall in Kansas City and contains 150 businesses, including shops, theaters, and restaurants.

Bannister Mall exemplifies both the positive and negative features of this kind of development. Shopping malls have generated criticism in recent years because of their sanitized, homogenous, and generally predictable character. Conversely, malls have also been praised for their uniformity of climate, their centralized services, and cleanliness. They have inspired interior landscape scenes that provide the shopper and casual stroller with visual relief uncharacteristic of an urban setting. Bannister Mall provides the public with one of the most unified decorative schemes yet accomplished in the Kansas City area, and the fountain treatment itself is noteworthy.

The architects purposefully designed the mall without resorting to the long, straight, shopping street approach which was employed in the Ward Parkway Shopping Center. They planned instead a multi-level mall with a curving floor plan and periodic openings between the levels which

Fig. 153

provided relief from an unbroken, continuous axis. Through the extensive use of skylights, natural wood, plants, fountains, and ever-present curves, considerable visual interest was added to the space.

The mall has four fountain pools, developed primarily in response to surveys which indicated that shoppers were making fewer trips to shopping centers but were staying longer. These fountain areas were designed to relieve the psychological and physical fatigue related to long shopping expeditions by providing soothing sounds and images which were restful.

The largest fountain area is in an ampitheater-type space near the center of the shopping mall. This central meeting area in the mall is the functional equivalent of a small town square. The sunken area is surrounded by low, curved carpeted steps that can be used as seating for viewing a variety of activities, including mall-sponsored productions and church services. They take place on two circular brick stages that project into pools of reflecting water. The pools are separated by a brick walkway, and a waterfall curves to form the rear wall, providing an elegant animated backdrop for the activities. The sculpture located in this amphitheater-space is a work by Rita Blitt, the wife of one of the mall's developers. The sculpture is a twenty-six foot tall, white steel formation in a shape which is also used as the mall's logo.

The other three fountain pools in the mall are smaller and literally wrap around and under stairways and escalators. They feature irregularly-shaped pools which are surrounded by greenery. The water effects are varied. In one, a ring of jets encircles a brick pier which serves as a stair support (Fig. 153). In another, a series of bubbler jets follows the irregular shape of the basin. One irregular brick basin has a contiguous series of five spray rings, each with a bubbler jet in the center. Underwater lights are used in all of the fountains, adding another dimension to the already pleasing visual display.

12 Contemporary Fountains

Traditionally, fountains have been constructed from certain basic components, such as retaining pools, basins, pedestals, and sculptural decoration. However, many contemporary fountains radically depart from this tradition and rely only upon the water itself to provide the impact and visual display.

From earliest times there have been examples of fountains which have either employed a minimum of sculptural elements or relied heavily on them for maximum dramatic effect. The choices of elements which decorate a fountain are often contingent upon the purpose of the fountain and the desires of its patrons.

In contemporary fountains, the sculptural decorations have embodied more abstract forms which, not surprisingly, reflect mainstream trends in modern art. Those that do not rely on sculpture for their artistic emphasis have carried the exploitation of water elements to its logical conclusions: the virtual elimination of any visible retaining receptacles or plumbing apparatus.

The Board of Trade

In 1966 (the fourth time in its history), the Board of Trade moved into a new headquarters building. Located at 4800-20 Main Street, it was designed by the architectural firm of Tanner, Linscott & Associates. A bridge entrance over a fountain moat is an important and unique feature of the building (Fig. 154).

The building sits on a slight grade which drops on the north. The fountain moat takes advantage of this situation as a stepped, rectangular pool runs almost the length of the building and follows the grade. "Miniature" waterfalls divide the rectangular moat into three levels. The central section is bridged over to provide access to the main entrance of the building on the east. The stair-step effect is created because the rectangular pool south of the central section is slightly higher than the central portion and the section to the north is slightly lower. The center section is twice as long as each of the end sections, which are approximately twelve feet long and six feet wide. The two end sections are equipped with traditional circular spray rings which agitate the water as the droplets fall to the surfaces of the pools.

Royals Stadium Fountain/Water Spectacular

Water assumes the role of sculpture in the *Royals Stadium Fountain*. The portrayal of water as animated sculpture is nowhere else as clearly evidenced; in fact, the designers of the fountain referred to it from its beginnings as a "water spectacular." While the *Royals Stadium Fountain*

Fig. 154

is contained within a series of retaining pools, the impact of the work derives primarily from the manipulation of hundreds of water producing nozzles. The *Royals Stadium Fountain* is not only the sole water display in a baseball stadium but is also the largest privately owned fountain in the United States.

The history of the *Royals Stadium Fountain* is in its broadest context a metaphor for the history of Jackson County itself, as it illustrates the aspirations and growing sophistication of its citizens in bringing national attention to the Midwest. The dedicated participation of citizens and legislators ensured the building of a sports complex worthy of a progressive metropolitan center.

In 1966, Gov. Warren Hearnes appointed five persons to the Jackson County Sports Complex Authority, which was responsible for the planning, operation, and maintenance of a sports complex. At that time, Jackson County was anxious to build a new sports arena for football and baseball franchises that were located in Kansas City.

In determining a possible site for the construction of a new facility, the authority had to consider both economical and political restrictions. They narrowed the potential sites to the downtown area of Kansas City and an area called Leeds, located in eastern Jackson County. The downtown area, in desperate need of economic revitalization, was studied carefully, leading eventually to the conclusion that the costs of land acquisition and building a parking structure would be prohibitive. Further, as the complex was to serve all of Jackson County (which included the neighboring cities of Raytown and Independence), it was felt that it would be politically expedient to construct the facility in a centralized location as nearly equidistant as possible for all citizens. The Leeds site offered acres of land on which to construct surface parking lots and was a more central location.

In 1966, there were two sports franchises that operated out of Kansas City: the Kansas City Chiefs Football Club, owned by Lamar Hunt, and the Kansas City Athletics Baseball Club, owned by Charles O. Finley. The success of the stadium would be in great part dependent upon finding suitable long-term tenants which could ensure a steady flow of revenue and use of the stadium. When first approached, Finley declined to discuss the matter with the sports authority, and Hunt expressed an initial reluctance because of the plans which would require him to share the facility with a baseball club. Though Finley moved the Athletics to Oakland, California, in 1967, Hunt kept alive the stadium idea but proposed that instead of constructing one facility, which tried to meet the special needs of both sports, that two facilities be erected. Hunt's promise of a multi-million dollar personal investment ultimately made possible the construction of two stadiums. The authority had concluded that two stadiums could actually be built at little additional cost to the taxpayers.

In June 1967, Jackson County made national headlines when voters approved by an overwhelming 69.9 percent margin a $102,350,000 bond improvement package, the largest ever to be passed in the history of Jackson County. Those bonds would finance the construction of roads, make highway improvements, and erect new health and recreation facilities, in addition to providing the $43 million earmarked for the construction of the stadiums.

Kansas City's baseball future made an enormous step forward when in 1968 Ewing Kauffman became the new owner of the American League's newest franchise, the Kansas City Royals Baseball Club. Kauffman, president of Marion Laboratories, was from the beginning very supportive of the plans to build the new stadiums. He expressed this support not only in his financial investment but also in his time and energies. In August 1969, Lamar Hunt and Ewing Kauffman signed twenty-five year lease agreements with the sports authority. Thus, with the funds and lease in hand the authority could proceed with the building of its stadiums.

The distinguished Kansas City architectural firm of Kivett and Myers, with Clarence Kivett and Ralph Myers as principals, were selected as project architects. Architect Charles Deaton of Denver, Colorado, was selected as a design associate. The football stadium, named "Arrowhead" in reference to the Indian theme of the Kansas City Chiefs, was designed to seat 75,000. The baseball stadium, appropriately named Royals Stadium for its tenant, would seat 40,613 persons. The Stadium Complex was named the Harry S. Truman Sports Complex in honor of the former president and native son.

The designs for the stadiums garnered accolades on a national level. They feature countless innovations that were calculated to provide the best playing conditions, to seat the fans comfortably, and to ensure good visibility within the stadium. Both stadiums employ ingenious structural supports that minimize the need for supporting columns and piers which might have impaired the spectator's view of the action. The spiraling walkways provide easy access to all levels and are so distinctive in appearance that they led one critic, Peter Gammons of the *Boston Globe*, to remark: "From the outside of the Harry S. Truman Sports Complex, Royals Stadium and Arrowhead Stadium look like a display of modern sculpture from a class at M.I.T."

Royals Stadium was to incorporate two unique features that would eclipse the attention already paid to the excellence of its design: an electronic, programmable scoreboard and an enormous water display. The scoreboard, twelve stories in height, could instantly show game statistics and animated cartoon images of the players and their plays. The water display would give spectators a visual treat never before encountered in any sports arena.

Ewing Kauffman made it clear that the stadium was to be the best equipped, the most spacious, and most dramatic in its overall design. He was instrumental in seeing that those goals were accomplished. In spite of the attention Kauffman lavished on the physical surroundings of the stadium, it was he who emphasized that baseball was the primary and only reason for the stadium's construction. He noted: "The scoreboard and water display are so totally spectacular that they will border on making the stadium a dream world. But they will only add to and never detract from our most important project which will always be baseball."

Kauffman assembled a cadre of highly talented individuals to implement his plans for the stadium. Architect Kenneth von Achen was employed as stadium consultant to the Royals in June 1970, replacing the late Noble Herzog. The American Information Corporation of New York City was selected to design the scoreboard. The concept for the gigantic water display actually grew out of the plans for the giant electronic scoreboard.

Arnold Holt, an industrial designer with the Stewart Warner Electronics Company of Chicago (a division of the American Information Corporation), was brought into the project to design the innovative scoreboard. In June 1971, Holt, who had proposed the building of the scoreboard in the shape of the Royals logo, a royal crown, presented Kauffman with conceptual drawings that depicted three rectangular advertising panels set into the scoreboard crown. The overwhelming consensus was that the panels distracted from the board's design, and Holt was asked to prepare an alternative plan. He decided to move the advertising panels to ground level, and his new drawings illustrated three panels set into rectangular boxes to the right of the scoreboard. His drawings illustrated, perhaps as an afterthought, a single column of water placed in back of each of the three panels.

Kauffman immediately saw the potential for a magnificent water display and requested that Holt refine the idea and pursue its further development. Holt complied by producing another set of sketches which illustrated the various forms the fountain might take. It was, however, von Achen's hastily drawn sketch that won Kauffman's approval and is essentially the way the fountain was actually constructed.

The initial cost estimates to produce the fountain were between

$150,000 and $275,000. As the plans progressed, that figure became so inflated that it appeared as if the fountain might not be constructed because of cost restrictions. It was Kauffman's own decision to invest over $1.5 million to produce the magnificent water display that now graces Royals Stadium (Plate 12, page 29).

Anthony C. Mifsud, who owned Canal Electric Motors, Incorporated of New York City, was brought in to design the fountain elements. He had a long and distinguished career and had designed the water displays for the New York World's Fair. Mifsud was to determine the fountain's programmed cycles of action. Peter Micha, owner of the Pem Fountain Company of Ontario, Canada, who designed and fabricated fountain components, developed the hydraulic and electronic controls and supplied the equipment. Royals Stadium opened on April 10, 1973. The fountain was first operated during a daytime game on July 21, 1973.

The shape of the water spectacular derives from the gradually curving ellipse created by the outfield wall, and it is composed of two wings that extend in opposite directions from the towering scoreboard. Although the total length of the fountain measured from centerfield to rightfield is 322 feet, the wings are not of equal length, as the east wing is considerably shorter. Kenneth von Achen explained that during the initial design of the fountain the sports authority had requested that an area beyond the outfield fence be left available for the construction of bleachers during a World Series event. The shorter wing was built to leave sufficient space for that purpose and thus is not strictly symmetrical.

The fountain is built on two tiers. The highest produces water sprays which cascade some ten feet into a lower pool, also equipped with a multitude of jets. The water falls from this tier one further time, another ten feet into a retaining basin for recirculation. The cascades produced on the lowest level fall over five semicircular cuts in the wall, in between the advertising panels, creating an interesting horseshoe pattern across the front. The *Royals Stadium Water Spectacular* combines every conceivable water effect in its displays. Though there are eight "shows" programmed as the fountains' primary cycles, there are at least 150 combinations possible from those basic sets.

Tony Mifsud laid out the over 600 nozzles of the fountain to allow for the manipulation of the height and shape of the displays produced. The heads of many of the nozzles are laid in tracks, which can create either geyser or bubbler jet patterns, and others are clustered in circles to produce "water castles" or cones of water. The nozzles for some of the jets are set at an angle either facing or opposing each other to produce another effect, a series of "water fingers."

Everything connected with the fountain is on a grand scale. It takes one-half million gallons of water to fill the basins, and nearly all the water can be thrust skyward at any one time.

Screened from the fans, a pump room which resembles a massive waterworks provides the mechanical equipment to produce the endless series of displays. Ken Pepin, who is employed to operate and maintain the fountain, rules over a kingdom which includes a maze of pipes, a road map of electronic circuitry, and nineteen pumps required to propel the water up to seventy feet.

A central computer console located in the pump room orchestrates the series of water displays, which may be time-sequenced. Other computer panels are located in the Stadium Club, the Central Computer Room which runs the scoreboard, and in Kauffman's suite, which may override the main system when desired.

The *Royals Stadium Water Spectacular* serves to highlight the ingenuity of the people tasked with its design and operation. Pepin, for example, fabricates nozzles or makes adjustments to the existing nozzles when he finds that the effect desired is not forthcoming.

Royals fans have come to look forward to one of the fountain's most unique water effects not only because of its special character but also because this special jet is only used when the Royals hit a home run. It is reportedly the only one of its kind. The pipe, which is bent at right angles, produces a column of water which, when rotated, creates a spiraling water shape not unlike a fireworks display. As the fans applaud ever louder, the operator causes the stream to grow until it reaches its maximum height.

The fountain is equipped with over 600 quartz lamps which add a visual dimension that makes a night game a noteworthy experience. Just as the series of water cycles changes, the colors of the lights awe the spectators with the variety of hues produced.

The *Royals Stadium Water Spectacular* is a *tour de force* in the use of water for its special effect and qualities. Unlike others designed for a more contemplative expression, it exploits the potentialities of water to the greatest degree.

Heritage Fountain

The first contribution that the City of Fountains Foundation was to make to Kansas City was a fountain commemorating the 200th anniversary of American independence. While other major metropolitan centers planned elaborate ceremonies for the occasion, Kansas City moved ahead with plans for a more permanent symbol. A bicentennial steering committee had been organized under the administration of Mayor Charles B. Wheeler to prepare for the city's festivities. The first project approved by that committee in January 1975 was for a fountain to be named the *Heritage Fountain*.

Harold D. Rice, then a vice-president of Hallmark Cards, Inc., organized the City of Fountains Foundation in 1973 with the goal of building one fountain per year, thus ensuring Kansas City's reputation as the "City of Fountains." The citizens and legislators of the city heartily endorsed that ambition, and the city council, along with the board of the foundation, set about exploring various sites around the city for the placement of these future fountains. Of the 100 sites originally recommended, the Operations Committee of the city council reduced that number to thirteen with the full council further reducing to three the suitable locations for this first fountain. The sites included in their recommendation were Blue Valley Park, in the east section of the city; Quality Hill, on the fringes of the Central Business District; and the intersection of Westport Road and Southwest Trafficway, in Westport.

The selection of Blue Valley Park as the location of the *Heritage*

Fountain was acclaimed by the public. In touring the locations in February 1975, there was a consensus among members of the Municipal Art Commission, the Board of Park Commissioners, and the city council that the Blue Valley Park location was the most desirable. They concluded that the Quality Hill location was less acceptable because of the problems with the visibility of a work in that location and that the intersection of Westport Road and Southwest Trafficway offered very little ground for the construction of a fountain.

Blue Valley Park at East Twenty-third Street and Topping Avenue is one of the city's most dramatic public parks. The topography is especially hilly, affording great views of the surrounding cityscape. In addition, the grounds incorporated into the park shared a piece of Kansas City's rich frontier history as the area was a part of the Santa Fe Trail route for wagon trains heading West. This made it especially appropriate as a place to commemorate the bicentennial of the United States.

The choice of location for the City of Fountains Foundation's first fountain had even more widespread implications. The majority of the major fountain works had been placed in other areas of the city, mainly the southern portion. The reasons for their placement are well known; many were the gifts of private donors, and many were placed as a systematic embellishment of planned developments. It was the City of Fountains Foundation's goal to distribute fountain works throughout the city. A newspaper editorial appearing in the *Kansas City Times* praised the location of the *Heritage Fountain* and the philosophy its choice expressed:

> While the City of Fountains Foundation will be supported by private donations, it is proceeding along another course and properly so. Its objective is to disperse the fountains citywide. Blue Valley Park was an ideal site. If this philosophy is continued, as it should be, in time it should be possible to have fountains at most of the prominent locations in Metropolitan Kansas City.

To select the form that the fountain would take, the City of Fountains Foundation advertised a competition. With a deadline for submissions of April 1, 1976, the foundation issued a call for designs, stipulating that the artist "must be able to conceive, design, and supervise completion of the $100,000 fountain." Further, the foundation specified that "emphasis should be placed on water display rather than on the sculptural elements." That criteria won the applause of the community, as a newspaper editorial proclaimed: "A water display of major proportions is planned. Anything of a lesser scope or quality would waste one of the finest potential sites in the community. Kansas City will soon have another stunning addition to its growing outdoor museum." By May 1976, Harold Rice announced that the $100,000 needed to construct the fountain had nearly been raised.

Twenty-one sculptors presented plans, and three finalists were each awarded $1,000 to accomplish the design work, build the model, and prepare cost estimates. The contract for the *Heritage Fountain* was ultimately awarded to the "sophisticated" design of Dale Eldred. Lynn Bauer, vice-chairman of the Municipal Art Commission, claimed: "It almost could be to Kansas City what the Arch is to St. Louis."

The sculptural works of Dale Eldred have inspired much critical acclaim. As Chairman of the Sculpture Department at the Kansas City Art Institute, Eldred had earned a reputation as a dedicated teacher. He had been honored in many ways, notably by the National Endowment for the Arts and the Ford Foundation. In 1974, he was awarded a fellowship from the Guggenheim Foundation. More recently, in the summer of 1979, Eldred garnered an enormous popular response with an exhibition entitled "Sun Structures and Time Incident" at the Nelson-Atkins Museum of Art.

In many of his works, he designed what could be considered "environmental sculpture" wherein the work of art takes on immeasurable implications from its surrounding environment. The effects of his light sculptures relied heavily on the sun and the changing atmospheric conditions. The sun reflected off his outdoor works to create dynamic expression, which at any given time would create effects quite unlike those of any other.

Eldred commented upon his theories of art in an interview conducted in 1977. In answer to "What does it mean?" (a question Eldred considered to be one most frequently asked about modern art), he asked, "What does it mean to you?" He added that from his point of view as an artist, "I want a response. I want a response from *people*. It doesn't have to be a favorable one, just a response. I like it when they say, 'Sheeeeeoo! Wow! Sonuvagun!' Sculpture should be an exciting thing."

The *Heritage Fountain* is an exciting work. Eldred conceived the fountain in terms of its environment, emphasizing the dramatic qualities of the site itself, which stands some 400 feet above the base of the park. The fountain consists of an eighty-five foot steel pylon which is centered in a 160x160 foot corrugated, concrete base (Plate 1, page 7). Water is propelled through the pylon to issue from sixteen jets placed at the summit. The concrete slab is tilted at an angle conforming to the slope of the hillside and is stepped so that the water falling over the risers appears as a multitude of tiny waterfalls. Particles of iron were imbedded in the concrete, which after oxidation turned a reddish-brown, creating streaks in the concrete. The metal of the pylon itself was alloyed so that it too would oxidize and the resulting coating would not only match the hues in the concrete but also protect the metal itself from the destructive qualities of the weather.

The water effects created by the *Heritage Fountain* express Eldred's theories regarding dynamism in a work of art. Changing weather and atmospheric conditions keep the work in a constant state of flux. Water falls from the top of the eighty-five foot pylon and breaks up at the base, creating mists of water that on sunny days produce rainbows. From its hillside location, it is visible for miles around and can be seen by the travelers of the many highways that surround the park. The *Heritage Fountain* foregoes traditional figural treatment in favor of the special effects that water can produce. Indeed, with Eldred as the sculptor, it could be nothing less than a soliloquy to one of nature's primal elements.

The fountain site was dedicated in July 1976, culminating a year of fundraising , site selection, and design selection. Fifty persons were on hand to watch the unveiling of a plaque on the site by Mayor Wheeler.

Construction began in September 1976, and the fountain was dedicated on October 5, 1977. Harold Rice presented the title of the fountain to Mayor Wheeler, who accepted it as a bicentennial gift to the city from the City of Fountains Foundation.

The fountain became a popular site from the beginning when children came to play in its showers, and adults came to be mystified by its ever-changing water effects. Of course, not everyone was satisfied with the final product. One disgruntled writer to the *Kansas City Star* complained that, "In order to see it, you have to climb up on a cement ridge almost three feet high just to watch water rolling down the hill over cement ridges to a foamy standstill."

The fountain has not been without its problems (perhaps caused in part by its bold design), which have included failure of equipment, malfunction of the tower, theft of the grating, water overflowing the retaining basin, and the build-up of algae that had necessitated weekly shutdowns of the fountain for cleaning. After all these problems were resolved, a new one developed. It was discovered that after only limited use, the impellers on the pump had worn away, and the city could not afford to replace them each year.

For many months the fountain has sat dry. The Park Department believes the design of the fountain is at fault, but Eldred disagrees. He says, "It's not a 747 airplane. Only three switches control it." Eldred believes the Park Department simply needs to train the operators of the fountain more carefully. It is a priority of the department to repair the fountain: it now has plans to hire a consultant, a specialist in fountain design, to analyze the past problems and recommend ways to bring the fountain back to operating condition. Regardless of where the fault lies, the people of Kansas City are the losers as long as the fountain cannot achieve the spectacular effect it was designed to create. It initiated a new era in fountain design in Kansas City.

Loose Park Rose Garden Fountains

Loose Park, located just south of the Country Club Plaza between Fifty-first and Fifty-fifth streets, Wornall Road, and Summit, was not originally a part of the park system. It was given to the city by Mrs. Jacob L. Loose in 1927 as a memorial to her husband Jacob, who died in 1923. Jacob Loose had been chairman of the board of directors of the Loose-Wiles Biscuit Company. He shared his wealth with his fellow citizens and was noted for his annual "shoe-giving" party for orphans as well as other charitable acts. At his death he left $1 million charity fund for the needy.

The east eighty acres of the property had once been the site of the Kansas City Country Club. Mrs. Loose purchased the property, which included a country club building and a small lake, from the Ward estate for $500,000. Mrs. Loose stipulated as a requirement for her gift to the city that the park be used primarily as a quiet, restful area rather than as a recreational area. Her intent was to provide a playground for young children and restful retreat for their elders. She wanted to avoid such active sports as baseball and golf, and motor cars were not to be allowed in the park except at a parking area near the entrance at the northeast

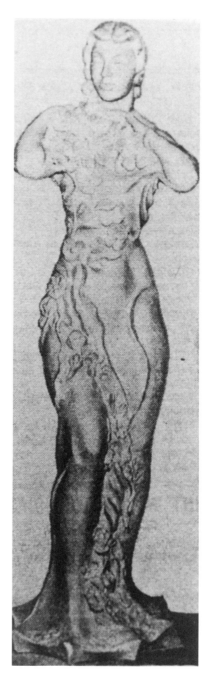

Fig. 155

corner of the park. She also specified that the city, within a reasonable time, remove the antiquated clubhouse on the land and replace it with a modern shelter house. Twelve years after receiving the park from Mrs. Loose, the city still had not allotted money for a shelter house, and Mrs. Loose donated her own funds to provide for this improvement.

The city's earliest proposals for the further improvements to the park pointed the direction that was to follow. The plan was to develop the park around a conservatory and surrounding gardens. The conservatory, however, was not constructed because of a lack of funds, although in 1931 the city did allot an acre and one-half of land for a rose garden, which was sponsored by the Kansas City Rose Society. The motivating force behind the creation of the rose garden was the president and founder of the Kansas City Rose Society, Mrs. Clifford B. Smith.* The development of the rose garden took a number of years and involved many organizations and individuals, among them the Kansas City Gardens Association, which in 1935 donated a native stone lily pond to the garden.

The rose garden was not formally dedicated until May 1938, eight years after its inception, with Mrs. Jacob L. Loose the guest of honor at the ceremonies. The dedication ceremonies included the presentation of a sculptural piece to the city by Mrs. Massey Holmes in memory of her late husband, which was to become the focal point of the park's earliest fountain. The piece was an unglazed terra cotta figure, *The Spirit of the Rose Garden*, modeled by Wallace Rosenbauer, head of the Department of Sculpture at the Kansas City Art Institute.** This life-size figure of a woman was depicted draped in roses and was modeled from a yellow-brown clay (Fig. 155). Rosenbauer had experimented with a glazed figure but felt that sunlight reflecting from the surface obscured the lines of the figure. He explained, "The neutral tone of the unglazed clay holds the light and prevents any reflection of the sun."

The figure was placed upon a low fluted base in the center of the lily pond, surrounded by eight low jets of water rising from the base which played into the water of the pond. The records concerning the later history of the fountain and its unfortunate disappearance have not been uncovered. Most probably the figure was broken or stolen sometime during the 1950s.

In 1939, a stone-pillared, circular pergola was placed at the perimeter of the rose garden. In May 1942, a Works Progress Administration project added an unusual wall fountain. The water effects of this fountain, however, are not currently in use.

A competition was held to select the sculptor for this wall fountain, and Jeannette Klein of Kansas City was awarded the commission. She created larger-than-life-size figures of a man and a woman, which were placed in semicircular niches on the south wall of a service building. They were unveiled during the 1942 Rose Day celebration. The kneeling figures each hold bowls from which water trickled into deep retaining basins at the base of the niches (Fig. 156). By 1946, the figures had undergone extensive deterioration and had to be reconstructed. The water elements were eliminated at that time.

In 1979, a new fountain was installed in the rose garden lily pond which had earlier contained the *Spirit of the Rose Garden*. This fountain was a gift of Florence Nelson from the Oscar and Florence L. Nelson Fund. Oscar Nelson had been president and chairman of the board of the Butler Manufacturing Company. This modern fountain, a dramatic departure from the earlier figural sculpture, features a retaining pool approximately thirty feet in diameter and four feet deep. Two concentric slabs of

*In recognition of Mrs. Smith's accomplishments, the garden was renamed in her honor in 1965, becoming officially the Laura Conyers Smith Municipal Rose Garden.

**Rosenbauer was associated with the Kansas City Art Institute from 1924 to 1949, serving many years as head of the Sculpture Department and briefly as the director of the school. He

Fig. 156

variegated pink granite ring the basin. The inner slabs, separated from the outer by a metal grill, are slightly tilted to the outside and set slightly higher than the outer circle of granite.

In the center of the pool are five aluminum cylinders of varying heights (Plate 19, page 43). Each is equipped with a mushroom jet that sprays out a circumference of water into the pool. The moving water flows over the inner circle of granite into the grill where it is recirculated. Underwater lights are grouped around the aluminum cylinders.

had studied at the St. Louis School of Fine Arts, with sculptor Alexander Archipenko, and at the Kansas City Art Institute with sculptor Robert Merrell Gage. His work was exhibited in New York City in 1947 and 1948 in the Whitney Museum Annual Exhibitions. Rosenbauer was commissioned to execute several works of sculpture in Kansas City, including a stone *Madonna of the Annunciation* for a chapel in St. Peter's Catholic Church in 1949.

Crown Center Fountains

One of the most exciting developments ever to occur in Kansas City and one of the nation's foremost urban renewal projects was the construction of Crown Center. It is an eighty-five acre, city-within-a-city complex of hotels, apartments, shopping facilities, offices, and entertainment spaces.

The founder of Hallmark, Inc., Joyce Hall, first conceived the project in the late 1950s. The location for the Crown Center development was especially vital to the Hallmark organization, which has been located in the general area of Grand Avenue and Twenty-sixth Street for over sixty years. In 1923, the company constructed its building at 2601 Walnut after seeking employees' opinions on a site. The employees favored the Twenty-sixth and Walnut site because of its proximity to Penn Valley Park.

Hallmark continued to expand its facilities near its first building. However, a hillside close by at the southeast corner of Pershing Road and Grand Avenue had grown increasingly unattractive and eventually became known as "Signboard Hill," a reference to the billboards placed there.

Plans for the Crown Center urban renewal project, which would remove Signboard Hill, were publicly announced in 1967, and the development was undertaken by the Crown Center Redevelopment Corporation, a wholly owned subsidiary of Hallmark, Inc. The project was planned for construction in four stages over a fifteen-year period, with completion set for 1983.

The master planner for the whole development was New York architect, Edward Larabee Barnes. He designed many buildings in the complex and the central focus of the area, Crown Center Square.

This ten-acre space features sculpture, fountains, benches, and trees. The square is used year-round for musical performances, folk festivals, art shows, and winter ice skating. It has become one of the most popular gathering places in the city.

The highlight of the square is an unusual fountain, also designed by Barnes. None of the elements traditionally associated with a fountain are present here. There is no sculpture, no retaining basin, and no visible plumbing or nozzles. The fountain takes up 2,000 square feet of space and consists of an area paved with cobblestones, surrounded by a twenty-three foot apron of granite paving (Plate 16, page 37). Forty-nine water jets, arranged in rows and spaced seven feet apart, are located underneath special grating in this floor. This paved area has an almost imperceptible incline that allows water expelled from the jets to drain and recirculate. The water height from each jet can be adjusted to any point up to a maximum height of thirty feet. Below each jet is a 300-watt colored light which can be programmed to automatically turn on at dusk to form colored patterns within the flowing water. Water can circulate through this fountain at a rate of 3,500 gallons per minute. The number and placement of the jets permit the creation of a great variety of water patterns. When the fountain is turned off, the floor and surrounding apron area become part of the larger square.

Crown Center Square, on the east side of Grand Avenue, is surrounded by buildings of the complex. Shopping areas are to the south and west and to the north and east are office buildings. The offices on the east side are on a higher grade than the square, further isolated from the activity of the square by three landscaped terraces. This transition from the public square to the office space is further enhanced by two rectangular fountains, one on the middle terrace at the south end and the other on the lower terrace at the north end. The fountains are identical, consisting of basins approximately five feet wide and twenty feet long. Five jets placed regularly down the center of each basin send streams of water skyward.

Prospect Plaza Fountain

Around 1980, the design staff of the Parks and Recreation Department created a modernistic fountain for the Prospect Plaza Park at Twelfth Street and Prospect. The fountain consisted of over fifteen concrete cylinders of varying height and diameter grouped to form a sculptural arrangement (Fig. 157). A variety of effects were employed to activate the water, which included jets that created vertical columns of water, bubbler jets, and weirs (pipes with obstructions to divert a stream of water) that caused the water to jump from one level to another. After the water was spent in the fountain, it eventually fell into a shallow basin where it was recirculated.

The fountain operated only briefly before being shut off because the mechanical system simply did not produce a sufficient water supply. The system is currently being redesigned, and it is anticipated that it may be in operation in the future.

 Fig. 157

Spirit of Freedom Fountain

The successful translation of symbol to monument rests solely with the creativity of its designers. The *Spirit of Freedom Fountain* stands as one of the city's most successful expressions of an idea that transcends the literal to create a greater reality. It serves as a monument to the contributions of the black population in Kansas City and its leaders past and present.

The idea for a commemorative fountain originated with Bruce R. Watkins in 1977 while he was serving as councilman for the Fifth District. He noted the lack of any tangible memorial or facility that was dedicated solely to the contributions of the black people of Kansas City and moved for the fountain's creation. He organized the Spirit of Freedom Foundation, Inc., to provide the motivation, the creative ideas, and the funding for the erection of such a monument. Watkins targeted the area from Benton Boulevard to Cleveland Avenue and from Fifty-first Street to Brush Creek as the location for a fountain, as well as for future improvements which would include a museum of black history and a recreational center.

A variety of fund-raising events were held. An auxiliary organization, the Ladies of the Fountain, helped raise funds by staging fashion shows and other events. Contributions from individuals and grants from corporations continued to grow as more and more people took an interest in Watkins' dream. The project, which was to ultimately cost over $400,000, was successfully funded through the marriage of those contributions with Community Development Block Grant funds and grants from the National Endowment for the Arts and the Missouri Arts Council. The City of Fountains Foundation aided in the project as consultants, assisting in its development and funding stages.

The location for the fountain at the southwest corner of Cleveland and Brush Creek Boulevard was approved by the Board of Parks and Recreation Commissioners in February 1978, thus ending a bitter controversy. In July 1977, a request had been made by the Southern Christian Leadership Conference to the commissioners asking that the name of Brush Creek Park be changed to King Park in honor of martyred civil rights leader, the Reverend Martin Luther King, Jr. Because the request for the name change was initiated at the same time that the board was to vote on the location of the fountain, the two requests were inextricably linked. Conflict over the name change perceived by some as too modest a proposal resulted in the delay of the start of the fountain for months. Ultimately, the board consented on both requests, approving the fountain site location and agreeing to rename a portion of the park as King Square.

With the location of the fountain determined, the next task which the Spirit of Freedom Foundation addressed was the form of the tribute. Watkins and members of the foundation's board of directors met with Director of the Parks and Recreation Department Frank Vaydik to discuss the concept of the fountain. It was decided that it should be combined with a wading pool, similar to the fountain in Gillham Park. Although water was to play a great role in the fountain, plans called for a centerpiece of sculpture that would be set within the pool.

Richard Hunt, a black Chicago sculptor, was engaged to provide the design for the sculptural ornament. Hunt, who graduated from the Chicago Art Institute in 1957, had gained a national reputation through the exhibition of his work. In July 1979, he traveled to Kansas City to display models of four designs that he had prepared for the *Spirit of Freedom*

Fountain. Three were abstract designs, and one depicted a three-figure family group. He explained his preference for the abstracted forms and indicated their suitability for the expression of a concept that was in itself a symbol and not a literal representation. He explained that the inspiration for his models, which consisted of curving, vertical projecting forms, was his flamelike image of freedom, coupled with his conception of the improvisational aspects of Kansas City jazz.

The design preferred by Hunt was selected for the fountain. It was determined that the proposed 5,000-pound form would sit atop a pedestal in the middle of a retaining pool that would be created by the design staff of the Parks and Recreation Department. The cost of Hunt's work would be $100,000, with $25,000 earmarked as the sculptor's fee and the remainder used for the material supplies and contract labor that would be necessary for the completion of the project. The city council voted to approve the contract with Hunt in February 1980. Despite outspoken objections of one councilman, the contract proposal passed overwhelmingly with a vote of eleven to one.

On June 9, 1980, Bruce Watkins delivered the keynote address for the ground-breaking ceremonies. His remarks called attention to the overwhelming obstacles that had been solved in the project thus far. He also noted that "this is a fountain that is not only coming into being physically but spiritually." He told his audience that the fountain was to be "dedicated to the men and women who came here a century ago, as slaves, who felled the trees, built the roads, launched their dreams."

On September 13, 1980, soon after an unsuccessful bid for election to mayor, Bruce R. Watkins died. The momentum he had generated to erect the *Spirit of Freedom Fountain*, however, was not to end. His family encouraged his mourners not to send flowers to the funeral but to send donations to the *Spirit of Freedom Fountain* project. Soon after his death, the Bruce R. Watkins Foundation was formed to pay for his unpaid campaign debts and to complete the projects that Watkins had envisioned. The fund-raising continued and contributions poured in. The result was that on September 13, 1981, exactly one year after his death, the *Spirit of Freedom Fountain* was dedicated.

The fountain roars out its message as water cascades, erupts, and fans out in a myriad of patterns. It stands as eloquent testimony to the spirit of its designer in its sculptural decoration, its placement and landscaping, the shape of the basin, and the arrangement of the jets within the collecting receptacle.

The design for the pool of the fountain respected the wishes of its benefactors and provided a wading pool and fountain that would actively engage its audience. The pool is roughly elliptical, and a series of irregularly shaped, raised platforms intrude into the pool to surround the focal point of the fountain, the nine-foot welded bronze sculpture, and to encircle the outside perimeter of the pool. Two of the platforms intrude into the pool itself (on the east and west ends), framing the sculpture and acting almost as theater wings to focus attention on the sculptural centerpiece (Plate 13, page 31).

The huge metallic sculpture is elevated and supported by a four-sided, truncated pyramid, faced with a gleaming pink granite. The pyramid is stepped with twelve risers, becoming progressively longer as they

descend from the summit to the base of the pedestal. As the water pours
forth from beneath the square platform of the pedestal, it falls over the
series of projecting steps to create a glittering pattern of water droplets, a
fitting accompaniment to Hunt's dramatic flamelike image. The natural
ease with which the water falls over the pyramid belies the efforts that
were made to create that surface pattern. Wallace Beasley, civil engineer
with the firm of Larkin & Associates who were consultants on the project,
explained that because of the ever-widening surface of the trapezoidal
pyramid a solution had to be found which would ensure that the water
falling from the summit would cover the entire length of the risers.
Beasley solved the problem by cambering the risers, which entailed
making them almost imperceptibly arch convexly to propel the water
outward from the center.

Six clusters of water jets are interspersed around the interior of the
basin. Within each group, four jets erupt at different heights to create a
frothy vertical column, while one jet spreads out in a mushrooming
shape. Because of the great pressure used to expel the water from the
nozzle and the relatively large diameter of the water outlet of each
nozzle, the fountain bursts with energy and creates a virtually deafening
symphony of sound effects. The water swirls in agitated movement
throughout the pool and is collected in outlets for its recirculation.

In November 1982, the Municipal Art Commission awarded the *Spirit
of Freedom Fountain* an Urban Design Award. The award, reserved for
those products of urban environment that greatly enhance the quality of
life in Kansas City, recognized the excellence of the fountain's design.
Watkins and the multitude of people who dedicated so much effort
toward its creation would indeed be proud.

A small bronze plaque, affixed to the back of the sculpture, reads:
"Richard Hunt, Sculptor. This work was inspired by civic and community
leader Bruce R. Watkins. March 20, 1924—September 13, 1980. Dedicat
ed September 13, 1981."

Rain Thicket Fountain

The late 1960s saw the reemergence of a policy which encouraged
systematic city planning. The legacy of urban renewal projects, which
were responsible for the wholesale clearing of land without regard for the
potentials of existing building stock, had made the public skeptical of any
new projects. The Central Business District had been especially victim-
ized. As one citizen noted, the downtown area of Kansas City looked as
though it "had once been the target of a wartime bombing raid." Surface
parking lots were scattered throughout the city where proposed developments had never materialized. Critical backlash resulting from these
abandoned projects caused new proposals to be scrutinized more closely.

In a city renowned for its parks and boulevard system, it was surprising
to find that not even one green space had originally been incorporated
into the downtown area. For unknown reasons, early planners had ignored the heart of the city, and contemporary citizens overwhelmingly
agreed that a change was long overdue. Public officials sensitive to the
image of the downtown sought to halt the trend toward the wholesale
demolition of buildings in the area and favored planned redevelopment.

As early as 1957 an ambitious master plan entitled "KC 80" had been formulated by the Kansas City Chapter of the American Institute of Architects. However, its systematic approach to development was never carried out. In 1966 and 1967 under the administration of Mayor Ilus Davis, an updating of that plan was requested. Frank Vaydik, Superintendent of Parks, was asked to consider ways to provide green spaces for the downtown area. Though many plans were discussed, no parks were forthcoming.

In 1977, progress on the creation of a downtown park was finally made. James M. Kemper, Jr., was instrumental in procuring the land which was ultimately transformed into the "Oppenstein Memorial Park." For years the building located at the northeast corner of Twelfth Street and Walnut, the site of the future park, had been occupied by the Oppenstein Jewelry Company. After the Oppenstein brothers vacated the property, it became underutilized and began to deteriorate. The heirs ultimately placed the property in trust with the Commerce Bank.

Kemper, then chairman of the board of the Commerce Bank, held a long-standing commitment to the downtown area. Sensitive to the need for a downtown green space, he saw an opportunity and contacted the Oppenstein heirs to ascertain their plans for the property. Learning that there were no plans to rehabilitate the building, Kemper suggested to the family that they donate one-half of the appraised value of the property to the public for use as a park. The heirs agreed to Kemper's proposal with only one stipulation: the park be named for the Oppenstein brothers who had been citizens and businessmen in the Kansas City community for many years.

Kemper moved quickly to put the next pieces of the project together, and he offered the land to Jackson County for its development into a public park. It was largely due to the efforts of Mike White, then Jackson County executive, that the park became a reality.

In February 1978, a resolution was submitted to the Jackson County legislature requesting a $128,000 appropriation for the purchase of the property. Several weeks later, Kansas City officials pledged their support, and the City of Fountains Foundation announced that the park would be the site for their next major fountain. It appeared that the city was soon to see its first public downtown park.

The space that the park was to occupy measured 86 by 110 feet and was commonly referred to as a "vest pocket" park, a small, heavily landscaped space. Immediately adjacent to the future park site on the north was a row of buildings that had been constructed at approximately the same time as the soon-to-be demolished Oppenstein Jewelry Building.

In February 1979, the Allright Parking Company announced that they had acquired the two buildings adjacent to the park on the north. Their plans called for the demolition of the buildings for the erection of a forty-four car surface parking lot.

It became clear that a surface parking lot abutting the northern edge of the park was unacceptable and would pose a serious threat to the success of a hard-won battle. A series of local newspaper articles ardently supported the purchase from Allright of those parcels which would allow the expansion of the park. William P. Landahl, director of the Jackson County

Parks and Recreation Department, announced that the county would submit a proposal to the federal government for a grant to purchase the property. The grant was to be issued on a matching funds basis, and the next task was to find the local funds to meet the federal share.

Under the leadership of James Kemper, private donations were solicited. After a swift and successful campaign, the money was raised and the land purchased. With this acquisition, the size of the future park doubled.

One of the most compelling reasons given for the need to acquire the land involved the park's centerpiece—a fountain. Before the acquisition, a newspaper account reported: "The mini-park is small, and there are those that believe that the fountain will have to be squeezed into the site, if it is to be accommodated at all." Harold Rice, president of the City of Fountains Foundation, had, in fact, been one of the influential parties in Allright's decision to sell the land they had just recently bought. Thus, the fountain was to have a suitable environment and one which would contribute to its artistic success.

Financed by an anonymous donor and matched with funds provided by the City of Fountains Foundation, the fountain was the design of William Severson and Saunders Schultz. They worked from their studio, Scopia, just outside St. Louis, founded in 1962. The duo since the early 1950s had been awarded sculptural commissions both in the United States and abroad.

The designers' work can be most appropriately classified as "architectural" sculpture. The definition derives more from how the form relates to its environment than a description of the actual components of the work. While maintaining their personal artistic integrity, Schultz and Severson have an ability to extrapolate from the environment in which their sculpture is to be located and to incorporate the flavor or feeling of that association in their work.

One of their successful designs illustrates their sensitivity to symbol, form, human interaction, environment, and setting. Scopia was commissioned to design works of art for the Blue Cross-Blue Shield Headquarters Building in Chapel Hill, North Carolina. To determine the form that their sculpture would take, the sculptors interviewed the architects and company officials and familiarized themselves with the company's operation. Recognizing the importance of the computer to successful operations, they derived the shape of the sculpture from a computer connector chip, which they set into a reflecting pool. Although the finished piece entitled *Computer Connectors* is an abstracted, personally inspired form, it is one that intentionally relates to its environment and to the purpose and the people which it serves.

The design process for the *Rain Thicket Fountain* in Oppenstein Memorial Park was virtually identical. The sculptors' regard for the appropriateness of the fountain form and its relationship to the environment and its public were key considerations in their design.

As the focal point of the downtown park, the sculpture had to relate to the urban landscape as well as to the lush landscaping planned as part of the park. In an interview conducted in 1980, Saunders Schultz explained, "Nature has been my main source of inspiration. Capturing the images around me in the natural world and restructuring them as art is endlessly fascinating. There can be no substitute for the quality of mystery and magic found in nature."

The design of the *Rain Thicket Fountain* consists of an eighteen and one-half foot stainless steel sculpture, constructed of branching tubing (Plate 4, page 13). The sculptors ingeniously designed the piece so that water would be carried through the tubing to transform it into a fountain. The water which flows from the tubing breaks into droplets, mists, or sprays which produce sun-catching visual effects. In describing their work on the *Rain Thicket*, the artists remarked that the treelike forms of the sculpture "serve as a metaphor valuing the randomness in nature symbolized in a rain thicket." The fountain's stylized tree form perfectly conveys the theme of the park itself. In combination with the diagonals created by the paved walkways that lead into the park, the fountain adds a dramatic centerpiece to the heart of the park.

The design of the fountain had initially prompted disproportionate criticism from the citizens of Kansas City. When the park was dedicated during an inhospitable winter day in 1981, the fountain was necessarily inoperable, and its nontraditional form caused many to dismiss it as an unsuitable appurtenance.

The *Rain Thicket Fountain* is modern, as it eliminates many of the traditional forms associated with a fountain's design. The stainless steel construction has allowed the designers a certain liberation from the less flexible materials of stone and hard metals and was essential in their successful translation of concept into substance. The stainless steel tubing is light and can be shaped into a variety of forms. Even the capricious breezes cause the tubing to vibrate, moving the *Rain Thicket Fountain* almost imperceptibly.

The containing elements of the fountain also radically depart from more customary means, as the twenty-five foot diameter basin for the fountain is gradually sloped so that the falling waters will run to the drain placed in its center. It seems almost inconceivable that the basin could accommodate the waters necessary for the fountain's operation.

As the trees and shrubbery of the Oppenstein Memorial Park have matured, the fountain has also grown into its space. Visitors to the park, now accustomed to this new form of expression, enjoy the delightful play of sun off the waters.

The Northland Fountain

The *Northland Fountain* might also be called the "Spirit of Cooperation," as it illustrates the unified effort of public and private sectors in achieving a common goal. In 1951, after a long and sometimes bitter controversy, a nineteen-square-mile area beyond the city limits and north of the Missouri River was annexed to Kansas City. Again, in 1959 and 1969, additional land areas north of the river became a part of Kansas City.

Since its annexation, a perceived "stepchild" attitude has been felt among many of the residents of Kansas City North. This attitude has been mitigated only through public improvements in the area, and has some basis in fact, as the initial development of the Northland posed special problems for city administrators. Unlike the rest of the city, which had to conform to zoning regulations that were implemented in the 1920s, the newly annexed area had grown without regulation, witnessing the sometimes incompatible mix of commercial, industrial, and residential areas.

After its annexation, City Manager L.P. Cookingham immediately called for a master plan for the development of the Northland and charged his staff with providing a well-founded, comprehensive program that would enhance living conditions. Kansas City North was growing at a phenomenal rate, and industry was beginning to further encroach residential areas. One immediate result of that growth was the formation of strong neighborhood associations that sought a development program which would be applied to commercial and industrial expansion. Growth also was the springboard for the *Northland Fountain,* located on a tract of land bordered by North Oak Trafficway, Interstate 71, and Northeast Vivion Road.

Northeast Vivion Road is one of two major traffic arteries north of the Missouri River. The street was named for Major Harvey Jackson Vivion, a Civil War officer who built his home in 1876 in the rolling farmlands of Clay County. A major landholder in the county, he generously gave a part of his holdings to the church. His daughter, Sheffa Vivion Foster, continued the tradition, as she not only gave or sold much of the family's land to the Southern Baptist Church at remarkably reduced prices but also deeded her home and the surrounding grounds to the Midwestern Baptist Theological Seminary. Today, the Vivion home, which was constructed in 1947 after a devastating fire destroyed the original homestead, is the home for the president of the seminary.

North Oak Trafficway which borders the seminary on the west, had become the dividing line that separated the existing commercial areas from the residential areas located on the east. When commercial interests began to expand facilities east of North Oak Trafficway, it became apparent that a major campaign needed to be waged to prevent this encroachment.

Robert Kipp, then director of the City Development Department, rallied to the issue and pledged his support to maintain a "corridor of green" in Northland. The city's continued commitment to that philosophy was to be vitally important in the events that were to follow. The Board of Parks and Recreation Commissioners and Director Frank Vaydik were also strongly in support of restricting the growth of commercial development to the west of North Oak Trafficway. With community leaders they began to effect a plan to acquire the land bordered on the north by Vivion Road, on the west by North Oak Trafficway, and on the south by Interstate 71 for use as public park land. The property that was under consideration for purchase was located directly south of the Baptist Seminary campus and was approximately eight and one-half acres.

Charles Garney, a Northlander with bold visions for his community, held a key role in the acquisition of the property then owned by the seminary. Garney first approached the seminary's president, Dr. Milton Ferguson, with a proposal for a park on the grounds, which would be accompanied by a monumental fountain (the first for the citizens north of the Missouri River). Garney believed in the project to such an extent that he guaranteed the construction of the fountain by placing $150,000 of his funds into an escrow account. The seminary's board, convinced by the compelling arguments presented by Ferguson and Garney, made a decision to sell the city five acres of land and to donate the remaining three and one-half acres with the stipulation that a fountain be erected on the site.

City Manager Robert Kipp and councilmen Harold Hamil and Edward Quick were instrumental in appropriating through the city council the $250,000 required to purchase the land. The council voted the funds during 1979 and 1980, and the title to the land was transferred to the Park Department in 1980. The only step then left in this grand scheme was to raise the $250,000 to build a fountain worthy of the new park to be named "North Gate."

Garney and another Northlander, Mrs. Gerald W. Gorman, who in 1979 became the first woman to serve on the Park Board since its beginnings in 1899, became co-chairmen of the Northland Fountain Committee and led a campaign to raise the required funds. What followed was beyond anyone's imagination. There was, as Mrs. Gorman expressed it, "a unanimity of purpose," which resulted in the generous contributions from schools, churches, industry, and political parties. Contributions ranged from $30,000 donated by Farmland Industries to three cents given by a Northland school child. Varied and imaginative fund-raising events were held, and the future of the *Northland Fountain* became a reality. Garney's guarantee had been made good.

Garney and Mrs. Gorman became members of the board of the City of Fountains Foundation, which was actively engaged in providing funds, technical expertise, and encouragement for the creation of *Northland Fountain*. The foundation was also responsible for underwriting future maintenance costs, a requirement necessary for the city's acceptance of a fountain to be erected on public property.

The City of Fountains Foundation has since its inception considered visibility and pedestrian access to be two important criteria for a fountain's success. The site of the *Northland Fountain*, located on a high elevation and surrounded by busy traffic arteries, was selected because of its highly visible potential. Pedestrian needs were met by turning the surrounding land into a public park which would eventually be lushly landscaped and have benches installed.

A design committee, chaired by Mrs. Frank Werner was formed to explore designs for the fountain. Wallace Beasley, a civil engineer with Larkin & Associates and intimately connected with the special concerns unique to fountains for many years, was hired as a consultant. Homer Williams, an architect with the Architects Design Collaborative, donated his services to the Northland Fountain Committee.

The decision to have a fountain operational year-round led the committee to evaluate proposals in a different light. For example, though sculptural decoration of the fountain was one of the first proposals considered, it was judged impractical since weather conditions would severely affect the material of the sculpture.

The committee studied Kansas City fountains and literature produced by major fountain component fabricators, suppliers, and designers. They were particularly impressed with a design by the Hydrel Company for a fountain installed in Stuttgart, Germany.

Several members of the committee made a trip to Hydrel's headquarters in Sun Valley, California, where they consulted with designers and engineers concerning the future *Northland Fountain*. The resulting decision made by the committee was to use the Hydrel design from Stuttgart, making only minimal changes.

Engineer Beasley then conceptualized the siting of the fountain to maximize its dramatic possibilities, and Homer Williams designed curving walkways which would lead the spectator to the pool's edge. The fountain was then ready for construction.

The Northland Fountain was dedicated on June 21, 1983, with a throng of spectators. Mayor Richard L. Berkley, one of the many dignitaries in attendance, called the new fountain "a north star in our constellation of fountains." Assisted by a drum roll and a countdown from the audience, Mrs. Gorman dramatically called forth the waters.

The fountain is composed of an eighty-foot diameter circular reflecting pool, equipped with multiple water jets (Plate 11, page 27). The highlight of the fountain is its central geyser which can propel water to a height of thirty-five feet, where it breaks into a fine mist of tiny droplets that are blown by the wind.

An inner circle of jets surrounding the central spout sprays water away from the center at a height of approximately ten feet. An outer circle, which has jets placed intermittently along the perimeter of the basin, casts its arcing water toward the center where it meets with the inner circle, creating a dramatic melding of the waters. Bubbler jets set in rings form an intermediate "layer" of the fountain, adding further visual interest.

The fountain and the fall of its waters create a din of roiling agitation. When the sun catches the diamondlike droplets or the mists produced by the sprays, the spectator is treated to a multitude of colorful rainbows. At night, underwater lights provide another source of color for the fountain.

The *Northland Fountain* is indeed a noteworthy addition to a long-overlooked segment of our city.

Fifty-ninth Street and Lydia Fountain

One of the most active and successful neighborhood groups in Kansas City is the 49-63 Neighborhood Coalition. Formed in 1970 to encompass an area between Troost and The Paseo from Forty-ninth to Sixty-third streets, the coalition has diligently worked to create a stable, integrated community.

In 1974, the neighborhood received $800,000 in federal revenue-sharing funds for major improvements of such items as street lighting and curbs. By the early part of 1980, $58,000 remained that the neighborhood council decided should be allocated for a fountain and markers to identify the neighborhood. Several delays stalled these projects, but by the summer of 1981 a site for the fountain was agreed upon by the neighborhood council and the Park Board, which was providing the land for the fountain's placement.

Initially it was thought the fountain would be placed on or immediately adjacent to The Paseo median strip. However, the funds allocated for the fountain project were not sufficient to create a monumental work, and

Fig. 158   the Park Department thought that only a substantial work would be
appropriate on this grand boulevard. Eventually, a site consisting of a
large traffic triangle adjacent to The Paseo was decided upon. The Paseo
runs along the east edge of the site, Lydia along the west edge, and Fifty-
ninth Street to the north. The fountain is placed on the east side of the
triangle at the furthest point from The Paseo.

A point for negotiation that delayed the project was the Park Department's insistence that a clause be inserted into an agreement with the 49-
63 Neighborhood Coalition that would require the neighborhood to
provide the maintenance. The neighborhood felt the Park Department
was changing the rules in the middle of the project, but the department
had instituted this new, informal policy to stretch an already tight budget.
The neighborhood finally agreed to the added clause, and construction of
the fountain began during the summer of 1983.

Kansas City sculptor William Nettleship was contracted to design both
the neighborhood markers and the fountain. His design had to adhere to
criteria specified by the neighborhood and the Park Department. The
neighborhood was interested in a fountain scaled for pedestrians, that
would not be a pool for bathing and would not be an empty basin during
the winter months. The Park Department insisted on a fountain with low
maintenance requirements, low operating costs, and little buildup of
algae. Nettleship had designed only one other fountain, although he had
designed numerous neighborhood markers for the city. He consulted
with Wallace Beasley in his design, and the resulting fountain meets the
criteria of both parties yet functions as a fluid, dynamic, and expressive
work of art.

Nettleship sees a relationship between the *Fifty-ninth Street and Lydia Fountain* and the fountains of the Moorish, North African cultures. They all rely on minimal water activity that results in peaceful, meditative drips and trickles. Nettleship also drew on his long-standing interest in landscape forms in his design for this fountain.* An undulating concrete form extends north and south of a sunken brick floor, resembling low concrete hills and a brick valley. The brick floor has a variegated surface to minimize the algae buildup. At the north end of this sunken floor, the brick extends upward, forming a "water wall." Five openings at the top of the wall permit water to flow over brick splashblocks, down zig-zag patterns formed by slightly elevated bricks, and into a drain at the base (Fig. 158). Unlike many fountains today, this is not a recirculating fountain but a "waste" fountain, in which the water is used only once. Because the water effects are so limited, little water is expended so the operating costs are minimal. Expenses are further reduced because the fountain does not need filters or electricity to run a recirculating pump.

Nettleship consciously tried to relate the fountain to the design of the markers for the neighborhood. He accomplished this by using identical materials (concrete and brick) and employing similar curving shapes.

Even a simple fountain like this can be vandalized. Soon after the water was turned on, Nettleship visited the site and discovered that children had already figured out how to manipulate the water and had greatly increased the flow. He sat down with them and discussed the economics and design of the fountain. He is considering visiting the neighborhood school to present a program about the fountain, hoping to create some understanding and pride in it. His commitment to the project has certainly exceeded his sculptor's fee.

Kingswood Manor

The *Kingswood Manor Fountain*, located at 103rd Street and Wornall Road in the southern part of Kansas City, was a gift from Mrs. Gerry Barrows as a memorial to her late husband, Raymond. The fountain was designed by Harold Rice, president of the City of Fountains Foundation, for the main entrance to this retirement complex which opened in 1982.

The brick buildings which compose Kingswood Manor are set well back from Wornall Road, a busy thoroughfare. The grade changes abruptly from the street and rises steeply up to the main entrance of the building. A circular drive aids in the transition from the road to the entrance and also defines a semicircular area used for a parking lot and as the site of the fountain.

The fountain's oval pool is located at the highest elevation and on a direct line with the main entrance to the building. Four aerated jets are placed in a line across the center of the pool, and their height is regulated with the center jet the tallest (Fig. 159).

---

*Nettleship studied at Columbia University in New York City and received an M.F.A. at the University of Arkansas. He has traveled to England to study blacksmithing and to India to study sculpture. Growing up in various national parks contributed to Nettleship's interest in landscape, and much of his work the past several years has been loosely based on landscape ideas. He says: "Forms grow, compress, repeat, alter and reverse, like musical material in the development section of a sonata."

Fig. 159

The pool is contained by a coursed stone basin which is approached by a flight of stairs leading from the parking lot. The basin is approximately four feet tall and features a ledge for the spillover of a higher fountain pool. That run-off creates a shimmering cascade of water before it is collected and recirculated in the pool beneath.

The *Kingswood Manor Fountain* is surrounded by luxuriously planted flower beds which radiate like spokes from the fountain basin. The red brick paving which surrounds the pool adds another dimension to this already colorful fountain construction.

13 What Might Have Been and What is Yet to Come

In past decades there have been several imaginative fountain proposals that never reached fruition. For some, the ideas were never fully developed, and others reached a more complete stage before being abandoned. For a few, only a germinal concept is recorded, but for others sketches or descriptions provide more complete ideas of what might have been. Why the proposals failed to be realized is frequently unknown. Unfortunately, the creation of works of art often falls prey to the realities of prevailing economic situations. Other proposals were probably doomed by lack of public support and interest, or they may have simply been ideas that were not fully examined to establish their viability and were therefore later abandoned. Some of these bear mentioning.

Swope Park Mall Proposal

One interesting proposal that failed to be realized because of monetary considerations was a fountain associated with the development of the Swope Park Mall. The park was a major addition to the park and boulevard system in 1896.

The Swope Park entrance at Meyer Boulevard and Swope Parkway and the nearby shelter house were constructed in 1904 from designs by Park Board architect John Van Brunt. Originally, a sunken garden was just behind (to the east) the shelter house, and beyond this was a golf course.

In 1914, the Park Board President, General Cusil Lechtman, and George Kessler, landscape architect for the Park Board, began to design a monumental pedestrian mall which would add an element of classical ornamentation to the natural topography of the park. A practical reason for the construction of the mall was to provide a strong line of demarcation along this edge of the park. A number of hot dog stands and "honky-tonks" lined Sixty-seventh Street, which paralleled the south edge of the park. The design of the mall would make it clear that these "unsightly" elements were not on park property and would provide a way to screen them from the view of those inside the park.

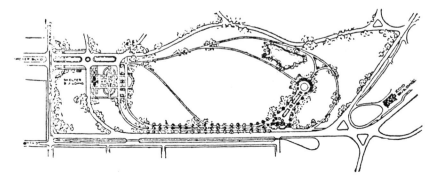

Fig. 160

Fig. 161

The inspiration for the design was the mall in New York's Central Park. The plans for the Swope Park Mall, first publicized in October 1915, illustrate a broad, landscaped mall 100 feet wide and 3,000 feet long (Fig. 160). Two parallel walkways were to extend along the southern edge, running from the sunken garden area behind the shelter house to a point immediately north of Elmwood Avenue. A row of shade trees was to line each side of the two walkways, forming an attractive screen. A massive pergola containing carved stone benches of Roman design was to be placed at the termination of the walkways, where weary strollers could rest and be treated to an array of flowers and shrubbery. At this point, the walkways would turn northeast into the park for a short distance and terminate at a fountain set on a circular platform, 220 feet in diameter, ringed with columns (Fig. 161). This fountain was probably designed or at least conceptualized by George Kessler.

Financial difficulties beset the mall project from its inception. The proposal was announced in 1915 but was then apparently shelved for several years. Surprisingly, the project was revived in 1919 as a result of Prohibition.

A concern about the effect Prohibition would have on leisure time prompted the frequently asked question, "What will take the place of the saloons?" The answer proposed by the Park Board was to improve the parks—make outdoor recreation and sports accessible to all. Swope Park was cited as being especially in need of improvements. The Park Board made plans to ask for the addition of $900,000 to the city budget for Swope Park alone. The majority of the park was still inaccessible to most visitors, and the public was beginning to accept its undeveloped state as a permanent condition. Evidently, the only step toward creating the mall was its grading in 1922.

In 1923, an attempt was made to adapt the original fountain concept to suit another function. After the grading was completed, 300 white elms were planted along the perimeter of the mall. For this new concept, the columned platform would be used for the placement of bronze plaques, rather than a fountain, honoring men of Kansas City and Jackson County who gave their lives in World War I. This plan was considered more economically expedient but was also unsuccessful because the funds necessary to accomplish the proposal were still not made available.

Other Early Proposals

Why other known proposals were not accomplished is much less clear. In general, their reported descriptions were less detailed, and they most probably never reached a final design stage. The proposals were memorial in nature and either were purely decorative or more functional drinking fountain forms. The plans do illustrate the imagination and concerns of the public in selecting fountain sites and the individuals those fountains would honor. Those selected for discussion show an amazing diversity.

In 1925, the James Kearney Chapter of the Daughters of 1817 proposed to spend $800 to erect a granite memorial drinking fountain to honor Andrew Jackson at Thirty-ninth Street and Gillham Road.

In 1930, a fountain described as "monumental and utilitarian" was proposed for erection in the northeast district near the Concourse at Benton and St. John as a memorial to William J. Bland, a brilliant young attorney killed during the First World War. Although a memorial drinking fountain in honor of Bland never materialized, he was memorialized in 1936 with the placement of a red granite boulder and plaque in Gillham Park near Forty-second Street.

The Board of Governors of the South Central Business Association recommended to the Park Board in 1926 that the traffic circle at Linwood Boulevard and The Paseo would be a good location for a memorial to George Kessler, one of the founding fathers of the city's park and boulevard system. They proposed erecting a statue of Kessler "surrounded by four beautiful fountains, growing plants, and flowers."

Fig. 162

The City Plan Commission passed a general resolution in 1928 calling for a monument to honor William Rockhill Nelson. The Nelson-Atkins Museum of Art was already in the planning stage at this time. In taking note of this resolution, the *Kansas City Star* believed the memorial deserved "long and intelligent study." The *Star* then made two tentative suggestions for the memorial: one that could be worked into the general setting of the art museum, or one that would cascade down the Liberty Memorial Hill.

The following year, leaders of Kansas City's electrical industry named a memorial fund committee to honor Thomas A. Edison. An electric fountain was proposed as a way of celebrating the fiftieth anniversary of Edison's invention of the incandescent lamp.

Another fountain proposal, tendered in 1929, was a facet of a ten-year development plan for the Forest Hill Cemetery at Sixty-ninth Street and Troost Avenue. An Egyptian-styled mausoleum facing Troost Avenue had been constructed in 1921. Three more mausoleum structures were planned to form a quadrangle which would have a mirror pool fountain as their centerpiece (Fig. 162). Only one of the three projected buildings was actually constructed, and likewise, the mirror pool did not materialize.

Rickey Sculpture Base Proposal

Late in 1972 the city was given an abstract piece of sculpture from an anonymous donor, later revealed to be the Sosland family. That gift required that the city resolve certain problems which were associated with the costs of its installation. Government officials were concerned about the public's reception of the sculpture, which was decidedly modern in its appearance. They also questioned how the city could justify spending money on art when the public was aware of more pressing needs. As expressed by Councilwoman Sarah Snow, "How do you accept a gift you can't afford?"

The gift was a kinetic sculpture created by George Rickey entitled *Two Planes Vertical-Horizontal Gyratory*, consisting of a thirty-foot high steel pole with a pair of six and one-half foot square panels of burnished steel mounted at the top.* The panels were designed to spin in the wind and rotate on the pole, catching rays of sunlight.

In December 1972, the City Council agreed to provide a location for the work at the intersection of Tenth and Main streets. Later, city money was earmarked for the construction of a base. After visiting the site, sculptor Rickey designed the base which incorporated the use of moving water. Preliminary plans called for the placement of the sculpture on an existing traffic island, an elongated triangle that extended up the hill on

---

*George Rickey has been called the major living proponent of kinetic sculpture. He was born in Indiana in 1907 and at age six moved with his family to Scotland. He studied at Oxford University and in Paris. Rickey was a painter before turning to sculpture in the 1940s. Around 1959, he began working with thin sheets of metal in vertical and horizontal configurations, designed to be driven by the wind. The Kansas City work was built in 1968 with a shorter stem, exhibited in Berlin, and then placed on a farm near East Chatham, New York. The Nelson-Atkins Museum of Art also has a work by Rickey, *Four Planes, Hanging* (1966).

Tenth Street west of Main. The water element was disassociated from the sculpture but was designed as a cascade. The water would flow downward from the narrow top of the triangular island, over three walled levels, each wider than the one above, to a pool at the bottom where it would be recirculated (Fig. 163).

Initial bids revealed that the cost of construction for the base would exceed the value of the piece itself. The value of Rickey's work was estimated at $35,000 and bids for a simple base were over $39,000. An additional $50,000 would be needed to install the fountain element.

It was decided to attempt to solicit private funds for the project. Joan Dillon, a member of the Municipal Art Commission, suggested that the City of Fountains Foundation might be persuaded to underwrite one-half the cost of the cascade base. However, by July 1973 these hopes had not been realized, and the city council voted to install the sculpture without the waterfall, even though they expressed a fear that without the water element, the piece would not be accepted by the general public.

George Rickey personally supervised the installation of the work in September 1973 but refused to make extensive comments about it, saying: "I have no theme—it's just what it is." Others were less reluctant to discuss the sculpture. Ralph T. Coe, then assistant director of the Nelson-Atkins Museum of Art, optimistically anticipated that the work would mark a visual renaissance for the downtown area:

Fig. 163

As his two planes hover and turn and move about the street scene and reflect blurred images and dynamic light from their metallic surfaces, an element of movement and festivity and action should be added to a rather static downtown environment.

Donald Hoffman, art critic for the *Kansas City Star* was less appreciative of the work, feeling that its placement was unsympathetic, having to compete with traffic lights, street lights, poles, signs, and the generally "nondescript" buildings that surrounded it.

The relative success of the work and its mixed reviews illustrate the difficulties inherent in decisions regarding public art. The Rickey sculpture has become less controversial as time has passed, but there are still those who believe that the lack of funding which scrapped plans for the fountain element prevented the addition of a truly noteworthy work of art within the downtown area.

Current Proposals

In 1973, the City of Fountains Foundation (in conjunction with the Municipal Art Commission and the Park and Recreation Department) published an extensive study that identified sites with the greatest potential for the location of future fountains. Many locations identified have since been used, while others await an imaginative proposal.

Westport Business Association Proposal

The Westport Business Association is actively pursuing the possibility of a fountain to be placed in the large traffic triangle at Westport Road and Southwest Trafficway. The association has engaged William Linscott of the Linscott, Wimmer & Wheat architectural firm to design a fountain and landscaping for the site and is in the process of raising the funds for such a project.

Bernard Powell Memorial Proposal

Plans are also underway for a memorial fountain to honor Bernard Powell, a social activist slain in 1979. The Park Department had designed a memorial consisting of a statue of Powell to be placed in the center of a fountain envisioned for the southwest corner of Spring Valley Park at Twenty-eighth Street and Brooklyn. Powell founded the Social Action Committee of 20 (now called the Action Committee for Social Change), and that organization is currently raising the funds to implement construction of the memorial.

Vietnam Veterans Memorial Fountain

The site at Forty-third Street and Broadway (J.C. Nichols Parkway) was identified in the 1973 study and is a highly visible spot between Westport and the Country Club Plaza. The fountain to be constructed there will serve as a memorial to area Vietnam veterans.

The plan for the fountain, which will cost over $250,000, was developed by the Kansas City Vietnam Veterans Memorial Fund, Inc. The

Fig. 164

steering committee of that organization is composed of Vietnam veterans. The fountain proposal was publicly unveiled on Memorial Day in May 1984.

Designed by architect David Baker, the fountain derives its form from the symbolism it expresses (Fig. 164). A series of rectangular, interconnected pools (some larger than others) with a serpentine path that leads around them creates a visual metaphor of America's involvement in the war, moving from a greater to lesser involvement in the conflict.

Behind and at the center of the arrangement of pools is a wall which will have the names of 451 casualties inscribed upon it. The pools will be equipped with a variety of fountain jets adding an animation to the otherwise still waters. Fund-raising efforts continue. It should be one of the most stunning as well as evocative fountain memorials in the city.

Epilogue

While it is interesting to visualize the fountains that had been dreamed for Kansas City, it is even more exciting to explore the proposals for fountains yet to be created. The increasing awareness of Kansas City as a "City of Fountains" has enhanced the interest in existing fountain works and has spurred further interest in building new ones.

Fountains will undoubtedly continue to be used in traditional ways: as memorials and decorative objects for a variety of settings. The ongoing popularity of the residential fountain is evident throughout practically any neighborhood in the city.

With their ability to soothe and pacify, fountains would easily have a greater therapeutic value as the stresses of modern life accelerate and Kansas City becomes more and more urban. Hospitals could incorporate the fountain into their designs, making soothing waters visible from patient rooms or family waiting rooms.

Fountains could certainly play a larger and more visible role in the downtown area. The large plaza in front of the Federal Building, for example, could easily contain a major fountain work. Some imaginative plan could be developed to create a cascading fountain down the side of the bluffs on the west edge of the downtown area.

Other excellent fountain sites are awaiting development. For example, the Kansas City International Airport would be an appropriate site for a major fountain to introduce the visitor to this "City of Fountains."

The only danger associated with Kansas City's love affair with fountains is the possibility that quantity could overpower quality. At this moment the sophistication the city has achieved in its thoughtful placement, maintenance provisions, and excellence of fountain design prompts the conclusion that this event is highly unlikely. The only certainty is that the development of fountains in Kansas City is just now reaching its most exciting moments.

Afterword

Kansas City's fountain story will continue.

While the pages of this manuscript are prepared for printing, a major fountain bordering Barney Allis Park on 12th Street nears completion. A fountain and memorial to Vietnam War dead have been designed for a site on Broadway near St. Luke's Hospital. The project is nearing the construction stage. The City of Fountains Foundation has been contacted by an association of homeowners interested in placing a fountain in Tower Park at 75th and Holmes. A director of the foundation has donated monies to be placed in escrow for use at some future date to build a visitors' fountain at K.C.I. Airport. And, the foundation has developed a concept and conferred with designers to create a carousel children's fountain to be placed in one of Kansas City's parks.

This book recounts the history of Kansas City's fountains, names those responsible for their existence and also tells of fountains, well-known in the past, that have been lost through neglect. The city's affection for its fountains is growing and has accelerated over the past ten years. The pride in this outstanding art collection continues to grow. Newspapers of other cities have admired this treasure, envious of the accomplishment of private funds applied year after year since before the turn of the century, knowing Kansas City's private sector has an ongoing program and other cities can never catch up.

When a sequel to this book is published 25 or 50 years from now, what additional fountains will be described? What individual and group efforts will be applauded? What will other cities then say about our fountains? How many people will come to Kansas City yearly just to see its water displays, and how will Kansas City then measure the value of what will surely be the most magnificent collection of fountains in the world?

Kansas City's fountain story will continue.

Harold D. Rice

Appendix I

Traditionally, the sculptor or the architect receives credit for the creation of a fountain. However, most fountains come into existence only through the efforts of numerous specialized talents. Where possible those other individuals who were not mentioned in the text are recognized here.

Chapter 6. Conventional Fountain Forms
The Fifteenth and The Paseo Fountain
Contractor: Dugan Cut Stone Company
Plumbing: Cotter, McDonnel & Company
Electrical wiring: W.T. Osburn & Company

Chapter 7. Memorial Fountains
American War Mothers Memorial Fountain
Contractor: C.P. Hucke

Pendergast Memorial Fountain
Casting: Florentine Brotherhood Foundry, Chicago

Alfred Benjamin Memorial Fountain
Casting: Rome Foundry, New York
Design of base: W.F. Fix, architect, New York City

William Volker Memorial Fountain
Structural engineer: Edwin Pfuhl
Mechanical engineer: William Cassell
Contractor for basins, walks, plumbing: Miller-Stauch Construction Company

Muse of the Missouri
Contractor: Winn-Senter Construction Company
Mechanical engineer: William Cassell
Structural engineer: E.K. Stevson

Chapter 9. Courtyard Fountains
Kansas City Star Fountain
Landscaping: Hare & Hare
Planting: Rosehill Gardens, Everett Asjes
Consulting mechanical and electrical engineers: John C. Fasnacht & Associates
Granite work: Guidici Brothers
General contractors: Callegari-Kahn Company

Chapter 11. The Fountain's Role in Planned Development
Pomona Fountain
Casting: Marinelli Studios, Florence, Italy

The Boar
Casting: Marinelli Studios, Florence, Italy
Setting (reflecting pool and coin collection area): Jac Bowen

Alameda Plaza Hotel
Landscaping: Sasaki-Walker

Court of the Penguins
Casting of Penguins: Johnson Atelier, School of Sculpture, Princeton, New Jersey

Bannister Mall
Fountain components: Kim Lighting Company

Chapter 12. Contemporary Fountains
Heritage Fountain
Mechanical engineer: U.S. Engineering
Electrical engineer: James Lacy

Fifty-ninth and Lydia Fountain
Concrete finisher: Leon Lickteig
Brick mason: John Hachmeister

Appendix II

Kansas City's vast number and diversity of fountains erected by individuals or commercial interests outside of the public's view necessarily limits our ability to identify all of them. Unquestionably, there are also a number of fountains that were obtained from catalogues, and a mention of all of them in the text would simply be redundant. In other cases, distinctive fountains that we have discovered are shrouded in mystery, as records pertaining to their design and history have not been forthcoming. We have provided the brief summary that follows in an effort at completeness.

Basin Fountains
Fountain of Life, Nazarene World Headquarters Building, 6315 The Paseo, installed ca. 1963.

Mission Hills Town Hall Fountain, 6300 State Line, installed 1962.

Westwood Hills Fountains, Fiftieth and State Line and Fiftieth and Ward Parkway, installed 1983.

Pedestal Fountains
D.W. Newcomer's Sons, 1331 Brush Creek Blvd., east lawn, installed ca. 1925.

Kansas City Art Institute grounds, 4415 Warwick, installed ca. 1927.

Muehlebach Funeral Home, 6800 Troost, date of installation unknown.

Parkway Towers, 4545 Wornall Road, installed ca. 1974.

Sixtieth Terrace and Huntington Road, date of installation unknown.

Sixtieth Terrace and Stratford Road, date of installation unknown.

Courtyard Fountains
D.W. Newcomer's Sons, 1331 Brush Creek Blvd., north lawn, installed ca. 1936.

Forest Hill Cemetery, Chapel of Memories, Sixty-ninth and Troost, installed 1964.

Fountain of the Three Graces, University of Missouri-Kansas City, north of Haag Hall Annex, installed 1940, removed ca. 1970. Designer: Wallace Rosenbauer. Replaced by a contemporary fountain treatment, date unknown, currently inoperable.

Contemporary Fountain Treatment
Mt. Moriah Cemetery, 10507 Holmes, mausoleum fountain installed 1963.

Vista International Hotel, 200 West Twelfth Street, lobby fountain, hotel opened 1984.

General Bibliography

Research materials which describe the history and personalities associated with Kansas City's fountain art have been gleaned from a number of sources. The following lists the repositories of some of the documentation we made use of and indicates those materials which were vital to our appreciation and understanding of Kansas City fountains.

Missouri Valley Room, Kansas City Public Library Newspaper clippings, vertical files, issues of the *Country Club Bulletin,* photographic collections, Park Department Reports

Western Historical Manuscript Collection *(University of Missouri-Kansas City General Library)*

J.C. Nichols Company scrapbooks and other related company materials

City of Kansas City, Missouri
Municipal Art Commission—historical files and official minutes of meetings

Park and Recreation Department—copies of original drawings and official minutes of meetings.

The following is a selected list of general sources of information:

Case, Theodore S., ed. *History of Kansas City, Missouri.* Syracuse: D. Mason & Co., 1888.
Cowtown 1890 Becomes City Beautiful 1962. Kansas City: Board of Park Commissioners, ca. 1962.
Craven, Wayne. *Sculpture in America.* New York: Crowell, 1968.
Mitchell, Giles Carroll. *There is No Limit: Architecture and Sculpture in Kansas City.* Kansas City: Brown-White Co., 1934.
Wilson, William H. *The City Beautiful Movement in Kansas City.* Columbia: University of Missouri Press, 1964.

Photo Credits

Kansas City Public Library, Missouri Valley Room, Figures 1, 2, 3, 4, 5, 6, 7, 8, 10, 11, 12, 13, 15, 16, 18, 19, 20, 21, 22, 23, 25, 32, 33, 36, 38, 39, 41, 42, 44, 45, 46, 47, 51, 53, 59, 60, 61, 63, 64, 65, 67, 69, 71, 74, 75, 81, 87, 88, 97, 113, 115, 121, 128, 155, 160, 161, 162, 163

Kansas City, Missouri, Parks and Recreation Department, Figures 9, 50

Ochsner, Hare & Hare, Landscape Architects and Land Planners, Kansas City, Missouri, Figures 24, 109

Kansas City, Missouri, Municipal Art Commission, Figures 98, 140

Authors (Piland & Uguccioni), Figures 14, 17, 26, 27, 28, 29, 30, 31, 34, 37, 40, 48, 49, 52, 54, 55, 57, 58, 62, 66, 68, 70, 72, 78, 79, 82, 83, 84, 85, 86, 89, 90, 91, 95, 96, 99, 100, 101, 102, 103, 104, 105, 106, 107, 110, 111, 114, 116, 117, 119, 120, 122, 123, 124, 125, 127, 129, 130, 132, 133, 134, 135, 136, 138, 139, 141, 142, 144, 145, 146, 147, 148, 149, 150, 153, 154, 156, 157, 158, 159,

J.C. Nichols Company, Figures 35, 56, 108, 112, 126, 131, 143, 151, 152

Charles Uguccioni, Figure 43

Landmarks Association of St. Louis, Inc., Figure 73

Kansas City Vietnam Veterans Memorial Fund, Inc., Figure 164

Yale University Press, Figure 76

Bryant Library, Roslyn, New York, Figure 77

Library of Congress, Historic American Building Survey, photographer: Cervin Robinson, Figure 80

Kansas City, Missouri, Landmarks Commission, Figures 92, 137

James Kemper, Jr., Figure 93

Business Mens Assurance Company, Figure 94

Wilborn & Associates, Photographers, Figure 118

All color photographs were taken by Fred Kautt except those on pages 7, 19, 21, and 23.

Production Credits

The talents and efforts of many individuals went into the making of this book. Grateful acknowledgement is made to the following: Joy Wightman for mechanicals and Barbara Leach for proofreading.

Typesetting was provided by the Photo Composition department at Hallmark Cards, Inc., including Alex Kreicbergs, Debbie Boan, Gale Boydston, Pam Leeds, Betty McDonald, Sandy Cooke, Jaye Miller, Karla Haas, Alvin Kern, Jan Ludecke and Herb Steffens.

Photo prints were made by the Jack Denzer Photo Service.

Index

References to photographs and drawings are printed in italic type.

Abend, Singleton & Associates, 206-207
Abend, Stephen
Alameda Plaza Hotel Fountains, 6, 181, 266-268, *267*
Alameda Waterfall, 267-268, *51*
Aleman Court Fountain, 85, 248, 250, *249*
Aleman, Miguel, 248
Allen, Earl Wilson, 259
Allen, Eleanor Nichols, 259
Allen Memorial Fountain, 259-260, *260*
Allis, Barney, 191
Allis, Barney, Plaza, 66, 188-192, *190, 53*
American Information Corporation (New York City), 280
American Legion Fountain, Ninth and Main Streets, 64, 67, 128-130, *128, 129*
American Legion Fountain, Swope Park, 127-128, *127*
American War Mothers Memorial, 134-135, *135*
Anderson, Dallas, 111, 112
Anderson, L.C. (Andy), 111, 112
Anderson, Orville, 111, 112
Anderson Photo Company, 111
Armour Center Fountain, 229-230, *230, 231*
Armour Green Fountain, 231-232, *232, 233*
Armour Hills, 229, 231

Bacchus, see Pan (Bacchus) Fountain
Balcony Building, 248
Baker, David, 308
Bales Lake, 90
Baltimore Hotel, 242-243
Bannister Mall, 275-276, *276*
Barnes, Edward Larabee, 186, 289
Barrows, Mrs. Gerry, 301
Barrows, Raymond, 301
Bartle Convention Center, H. Roe, 191
Bartle, Mayor H. Roe, 156, 163, 164, 258
Beals, David T., residence, 78
Beardsley, Mayor, 124
Beasley, Wallace, 99, 293, 298, 299, 300
Belinder Court Fountain, 240-241, *240*
Benelli, 258
Benjamin Memorial Fountain, Alfred, 145-147, *147*
Berkebile, Robert, 266
Berkley, Mayor Richard, 299
Bernini, Giovanni Lorenzo, 164, 165
Bitter, Karl, 141
Bixby, Mrs. Harry, 148
Black & Veatch, 160, 172
Blitt, Rita, 276
Bloch, Mr. and Mrs. Richard, 92
Block Company Fountain, H & R, 210, *210*
Blue Valley Park, 66, 90, 282, 283
Boar Fountain, 258-259, *258*
Board of Trade, 277, *278*
Boatman's Bank Fountain, 214

Boller Brothers, 253
Bovard, William R., 202
Bowen, Jac, 180, 258, 274
Boy and Fish Fountain, 247-248, *247*
Boy and Frog Fountain, 250-251, *251*
Bromsgrove Guild (Worchestershire, England), 256, 261, 268
Brookwood Fountain, 238, *238*
Brunelli, Norman, 265, 266
Business Men's Assurance Company Fountains, 194, *194*

Central Park (New York City), 62, 303
Chandler, Clarence, 261
Chandler Court, 261-264
Children's Mercy Hospital, 147, 148, 254, 258, 259
Cipriani, 250
City Center Square Fountains, 213-214, *213*
City Hall Fountains, 65, 199-205, *200, 9*
City Hall Fountain, proposal, 201-203, *202*
"City of Fountains," 1, 65, 282
City of Fountains Foundation, 66-67, 192, 282, 283, 285, 294, 295, 298, 301, 308
Cliff Spring, 181, *182, 183*
Colgrove, Tom, 195, 196, 205
Colonial Court Fountain, 237-238, *237*
Colonnade Fountain, 110, *111*
Columbian Exposition (Chicago), 70, 79
Commerce Tower Building, 167, 197
Commerce Tower Sunken Garden, 197-199, *41*
Commerce Trust Arcade Fountain, 65, 193-194, *193*
Community Federal Savings and Loan Fountain, 265-266, *265*
Convention Hall, 189
Conservatories, 71-72, *71, 72*
Cookingham, L.P., 189, 297
Copaken, White & Blitt, 275
Corwin, E.W. (Rusty), 98
Country Club Plaza, 122, 219
Country Club Plaza Fountains, 245-272
Country Club Residential District, 163, 219-222, 232, 245, 259
Court of the Penguins Fountains, 270-272, *271*
Cowgill, Mayor James, 127
Cranes Rising, 175
Crawley, Kenneth, 85
Crown Center Fountains, 186, 289-290, *37*
Crystal Palace (London), 69, 70
Curtiss, Louis, 242

Darter, Jerry, 66
Daughters of the Confederacy Monument, 163
Davis, Mayor Ilus W., 124, 226, 294
Deaton, Charles, 279

Delk, Edward Buehler, 122, 135, 155, 156, 178, 224, 245
Diana of Alameda Plaza, 268
Diane: Sitting, 269-270, *270*
Dreyer, Jorgen, 81, 82, 101, 126
Drinking Fountains, 64, *63, 65*
Dunlap, Matthew, 74
Dunn, W.H., 91, 101, 133
Dyer, Daniel B., residence, 79-80, *80*

Eagle Scout Memorial Fountain, 170-173, *172, 21*
Eisenhower Lake, see Lake Willow
Eldred, Dale, 283, 284, 285
Electric Park, 59-60
Electric Park Fountain, 60, *61*
Elmwood Cemetery Lake, 89
Embassy Suites, see Granada Royale Hometel
Epperson, U.S., residence, 82-83, 85, *84*

Farragut Monument (New York City), 123
Faxon Fountain, 56-57, *56*
Faxon, Frank, 56
Federal Building, 202, 203, 204
Ferguson, Dr. Milton, 297, 298
Fifteenth Street and The Paseo Fountain, 105-108, 110, *107*
Fifty-second and Brookside Fountain, 234-235, 236, *234*
Fifty-ninth Street and Lydia Fountain, 299-301, *300*
Fitzsimons Memorial Fountain, William, 6, 114, 115, 124, 125-127, *126*
Flame Fountain, see Pegasus/Flame Fountain
Foley, Margaret, 69
Folke Filbyter, see Fountain and Water Trough of Folke Filbyter
Forest Hill Cemetery, 140, 305, *306*
Fountain and Water Trough of Folke Filbyter, 156, *157*
Fountain of the Animals, 216, 218, *217*
Fountain of Faith (Falls Church, Virginia), 158
Fountain of Life, 65, 197-199, *4*
Fountain of Latona (Versailles, France), 105, 108, *106*
Fountain of the Four Rivers (Rome, Italy), 164-165, *165*
Fountain of Trevi (Rome, Italy), 5, 114
Four Fauns Fountain, 251-252, *252*
Franklin, G.B., 129
Fraser Memorial Fountain, Mary, 177-178, 179, *177*
French, Daniel Chester, 123
Furlong, Jack, 112

Gabrielli, Donatello, 255
Gage, Robert Merrell, 127, 129, 130
Garney, Charles, 297, 298
Gaston Park, 58
Gemignani, S., 259
Gentry & Voskamp, 189
Gentry, Voskamp & Neville, 118
Gillham Park, 98, 172, 291
Gilham Park Wading Pool and Fountain, 97-100, *100*
Giralda Tower, 260, 261, 264, 265
Goodin, James, 70
Gordon Fountain, June Hemingway, 175, 177, *176*
Gorman, Mrs. Gerald W., 298, 299

Grace & Holy Trinity Cathedral Courtyard Fountain, 206-209, *208, 209*
Granada Royale Hometel Atrium Fountain, 214-216, *216*
Great Exhibition of the Works of Industry of All Nations, 69
Greber, Henri, 161, 164, 165, 167
Greenebaum, Hardy & Schumacher, 144
Grove, The, 90, 106
Guggenheim Museum (New York City), 211
Gumersen, W. Dow, 174

Haff Circle Mirror Pool and Fountain, 100-102, *103*
Haff, Delbert, 100-101
Hall, Joyce, 289
Hallmark Cards, Inc., 185, 289
Hallmark Corporate Entrance, 185-186, *186*
Hall's Plaza Fountains, 116-117, *117*
Halprin, Lawrence, 203, 204, 205
Halprin Plan, 203-205, *205*
Hamil, Harold, 298
Happy Woods Park, 92, *93*
Hare and Hare, 81, 94, 95, 169, 195, 203, 205, 227, 228, 237, 238, 239, 245
Hare, S. Herbert, 133, 144, 155, 156, 224, 227, 238, 239
Hare, Sidney, 239
Harrington, Howard & Ash, 90
Hartwig, Dr. & Mrs. Raymond W., residence, 85-86, *85, 86*
Haskell, Henry J., 149, 151
Heim Brewing Company, 59
Heim Brothers, 59
Heritage Fountain, 66, 282-285, *7*
Herzog, Noble, 280
Hibbard, Frederick, 136, 137, 138
Hilton Plaza Inn, 184-185, *184*
Hogg, James Oliver, 79
Hoit, Henry, 72, 224
Holmes, Mayor Benjamin, 60
Holmes, Mrs. Massey, 287
Holt, Arnold, 280
Horse Trough Fountain, 55, 113, *55*
Horticulture Hall (Philadelphia), 69, *68*
Hunt, Jarvis, 195, 196
Hunt, Lamar, 279
Hunt, Richard, 291, 292, 293
Hunt Memorial, Richard M. (New York City), 123
Huntington, Anna Hyatt, 175, 177
Hutchison, Stuart, 175
Hyde, Dr. Bennett Clark, 140
Hydrel Company, 298, 299

Indian Hills, 94, 220
Industrial Exposition Association, 70

Jackson County Courthouse, 199, 201, 202, 203
Jackson, Davis K., 260
Jackson, Jerome D., 215
Jarchow, Gordon, 269
Johnson, Alba, 256
Jost, Mayor Henry, 136, 141
Junior League of Kansas City, 91

Kansas City Bait and Fly Casting Club, 97
Kansas City Bar Association Fountain, 130-131, *130*
Kansas City Casting Pool, 97-98, *99*
Kansas City Exposition Building, 70, *70*

Kansas City Public Library, Plaza Branch, Fountain, 211-212, *212*
Kansas City Star Fountain, 195-197, *39*
Kansas City Zoo Memorial Fountains, 177-180
Kauffman, Ewing, 87, 279, 280
Kauffman, Ewing, residence, 86-88, *86, 87, 88*
Keck, Charles, 143
Keene & Simpson, 111
Keene, Simpson & Murphy, 169, 197
Keith, Charles S., residence, 81, *82*
Kemp, Mayor William, 149, 190
Kemper, David Woods, 167
Kemper, James Jr., 193, 199, 294, 295
Kemper, James M. Sr., 167, 168, 169
Kemper, R. Crosby Jr., 184
Kessler, George, 62, 63, 101, 105, 106, 109, 110, 132, 141, 142, 143, 219, 237, 245, 303, 304, 305, *62*
Kiene & Bradley, 269
Kingswood Manor Fountain, 301-302, *302*
Kipp, Robert, 297, 298
Kivett, Clarence, 279
Kivett & Myers, 266, 269, 279
Klein, Jeannette, 178, 287
Kraft, Arthur, 193, 271
Kroh Brothers, 272

Lake Hiwassee, 94, *94*
Lake Willow, 94, *95*
Land Memorial Fountain, Frank, 173-174, *174*
Landahl, William P., 294
Landing Shopping Center, 273-275, *274, 275*
Landscape Associates, Inc. (Little Rock), 185
La Pierre, Horace, 82
Larkin and Associates, 99, 293, 298
Lechtman, Cusil, 303
Lewis, J.V., 108, 129, 159, 225
Liberty Memorial, 124, 132, 134
Liberty Memorial Fountains, 65, 132-134, *132, 17*
Lincoln Memorial (Washington, D.C.), 152
Linscott, Haylett, Wimmer & Wheat, 272
Linscott, Kiene & Haylett, 257
Linscott, Mayol, 201, 203
Linscott Plan, 201-203, *202*
Linscott, William, 308
Linscott, Wimmer & Wheat, 308
Linwood Presbyterian Church, 67, 144
Livestock Exchange Building, 57, *57*
Long, Robert Alexander, 132
Loose, Jacob, 285
Loose, Mrs. Jacob, 91, 285, 286, 287
Loose Park, 91, 285
Loose Park Lake, 91-92, *92*
Loose Park Rose Garden Fountains, 285-288, *43*
Loose Park Rose Garden Wall Fountain, 287, *288*
Louisiana Purchase Exposition (St. Louis), 79
Lowell, Guy, 161
Lowry Memorial Fountain, George H., 67, 144-145, *145*

McArthur, Charles, 85
McArthur, Jarchow and Associates, 255
McCoy, Hutchison & Stone, 175
McElroy, H.F., 118, 189, 199

McIlvain, Frederick, 146
McKim, Mead & White, 161, 170
McMullen, Maurice D., 172, 173

Mackay, Clarence, estate, 160, 161, 162, 164, *162*
Macy's Department Store, 273-274
Madison Square Garden (New York City), 170
Magonigle, Edith, 132, 133
Magonigle, H. Van Buren, 132, 133
Malyn, Michael, 180
Marinelli Studio, 218, 259
Marshall & Brown, 191, 197, 210
Masonic Veterans, Proposed Fountain, 131, *131*
Medical Office Building Fountain (4706 Broadway), 250, *249*
Meeting of the Rivers Fountain (St. Louis), 150, 152, 153, 158, *151*
Mercy Hospital Century Club Memorial Drinking Fountain, 147-148, *148*
Mermaid Fountain, 253-254, *254*
Meyer, August R., 101, 224
Meyer Circle "Sea Horse" Fountain, 65, 67, 85, 223-227, 240, *35*
Micha, Peter, 281
Mifsud, Anthony, 281
Millcreek Building, 246
Miller, Richard McDermott, 270
Milles, Carl, 150-160
Minty Memorial Fountain, Harry Evans, 179, *178*
Mirror Lake, 152, *152, 154*
Mission Hills, 94, 95, 96, 220, 272
Mission Hills Fountains, 237-245
Mission Hills Rock Garden, 95-96, *96*
Missouri State Office Building, 202, 203, 204
Moore, L.T., residence, 74, *74*
Mott Iron Works, J.L., (New York City), 75, *75*
Mt. Moriah Cemetery, 131
Mulkey Park, 139
Municipal Art Commission (Kansas City), 56, 66, 124, 146, 168, 197, 202, 203, 204, 224, 264, 272, 283, 293, 307, 308
Municipal Art Commission (New York City), 123
Municipal Auditorium, 118, 189, 190, 191
Municipal Courts/Police Headquarters Building, 199, 203, 204
Murphy, John, 169
Muse of the Missouri Fountain, 64, 167-169, 179, 257, *19*
Myers, Ralph, 261, 269, 279

Nelson-Atkins Museum of Art, 142, 152, 153, 155, 164, 175, 187, 188, 205, 219, 259, 284, 305
Nelson, Florence, 287
Nelson Fountain, Mack, 72-73, *73*
Nelson Gallery of Art, see Nelson-Atkins Museum of Art
Nelson, Mack B., 72
Nelson, Oscar, 287
Nelson, William Rockhill, 155, 187, 195, 219, 305
Neptune Fountain, 256, *45*
Nettleship, William, 300, 301
Neville, Homer, 118
Neville, Sharp & Simon, 173
Newcomer's Sons Funeral Home, D.W.,

121, 122, *121, 122*
Newport Apartment Fountain, 113, *113*
Nichols, Clyde, 221, 259
Nichols Company, J.C., 95, 96, 102, 120, 163, 216, 219-224, 227-232, 235, 237-241, 245, 250-252, 254, 259, 264, 266, 268-270, 272-274
Nichols Company Fountain, J.C., 120-121, *120*
Nichols, Frank, 120
Nichols, Jesse Clyde, 64, 80, 92, 94, 133, 149, 161, 164, 187, 219-222, 224, 225, 227, 229-231, 234, 239, 243, 245-247, 252, 259, 260, *220*
Nichols Memorial Fountain, J.C., 64, 65, 160-167, 169, *166, 11*
Nichols, J.C., residence, 81, *82*
Nichols, Jessie Eleanor, 221
Nichols, Jimmie, 120
Nichols, Miller, 87, 162, 218, 245, 246, 256, 258, 259, 260, 262, 272
Nichols Restaurant Fountain, 119-120, *119*
Ninth Street and The Paseo Fountain, 109-110, *108-109*
"Noah's Ark," 274, *275*
Nolen, John, 237
Northeast Concourse Casting Pool/Fountain, 101, 103-104, *103, 49*
Northland Fountain, 66, 296-299, *27*
North Terrace Park, 110, 181
Norton, Edith A., 177
Nurses Memorial Fountain, 174-175
Nymph, The, 245, *244*

Observation Park, 58, 97
Observation Park Fountain, 115-116, *115*
Old American Insurance Company Fountain, 119, *119*
Oliver, Norwood, 269
Olmsted, Frederick Law, 62, 239
Olmsted, Frederick Law, Jr., 133
Oppenstein Memorial Park, 6, 294, 295, 296
Out in the Rain, 78, *78*

Packer, Francis H., 146
Pan (Bacchus) Fountain, 261-264, *262, 263*
Paris Exhibition (1867), 69
Paris Exposition (1889), 69
Parsons, Harold Woodbury, 188
Paseo and Seventy-ninth Street Fountain, The, 65, 247, *248*
Paseo Lake, 89, 106, 108, *90*
Patriot's and Pioneer's Foundation, 101
Paxton, John, 141
Paxton, Joseph, 69
PBNA Architects, Inc., 265
Pegasus/Flame Fountain, 256-257, *257*
Pelican Fountain, 228-229, *229*
Pendergast, James T., 136, 137
Pendergast Memorial Fountain, James T., 136-139, *137*
Pendergast, Tom, 136
Pennsylvania Station (New York City), 170, 172, 173, *171*
Penntower Building Fountain, 214, *215*
Penn Valley Park, 90, 118, 132, 224
Pershing Road Fountain, Proposed, 118, *118*
Philadelphia Centennial Exposition, 69, 75, 78
Pierson, Elmer F., 205, 206
Pierson Sculpture Garden Fountain, E.F., 175, 205-206, *206*

Plaza Theater, 252-253, *253*
Plaza III, 257
Plaza Wall Fountains, 248, 250
Pomona Fountain, 253-256, *255*
Pompeiian Room, 242
Pompeiian Urn, 242-243, *243*
Portman, John, 212
Powell Memorial, Bernard, Proposed, 308
Prairie Village Shopping Center, 272, *273*
Prospect Park (Brooklyn), 70
Prospect Plaza Fountain, 290, *290*
Putto With A Dolphin, 88

Quick, Edward, 298

Rain Thicket Fountain, 6, 66, 293-296, *13*
Ramos Group, 275
Residential Fountain (2118 Independence Avenue), 76-78, 77
Residential Fountain (1211 West 64th Street), 85-86
Rhind, John Massey, 140
Rice, Harold, 282, 283, 285, 295, 301
Rickey, George, 306, 307
Rickey Sculpture Base Proposal, 306-308, *307*
Roanoke Park, 90
Rocha, Elpidio, 156, 159, 202
Rodin, Auguste, 150, 227
Romanelli Gardens, 227, 228
Romanelli Park Fountain, 227-228, 230, *228*
Romanelli, Pasquale, 227
Romanelli, Raffaello, 245, 250
Romanelli Studios, 87, 227, 250
Romany Road Fountain, 6, 236-237, *236*
Rosenbauer, Wallace, 287
Royals Stadium Fountain/Water Spectacular, 6, 277-282, *29*
Rozzelle Court Fountain, 187-188, *15*
Rozelle, Frank F., 187

St. Gaudens, 123
St. Joseph Hospital, 113
St. Martin of Tours, 153, 154, 155, 156, 157, 159
Scarritt, Rev. Nathan, 181
Scarritt Spring, 181-183, *182, 183*
Schultz, Saunders, 295
Schiwetz, Peter Berthold, 156
Scopia, 295
Scott, Henry, 202, 264
Scottish Rite Temple Fountain, 111-112, *112*
"Sea Horse" Fountain, see Meyer Circle "Sea Horse" Fountain
Severson, William, 295
Seville Light Fountain, 65, 247, 264-265, *23*
Seville Square Fountains, 269, *268*
Shaheen, Robert L., (Little Rock), 185
Sickman, Laurence, 163, 164, 166
Simon, Herman Frederick, 163
Sittenfeld Memorial Fountain, 179-180, *179*
Sixty-eighth Terrace and Ward Parkway Fountain, 235-236, *235*
Sixty-seventh and Wornall Road Fountain, 222, *222, 223*
Skidmore, Owings & Merrill (Chicago), 194, 213
Sloan, Clifton, 72
Smith, Mayor Bryce B., 118
Smith, William J., residence, 78-79, *79*
Spirit of Freedom Fountain, 66, 290-293, *31*
Spirit of the Rose Garden, 287, *286*

Spring Valley Park, 90, 308, *91*
Stalcup Company, 118
Starr, John, 171, 173
Stratford Garden Park Fountain, 232-233, *233*
Sutermeister, Arnold, 109
Suydam Building, see Millcreek Building
SWA, 191
Swan Fountain/Verona Columns, 238-240, *239*
Swansons Building, 261, 264
Sweeney, Emory J., residence, 81-82, *83*
Swope, Frances, 140
Swope Mausoleum, 142-143, *142*
Swope Memorial Fountain, Thomas, 6, 123, 131, 139-144, *143*
Swope Park, 101, 123, 146, 152, 181, 304
Swope Park Lagoon, 90
Swope Park Mall, Proposal, 303-304, *304*, *305*
Swope, Thomas H., 139, 140, 143

Tacca, Pietro, **258**
Taft, Lorado, 137
Tanner and Associates, Edward, 163, 273
Tanner, Edward, 87, 156, 159, 163, 164, 253
Tanner, Linscott & Associates, 211, 259, 277
Taylor, John C., 250, 251
Theis, Frank, 162, 258
Theis Memorial Mall, Frank, 160
Tiffany, Dr. Flavel, 72
Tofanari, Sirio, 216, 218
Tomahawk/Wenonga Road Fountain, 241-242, *241*, *242*
Trinity Lutheran Hospital, 174, 175
Troost Lake, 90
Truman Sports Complex, Harry S., 279, 280
Tsutakawa, George, 198, 199
Turkey Creek Pumping Station, 97, 115
Two Planes Vertical-Horizontal Gyratory, 306

Union Station, **118, 132, 133**
United Missouri Garden Bank Fountain, 183-184, *184*
University of Missouri-Kansas City, 85, 149, 152, 197, 202
University of Missouri-Kansas City Library Fountains, 197, *196*

Van Brunt, Adriance, **101, 125, 139**
Van Brunt, John, 64, 109, 114, 115, 116, 125, 126, 303

Vaydik, Frank, 65, 66, 98, 102, 291, 294, 297
Verrocchio, 88
Vietnam Veterans Memorial Fountain, 308-309, *309*
Vivion, Major Harvey Jackson, 297
Volker Memorial Fountain, William, 64, 65, 67, 148-160, 205, *33*
Volker, William, 146, 148, 149, 153, 160
Von Achen, Kenneth, 280, 281
Voskamp & Slezak, 119, 183

Wall Fountain, Proposal (John Van Brunt), **114**, *114*
Ward, Seth, residence, 75-76, *76*
Ward Parkway, 219, 223, 224, 225, 266
Ward Parkway Mirror Pool and Fountain, 102-103, *102*, *47*
Ward Parkway Shopping Center, 272-273, 275
Washington Cemetery, 59
Washington Park, 59, *59*
Waterworks, 57, *58*
Watkins, Bruce R., 291, 292, 293
Weeks, Edwin, 56
Weese, Harry, 185
Wellesley Garden Tours, 81, 175
Westin Crown Center Hotel, 6, 181
Westin Crown Center Hotel Lobby, 185, *25*
Westport Business Association Proposal, 308
West Terrace Park, 63
WET Enterprises, 192
Wheeler, Mayor Charles B., 282, 284, 285
Whewell, G.H., 256, 262
White, Mike, 294
Whyte, William H., 191
Wiedenmann, Mary, 274
Wight, Thomas, 133, 188
Wight & Wight, 130, 133, 141, 142, 143, 152, 188
Wight, William Drewin, 224
Wilkinson & Crans, 129
Williams, Homer, 298, 299
Williams, Wheeler, 168, 169, 179, 257
Wimmer, Ed, 272
Winner, Willard E., 59
Winters, Ernest C., residence, 87
Wooley, Dr. Paul, 124, 125
Woolf Brothers, 253, 254
Wright, Frank Lloyd, 211
Wright, Henry, 110

Zuckerman, Bernhard, **264, 268**

Fountains of Kansas City was typeset in ITC Garamond Light and Book weights by the Photo Composition department at Hallmark Cards, Inc., and printed on Lustro Offset Enamel Dull by The Lowell Press.

Book design by Rick Cusick.